Crossroads
Of Us

Bianca Beck

Copyright © Bianca Beck

crossroads.series@outlook.com

Cover Design: Alta H Haffner – Sakura Book Publishing

Cover Illustration: Sonia Naidoo, Durban

Published by Bianca Beck using the services of Sakura Book Publishing, Durban, South Africa

alta@sakurabookpublishing.com

ISBN: 978-1-0370-6046-5(print)

978-1-0370-6047-2(e-book)

All rights reserved. No part of this publication may be reproduced, distributed, or transmitted in any form or any means, including photocopying, recordings, or other electronic or mechanical methods without the prior written permission of the author, except in the case of brief quotations embodied in critical reviews and certain non-commercial uses permitted by copyright law.

Crossroads Series

Crossroads

Crossroads of Us

Acknowledgements

My dearest Nixie Pixie, my heart is broken by the loss of your beautiful light in this world. Thank you for being an incredible friend and one of the most fearless and amazing women I have had the privilege of knowing.

I'm sorry I didn't finish this book in time for you to read it, so I am dedicating it to you and all the other beautiful souls who came into my life and then left far too soon.

Ryan G

Arthur H

Brandon N

Frankie C

Candy O

Leslie R

Jono S

Nicola J

I will hold my memories of you in my heart until we meet again.

CROSSROADS OF US
Chapter 1

"I nominate Kalen to go fetch takeout." Jake Landers shouted from the floating lounger in the pool.

"Fetch your own food you lazy ass." Kalen Carter sniped back from the games room. Kendra Landers shook her wavy blonde hair as she pushed the folding doors fully open and narrowed her dark brown eyes at her brother.

"We're in the middle of a game. Why don't you just phone in a delivery order?"

"I want pizza but Meg wants sushi. They don't collect from two places." He whined as he wrapped his arm around the shoulders of Megan Cole, who was lazing on the lounger next to him.

"So do two orders then dumbass." Megan snapped at him as she shoved him off the lounger into the cool blue water.

"I could really go for a burger right about now." Mark McAllister admitted as he aimed at the dartboard.

"Actually, I could too." Christian Carter mumbled as he inspected his darts.

Mark glanced over at him. "Your darts are fine Carter, it's your aim that's the issue." He smirked as Christian aimed one at him.

"I wouldn't mind some sushi." Ciara Rivers added as she handed Mark and Christian each a beer.

"Let's take a bet. If Kendra beats Kalen in this game of pool, he has to collect the food with whoever backs him." Robbie Harris said grinning at Kalen, mischief glinting in his brown eyes.

"And if I beat Kendra?" Kalen flashed him a cocky grin in return.

"In the *unlikely* event that happens, then Jake has to collect with whoever backed Kenz." Blaine Matthews offered from his spot on one of the poolside sun loungers.

"Ok, so who will bet on me beating Kendra?" Kalen crossed his arms and leaned against the door, the breeze blowing through his dark brown curly hair.

"I'll take that bet." A familiar voice replied.

"Lia." Kalen straightened up and stared at her. Angelia Ryan smiled at her friends as she dropped her bag onto one of the chairs.

"Hey." She said softly. Blaine covered the distance to her in two steps. He wrapped her in his arms and lifted her off the ground.

"You are a sight for sore eyes my little sister." He lowered her to the ground and held her face in his hands as he rested his head against hers. She reached up and put her hands over his as she smiled.

"Do you know how much I love you?" Tears glimmered in her green eyes.

"As much as I love you, silly girl." He laughed as he hugged her again.

"Stop hogging her." Kalen complained. "You've been gone for way too long Lia. I missed you so much." He said quietly, she could hear the tears in his voice and she hugged him tighter.

"I missed you too Kale. I missed your hugs and I realised how much I take your friendship for granted. I love you, more than you know."

"Love you too LiLi." He chuckled as she groaned. Christian walked up and wrapped his arms around Angelia and his brother.

"Hey, come on, it's my turn." Robbie protested as he pulled her into a bone-crunching hug. "Don't you ever disappear on us again Lia." He whispered to her. "We missed you."

"We really did, four months with these clowns without you was torture," Kalen grumbled as Ciara looked at him with daggers in her light brown eyes.

"Thanks Kalen."

"No, I meant the guys I swear." He gave her an innocent wide-eyed look.

"Some things never change." Angelia chuckled.

"Well, some things do change." Ciara lifted her hand. "Christian proposed. Finally." Angelia looked at the ring on her finger before pulling her into a hug.

"Congratulations." She said beaming. "I knew you would make an honest man out of this scruffy thug one day."

"Excuse me." Christian gave her an offended look.

"Hi, Lia." She heard a hesitant voice behind her. She turned slowly as Kendra watched her uncertainly. Angelia smiled and wrapped her into a hug. "I missed you, my Kenz." She whispered and Kendra's eyes filled with tears as she clung tightly to her.

"I missed you too." She pulled away and wiped at her tears. "I thought I lost you forever." She admitted sadly.

"You could never lose me. I just needed some time." Angelia squeezed her hand. She smiled at everyone and glanced around as though she was looking for someone. Mark shot a look at Kalen who met his eyes briefly before looking away and shaking his head. Her eyes landed on Mark and she smiled brightly as she walked up and threw her arms around him.

"You have no idea how much I missed you, Lia. If I knew where you were, I would have jumped in my car to fetch you and bring you home." He held her tightly.

"I know. That's why I didn't want anyone to know." She pulled away and reached for his hands, looking around at her friends.

"I missed you all so much, I'm happy to be back." She smiled. "So, tell me what I've missed."

"I could do with a burger. Why doesn't everyone put their order in and Lia, Kenz and I will run out and collect the food, then we can eat lunch and catch up." Kalen looked at Angelia and shrugged. "If you want?"

"Why not? I was going to lose the bet anyway." She laughed as Kalen gave her an offended look. He passed a pen and a piece of paper to her and pulled his phone out to dial as Angelia took down everyone's orders.

"All the food has been ordered, so I guess we will be on our way to pick everything up." Kalen looked at his brother. "Can I borrow your car, Chris?"

"We can take mine. I'll drive." Angelia offered as she picked up her bag.

"Yeah. No." Kalen said holding out his hand to her. "We'll take your car but I'm driving."

"What's wrong with my driving?" She asked indignantly.

"You don't drive, you fly and I want to eat the food I ordered, not hospital food thank you very much." He motioned for the keys with his fingers. She crossed her arms over her chest and smirked at him.

"Is that right?"

"Yeah, the last time I drove with you we were doing 160 in a 100 zone, we ran three red lights, a stop street and played chicken with a truck."

"But did you die?" She asked smugly.

"Staring at that oncoming truck I think I did die for a few seconds." He stated, giving her a solemn look. She sighed and handed him her keys before linking her arm with Kendra's and following Kalen through the door.

"Did you buy your licence?" Angelia looked at Kalen with a raised eyebrow. "Wait, do you even have a licence?"

"I got mine a year before you got yours, smart ass." He pulled into the shopping centre. "We divide and conquer." He announced. "Lia you're doing the sushi run, Kendra the pizza and I will grab the burgers."

"Look at you, Mr. Efficient."

"When it comes to food, always." Kalen climbed out of the car. "We meet back here in five minutes, ok?"

"Sure, I'm just going to pop in and grab some groceries though. My milk has become a science project and my coffee, sugar, cereal and fruit juice has mysteriously disappeared." She said, arching an eyebrow.

"That *is* a mystery." Kalen mused.

"Hi." Angelia greeted the cashier. "I'm picking up a sushi order for Lia Ryan." She waited patiently as the cashier rummaged through the receipts before handing her the one for her order. She pulled money out of her purse and handed it over, taking her receipt. The cashier headed to the kitchen to collect the order.

Angelia's eyes scanned through the restaurant while she waited. Her heart skipped a beat as her eyes landed on a familiar figure. Kyle McAllister was seated at a table holding hands with a dark blonde woman. Angelia breathed in sharply. Kyle glanced up at her, she watched as recognition turned to surprise in his caramel-brown eyes. He attempted to stand as Angelia turned her eyes back to the cashier who handed her two packets. She smiled her thanks and turned to walk swiftly out of the restaurant. She arrived at her car and said a quick thanks that Kalen and Kendra were already inside waiting for her. She opened the passenger door and glanced back at the restaurant where Kyle stood at the entrance staring at her. She climbed quickly into the car and shut the door.

"I thought you were getting groceries?"

"I decided to get them on my way home. It's hot and I don't want the milk to go bad." She explained. Kalen looked at Kendra who shrugged.

"LiLi." Kendra sang out. Angelia looked up startled to see all her friends watching her.

"What?"

"I asked where you were the last four months." Blaine explained with a concerned smile.

"Oh, um. I volunteered at a wildlife rehabilitation centre. They rescue animals from snares and poachers, rehabilitate and release them. Those that can be released. It was fascinating working so closely with wild animals and I learned so much. I have a new respect for our wildlife and the dedicated and selfless people who work so hard to help and protect them."

"Did you meet any interesting people?" Kendra asked.

"Yes, I did. There are a lot of people who come from all over the world to volunteer. Some are trying to earn credit for their studies and others do it for work experience. I was with a fun bunch of girls, we all got on well which helped a lot. I was extremely homesick for a while." She stood and collected her empty dishes before walking over to the bin and dumping them. "Where are your parents this time?" She asked Kendra.

"They're back in Switzerland, they absolutely love it there. They've just bought a villa or apartment or something. We barely see them anymore. Jake's moved back into the cottage so at least I am not alone in this huge house " Angelia's eyes flicked to Jake at the mention of the cottage. He scowled and looked away from her as he rubbed the scar on his cheek.

"Lia." She heard a familiar voice behind her. Her heart raced and she closed her eyes for a second. She turned around and looked at Kyle.

"Hey, um, hi."

"You look amazing." He took a few steps towards her.

"Thank you. I'm tired, it was a hella long drive. I think I'm just going to head home and have an early night. I need to get some groceries and start unpacking." She flashed a quick smile at her friends as she reached for her bag.

"Please can we talk?" Kyle asked. "Not now obviously, I know you just said you're tired but sometime soon."

"Yeah, I guess so." She said dismissively as she tried to walk past him.

"Lia." He caught hold of her arm.

"Don't touch me, Kyle." She snapped at him as she jerked her arm away.

"I just want to talk to you Lia." He gave her a wounded look.

"You know what Kyle? I don't feel like talking to *you*." She turned to walk away.

"I missed you."

She spun around and glared at him. "You missed me? Are you being serious right now? I just saw you having lunch and holding hands with another woman. How the hell is that missing me?" She shouted at him.

"What did you expect Lia? You left without so much as a goodbye." He shouted back at her. "All I got was a few lousy lines in a letter telling me that you're not giving up on us and then you disappeared for months on end. I tried to call you, message you and nothing. Most of the time all I got was your voicemail. I didn't know where you were or if you were even ok."

"I was not *ok*, Kyle. I found out that you slept with my best friend and lied to me about it. All I wanted was some space to think."

"You had plenty of space, considering that none of us knew where the hell you were. You walked away from all of us Lia and we were left here worrying about and missing you. *Especially* me, all I wanted to do was hold you and say sorry and beg you for another chance and you just disappeared out of my life. You didn't give me the opportunity to apologise or beg you for forgiveness. What you did was incredibly selfish. You wanted space? Well, that is *exactly* what you got."

"I wanted space Kyle; I didn't want you to find someone else."

"I moved on. I can't keep putting my life on hold waiting for you to decide what you want. You want me. You don't want me. Do you want to work things out or do you want to run away? Do you even know what it is that you want anymore Lia?"

"I want you." She shouted as tears welled in her eyes. "All I ever wanted was you but I was hurt. I wanted to leave so I didn't say something I didn't mean, something I couldn't take back and lose you forever. I left so we would have a fighting chance to work this out. I was broken and I was angry because I was betrayed by two of the people I love most in this world. So yes, I needed space and time to calm down and to clear my mind because every time I closed my eyes, I pictured you and Kendra together and it *hurt* Kyle. The whole time I was away I thought about you and all I wanted to do was come back, hug you and never leave your arms, but I knew if I came back before I was ready, we would end up fighting again. Just like we are now." Tears tumbled down her cheeks.

"Kyle, what the hell is going on?" Everyone turned to look at the door where Kyle's girlfriend was standing with her arms folded glaring at him. Angelia turned away, wiped at her tears and grabbed her bag. She pushed past Kyle's girlfriend and ran to her car. He watched her leave then looked at Kalen who shot to his feet to follow his friend. Angelia drove off as he got to the door. He walked back and shook his head.

"She left. Again." He announced as he sat back down.

"Who was that?" Kyle looked up at his girlfriend, he could see the anger in her eyes.

"She's umm, she…it's a long story." He sighed.

"I have time."

"Not now Laura, please. I'm just going to take you home. Can we talk about this later?"

"Halfway through lunch you looked like you saw a ghost and went bolting out of the restaurant with no explanation. Then you insisted on driving here straight after lunch and ordered me to stay in the car so I decided to come in here to find out what's going on only to hear you and that girl declaring your love for each other at the top of your voices. I'd like to know who she is and what the hell is going on." She demanded. Kyle pulled his keys out of his pocket and pushed past her to get inside. She glared at the group of friends before turning to follow him.

"Has anyone noticed that their fights get louder, nastier and more frequent?" Blaine asked quietly. "They were never like this in the beginning."

"It's almost like the more they love each other the more they hurt each other." Megan said sadly.

"How long before it blows up and our friendships become collateral damage?" Kalen asked frowning. Christian and Mark looked at each other as Mark shook his head.

****

"Lia. Please let me in." Kyle called out as he knocked loudly on her door. She swung it open and glowered at him. He gave her a half smile as he took in her black satin and lace lingerie. "Hey, you."

She hesitated for a moment before stepping forward to grab the front of his shirt and dragging him into the apartment, slamming the door behind him. He looked at her in surprise. She wrapped her arms around his neck, burying her hands in his hair and drawing his face down to hers. His lips met hers as his hands went instinctively to her waist, holding her tightly against him. She pulled away and brought her hands down to his shirt, gripping it in her hands. She walked backwards a few steps pulling him with her before letting go and walking to her room. She stopped at the door, smiled and inclined her head to the inside of the room. He walked up to her and pulled her into his arms. She wrapped her arms around his shoulders and kissed his neck before whispering,

"I want you. Now." Into his ear. He moaned softly before finding her lips as he ran his hands down her back to her thighs and lifted her up easily in his arms to carry her to the bed.

Kyle took a few deep breaths to calm his breathing. He smiled, tugged Angelia against his chest and kissed the side of her head.

"Wow." He whispered. "That was..."

"Incredible?" She asked with a giggle. "It was." She cuddled up to him, planting small kisses on his neck. He wrapped his arms around her.

"That was not what I was expecting."

"Me neither. I opened the door, ready to carry on our earlier screaming match and I realised that all I wanted to do was kiss you." She sighed, running her fingers over his chest.

"All you wanted to do was kiss me, huh?" He rolled her onto her back and lay over her. "I think we did a little more than kiss babe." He ran his fingers through her hair.

"I think we did a *lot* more than kiss. Maybe there is something to this whole angry sex thing." She mused thoughtfully

"Angry sex?"

"Yeah, it's when you are so angry with someone that all you want to do is fuck them." Kyle's eyebrows shot up. "What?" She asked him wide-eyed.

"I'm not used to hearing you talk like that." He confessed.

"I'm not used to talking like that." She admitted as her cheeks flushed red.

"I like it." He whispered in her ear before pressing his lips to hers. She wrapped her legs around his and hungrily met his lips. She pushed him over onto his back and sat on his hips.

"Who are you and what have you done with my sweet little Lia?" He asked laughing as he ran his hands up and down her thighs.

"I learnt a little something, something in my time away." She flashed him a coy smile.

"Is that right?" He gripped her hips, wrestled her to the bed and rested his forehead against hers. "I have missed you so much." He whispered.

"I missed you too. I missed this. I missed us." She brushed his hair back with her fingers. "So, tell me, what exactly did you miss?" She asked, biting the side of her bottom lip.

"What do you mean?" He gave her a confused look.

"What exactly did you miss? About me?"

"Oh, right. Well, I missed your beautiful green eyes. I missed this cute little nose." He said as he kissed the tip of her nose. "I missed these soft kissable lips." He brushed his lips lightly over hers and looked down to see her staring at him intensely. "What?"

"Your heart is my home." She placed her hand on his chest. "I love you." She whispered as she ran her hand from his chest to his cheek. He closed his eyes and caught his breath. "Kyle?" She looked at him with concern. He turned his head to kiss her palm before looking down at her.

"You have no idea how long I have waited to hear that. I love you too."

"Do you?" She asked with a raised eyebrow.

"Excuse me."

"Show me how much you love me." She commanded as she raked her nails slowly down his back.

"Yes, maam." He smiled and bent down to meet her lips as he ran his hands down the sides of her body to her thighs.

CHAPTER 2

"Morning sleepyhead." Kyle heard a cheerful voice next to him. He opened his eyes and squinted to see Angelia sitting cross-legged next to him on the bed smiling.

"Morning." He rubbed his eyes and sat up. "You look so sexy." He reached for her and pulled her onto his lap. "But you're wearing too many clothes."

"I made breakfast." She flashed him a grin as he looked at her suspiciously.

"You don't cook."

"I am highly offended." She crossed her arms over her chest as she gave him a snooty look.

"What's for breakfast then?"

"Croissants with bacon and cheese." She announced proudly.

"Uh-huh." He looked at her with a raised eyebrow.

"Freshly made I will have you know." She gave him a haughty look while trying to suppress a smile.

"Uh-huh."

"By the bakery around the corner." She laughed. "But I did cut them open, put extra cheese on and put them in the oven to heat up so technically…"

"Technically, the bakery made them, and you just heated them with a side of cheese." He reached out and dragged her down to the bed tickling her sides.

"Stop, stop, ok fine. I don't cook. I admit it." She giggled breathlessly.

"I love that sound." He lay on his back and pulled her onto his chest. He ran his hands lightly up and down her back.

"What sound? Me being tortured by the man who claims to love me?" She asked indignantly.

"No, your laugh. We call it the Lia laugh."

"What?" She propped herself up on her elbow to look at him.

"It's when you laugh and I mean *really* laugh and your eyes light up. You look so happy and beautiful when you laugh like that."

"I am happy."

"Good." He reached out and ran his fingers gently over her cheek. She smiled and leaned over to trail kisses down his neck. He reached down to tug on her shorts. "I think you need to take some of these clothes off." He mumbled as she ran her hand gently over his chest before swinging her leg over him and straddling his hips. She gripped the bottom of her shirt and started to lift it when Kyle's phone buzzed on the bedside table. She looked at him, let go of her shirt and shook her head as she laughed. He sighed and reached over to pick up his phone, he looked at the screen and groaned.

"It's Kalen. He got an iPhone last month and now every call is a video call. Like I need to see his ugly mug more than normal."

Angelia rolled over onto the bed next to him, put her head on his shoulder and pressed answer.

"Hey Kyle, uh Lia." Kalen looked confused.

"Hey, Kale." Angelia smiled brightly. "What's going on?"

"Where are you?"

"My place."

"We're kind of busy right now. What do you want?"

"Busy with what? Looks like you two are still in bed."

"Exactly." Kyle grinned as Angelia nodded with an innocent look on her face.

"We're busy…doing stuff." She added.

"What stuff?"

"They're having sex you idiot." Robbie yelled to him.

"Kyle, I really don't want to picture you doing unspeakable things to my little sister," Blaine grumbled in the background.

"Pay up everyone who bet that Kyle *wasn't* with Lia last night." Mark laughed.

"You mean all two of us." Robbie groaned. "Lia I am so disappointed in you."

"Kalen, did you Facetime me in a room full of people?" Kyle covered his face with his hand.

"Not people. My brother, your brother, Lia's brother and our friends. Finish doing unspeakable things to Lia and come join us for brunch."

"Kalen." Kyle groaned as Angelia laughed.

"We'll be there in two hours." She said with a smug smile.

"Two hours woman? I'm not a machine." Kyle rolled over on top of her and looked down at her with a smile.

"Umm, Kyle. I'm still on the phone. And you're not wearing any clothes." Kalen said in a pained voice. Kyle clicked the end call button and threw his phone to the other side of the bed as he bent down to kiss Angelia.

****

"Hi everyone." Kyle walked through the door holding a packet in one hand and Angelia's hand in the other.

"We come bearing gifts." Angelia held out a packet to Ciara.

"Smells divine. What is it?" She peered in at the boxes.

"My famous bacon and cheese croissants." Angelia replied with a bright smile as Kyle snorted.

"Made by the little bakery next to Give Me Coffee." He informed them.

"Thanks, babe, I wanted them to believe that I made them." She sniped at him as Blaine burst into laughter.

"Yeah, no one was going to believe that, Lia."

"Especially when the boxes have the bakery's name on them." Ciara raised an eyebrow at her as she held up one of the boxes.

"Damn, I missed that."

"I hope you guys are hungry." Christian said as he brought plates through.

"Starving, we didn't have breakfast." Kyle confessed as he handed Kalen his packet. "We brought some orange juice and champagne to make mimosas." Kalen nodded and took the packet to the kitchen.

"I guess you guys were too busy *doing stuff* to remember to have breakfast." Robbie gave him a sly grin.

"No, we didn't forget to have breakfast." Kyle laughed and looked at Angelia. "Someone put our food into the oven and then proceeded to seduce me while our breakfast was reduced to smoke and ashes. I'm surprised the neighbours didn't call the fire department." He laughed.

"I seduced you?" She looked at him with raised eyebrows.

"That's how I remember it." He said with a grin as he held out a chair for her.

"I think you have selective memory issues, babe." She sniffed as she sat down. He sat next to her and leaned over to kiss her cheek.

"Do I really?" He asked smugly. He turned back to their friends. "She can't keep her hands off me."

"Kyle." Mark shook his head at his brother. Angelia shrugged her shoulders and gave Mark a mischievous smile.

"He's not wrong." She leaned over to kiss Kyle's cheek. He smiled and reached over to take her hand in his.

***

Kyle wrapped his arms around Angelia's waist and pulled her back against his chest. She giggled and half-turned to feed him a crumbed chicken strip. He took a bite and she kissed his cheek.

"There are plenty of chairs to sit on Lia. You don't have to sit on poor Kyle's lap." Christian raised an eyebrow.

"She's not going anywhere." Kyle kissed her neck and hugged her tighter. Angelia pulled a tongue at Christian who smiled and shook his head at her. Seeing the two of them so happy filled him with relief. The last four months had been hell wondering where she was, getting the odd text message every few weeks had not made him worry any less

"She looks happy." Ciara whispered to him. He looked at her, smiled and nodded.

"Kyle, you're up." Robbie called him from the games room.

"I'm not playing."

"Chicken," Kalen yelled. Kyle's phone buzzed on the table, Angelia reached for it and picked it up. Her smile faded.

"Why is Laura phoning you?" She asked, turning to look at him.

"Oh shit." He reached for the phone. She pulled it away and answered it.

"Hello."

"Oh hi." Laura sounded confused. "I was looking for Kyle."

"He's very busy at the moment." Angelia replied in an icy voice pushing Kyle's hand away as he reached for the phone.

"Put him on the line right now." Laura's icy tone matched Angelia's.

"Who may I say is calling?" She asked in a sickly-sweet voice.

"It's Laura, his girlfriend."

"I'm sorry Laura, I think you may be a little confused. His girlfriend is right here with him, sitting on his lap."

"Lia that's enough." Kyle lifted her up, set her down on the ground and took the phone from her.

"Hi, Laura. I'm so sorry, I wasn't sure exactly when you were getting back. I was going to give you a call over the weekend." He turned to walk off as a fuming Angelia dropped into his chair and glared at him while their friends exchanged worried looks. Kyle listened to Laura for a while before speaking briefly and ending the call. He rubbed his forehead with his free hand and tapped his phone against his thigh as he walked back to Angelia. He dropped his phone on the table and looked at her warily.

"What was that about?" She asked, her anger simmering.

"Don't turn this into a fight Lia. We have managed to get through almost an entire week without fighting so please listen to what I have to say and let's talk instead of shouting at each other." She looked up at him and nodded. He grabbed her hands and pulled her up onto her feet.
"I was so caught up in you and being happy you were back and giving us another chance that I completely forgot about Laura. She was pissed off with me after seeing us fight so we weren't on speaking terms when she left for her work conference. She got back late last night and called now to make plans for this weekend. I know I should have called or messaged her to tell her about us and that she and I are over, but I completely forgot about her and I am sorry. Ok?" He ran his hands up and down her sides gently. She bit her lip and looked up at him with a shy smile.

"Ok." She wrapped her arms around his waist and buried her face in his chest. "I'm sorry." She said in a muffled voice. "I just felt a bit jealous." She looked up at him. He cupped her face in his hands and bent down to kiss her nose.

"You have no reason to be jealous of anyone. Ok? I am with you, Lia. I only want to be with you." He said softly. She smiled up at him and hugged him tighter.

"Let's go kick Rob and Kalen's asses at pool." She let go of him and reached for his hand. He bumped his hip against hers.

"So, you'll be on my team?" She nodded as they walked towards the game room.

Ciara exhaled and looked at Mark with wide eyes.

"That's an improvement. I was waiting for the screaming match we saw a week ago."

"Me too." Blaine said quietly. He watched the couple as they joined Kalen and Robbie at the pool table. "Do you really think she's put the whole thing with Kyle and Kendra behind her? I know four months is a long time, but I have *never* seen Lia get jealous like that."

Christian shook his head as he exchanged a look with Mark.

"I don't know. That was one helluva swing in moods in such a short time. Happy to jealous to pissed to forgiving and apologetic. Does anyone else feel like they have whiplash?" He asked with a forced smile.

They looked up as Angelia walked back and sprawled across Mark's lap. He gave her an amused smile and wrapped his arm around her back.

"Hello, hon."

"Marky Mark." She grinned. "It's Kyle's birthday in a couple of months and I wanted to get him something special, can we meet for coffee so I can run some ideas past you?"

"Yeah of course. Are you two going to do something on your own or are we going to do our traditional bar hopping?"

"Just the two of us for dinner but I think we should all meet up afterwards for a few drinks. No getting him hopelessly drunk." She said sternly looking at Blaine with a raised eyebrow. He gave her an innocent 'Who? Me?' look and she laughed and shook her head. She looked up as Kyle joined them.

"What the hell is going on here?" He crossed his arms over his chest. Lia wrapped her arms around Mark's neck.

"I'm sorry baby, I think it's time I told you. I am leaving you for your younger and hotter brother." Angelia smiled up at him.

"Is that right?"

"Sorry Kyle, we just can't stay away from each other. We tried to fight it, but she just finds me irresistible. I told her no because you're my little brother and I love you, but she just can't keep her hands off me." Mark said with a serious look on his face. Angelia's jaw dropped.

"Jerk." She punched his shoulder gently. Kyle walked up to them, picked her up and threw her over his shoulder.

"I think someone needs a swim." He started walking towards the pool.

"No don't you dare, put me down this instant."

"Oh, I will put you down, in the deep end of the pool."

"Do that and you will never have sex again." She threatened while he hesitated for a second.

"It may be worth it."

"You are such an ass."

He laughed and set her down on the ground. She flicked her hair off her face and folded her arms over her chest and glared at him. He smiled at her as she laughed and threw her arms around his neck. He lifted her off the ground briefly before resting his forehead against hers.

"You make me so unbelievably happy." He said quietly. She tilted her head slightly and the tip of her nose touched his.

"I know." She whispered as she let go of him and started walking away. He stood stunned for a moment before turning around, grabbing her from behind and holding her over the edge of the pool.

"You know? I tell you that you make me unbelievably happy and all you can say is you know." He said incredulously. She started giggling and squirming to get back to the ground.

"Ok. Ok. I'm sorry, you make me unbelievably happy too."

"That's better." He smirked, setting her back down on the ground. She pulled him close and slipped her hands into his back pockets. She leaned up to kiss him and whispered.

"If we find an empty room, I'll show you *how* happy you make me." She looked up at him with an innocent smile. He cleared his throat and smiled back.

"I think I know where there's an empty room."

"Lia, Kyle, we're in the middle of a game." Kalen protested. Kyle groaned and looked down at her.

"Let's go finish our game." She said with a laugh. He draped his arm over her shoulders as they joined their friends.

"They seem really happy." Mark said. "Maybe this time it will work out." Christian smiled and raised his glass.

"I'll drink to that."

CHAPTER 3

Kyle groaned and leaned back in his chair at his desk. Angelia looked up from his bed, sitting cross-legged and reading a magazine.

"What's wrong?"

"My company is pushing me to go to their New York office for two weeks. There's a job opening there and they want me to take it. I turned it down, but they want me to go anyway and have a look. I agreed so they started all the paperwork. I hadn't heard anything for the last four months so I thought they had dropped it, but they've now emailed me all the details, I leave in just under three months."

"It's just a couple of weeks babe and then you'll be back" She shrugged. "You *will* be back, right?" She added with concern.

"Of course I will. I don't want to go. The last two months with you have been amazing and I don't want to leave you." He explained. She smiled and went back to her magazine.

"Why did you turn it down?"

He glanced up at her briefly. "My home is here. Why would I want to move?" He mumbled. He could feel her eyes on him. He sighed and looked up.

"Don't make this into a thing Lia."

She narrowed her eyes. "Kyle."

"I turned it down because I hoped you would eventually come back to me." He confessed.

"You based a huge decision like that on me coming back to you?" She looked at him wide-eyed with surprise.

"Yeah." He looked back at his laptop, and he heard her get up and walk to him. She sat across his lap and ran her fingers through his hair.

"Do you know how much I love you?" She asked quietly. He looked at her in surprise.

"Of course I do." He said as she smiled and rested her head against his.

"You're supposed to say 'As much as I love you'."

He smiled and ran his fingers down her cheek. "As much as I love you." He said smiling tenderly at her.

"The time will go quickly. You'll be so busy and you will be home before you know it." She glanced at the time on his computer. "We need to get ready for dinner. I'm going to shower quickly." She said as she stood up. He hooked his arm around her waist.

"Want some company?" He wiggled his eyebrows suggestively.

"Hells no." She laughed, "We'll never make our dinner reservations."

****

"Have I told you that you look stunning tonight?" Kyle kissed the back of Angelia's hand. She looked at him and smiled.

"About a hundred times, but I don't mind hearing it again." She squeezed his hand gently before turning her attention to the waiter who had appeared at their table.

"I'll have the lasagne and my beautiful lady will have the spinach and ricotta cannelloni." Kyle ordered as he handed his menu to the waiter. Angelia looked at him with a raised eyebrow.

"What?" He asked as he took a sip of his water.

"What makes you think I was going to order the cannelloni?"

"Because you order it every time you order Italian."

"Maybe I was going to try something different this time?"

"Were you?" He asked sceptically. She took a sip of her wine to hide her smile.

"No." She admitted and shook her head before looking down at the table. "I like it that you know me so well. It may not be a good thing, but I like it." He reached out and put his hand over hers.

"I know you a lot better than you think I do." He gave her a smug smile.

"Is that right?" He nodded as she narrowed her eyes. "You seem fairly confident about that."

"Oh, I am."

"So, tell me. What do you know about me?"

"I know that you have a killer sense of humour, I know that you secretly like love stories even though you publicly detest them. If you could, you would rescue all the dogs who need help because you hate the thought of even one of them being hurt. I know that you love your friends more than anything in this world and you are loyal and fiercely protective over the people you hold closest to your heart. I also know that you will lie to defend the people you care about if you feel it is justified."

"Who have I defended by lying?"

"Me." He replied, squeezing her hand.

"You? When?"

"When we were working together at Connell's, after the first time we hooked up. You told the waitresses who were being bitchy about me that I was an amazing kisser and phenomenal in bed." He arched an eyebrow. "I know for a fact that you remember very little from that night, but I was touched that you lied to defend me." She blushed and smiled at him.

"It wasn't a complete lie. You are an amazing kisser." She blushed again. "The first time you kissed me, my legs went weak, and I had butterflies in my stomach and I remember thinking 'How is this man still single when he kisses like that'?" She laughed. "It wasn't a far stretch of the imagination to deduce from those kisses that you would be phenomenal in bed." She leaned forward and whispered. "Do you know what? I was right." She gave him a shy smile.

"You are too much." He laughed and shook his head. She reached for her bag and pulled a wrapped box from it.

"Happy Birthday, babe." She said as she handed it to him.

"What's this?" He asked as he took it from her.

"Your birthday present."

"Lia. You didn't have to get me anything." He protested.

"I wanted to."

He opened the box and pulled out a silver chain with a round pendant.

"It's perfect."

"Turn it over." He looked at her before turning the pendant over and looking at the inscription.

"Love you 4ever. Your Lia." He read it out loud and then looked up at her. "I love it, Lia. Thank you." He slipped it over his head before reaching out for her hand and kissing the back of it.

"It's a St Christopher pendant. Ironically, he's the patron saint of travellers."

"I'll never take it off." He promised as the waiter arrived with their food.

"Dinner was amazing." Kyle squeezed her hand as they walked out of the restaurant to his car. "Do we have to go and join those hooligans we call friends now?"

"Yes, I promised them we would meet them for drinks. I've been hogging you all to myself for almost two months. I told them I would share you for a little while tonight."

"I don't want to get drunk." He pleaded.

"You won't. I have made them a promise that serious bodily harm will be inflicted on whoever tries to get you drunk. And I keep my promises." She said with a smirk. He laughed as he opened the door for her.

"Do you realise that we could walk to Connell's from here?"

"In these heels, I don't think so." She sniffed as she climbed into the car.

"They are very nice heels." He chuckled as he climbed into his side and started his car for the short drive. He pulled into a parking bay close to the entrance and climbed out to open her door. He caught her hand as she tried to walk off and pulled her close to him.

"So, you don't want me getting drunk tonight huh?" He asked with a raised eyebrow.

"No, I need you sober for later." She gave him a coy smile.

"Any particular reason why?" He asked innocently. She leaned up, kissed his cheek and whispered.

"I bought whipped cream." He groaned and reached behind her to open the door. "What are you doing?"

"Screw drinks, we're going home right now." He replied.

She laughed and pushed him back. "We are going to go inside, have a few drinks, spend time with our friends and then we can go home and do whipped cream bad things to each other all night."

"Lia." She heard a pained voice behind them. She peered around Kyle to look at a horrified Christian and a smirking Blaine. "Please check if there are people around before saying things like that, especially in front of your brothers." Christian said shaking his head. Angelia blushed and buried her head in Kyle's chest.

"Sorry Chris." She said laughing. Kyle draped his arm around her shoulder trying not to laugh as he followed them up the ramp to the pub.

"There you are birthday boy." Kalen yelled as he saw them walk into the bar. "Where've you been."

"In the car park shouting to the world about the whipped cream sex games they're going to play later." Blaine laughed.

"Ooooh, I want details." Kalen grinned. "Ow." He exclaimed as his brother gave him a swift punch to the ribs. "What was that for Chris?"

"I do not need to know the bad things Kyle does to Lia, with or without whipped cream." Christian grumbled. "I need a beer and a tray of tequilas to erase those thoughts." He said waving to Beth the barlady.

"No tequilas for us."

"Why not?" Mark asked as he joined them.

"Don't ask." Christian warned him.

Chapter 4

"Do you still have work to do?" Angelia sprawled herself across Kyle's lap.

"No, I'm finished. Why?"

"It's late and I need to get to bed, I like falling asleep in your arms." She nestled her face in his neck. He leaned over to close his laptop. She stood and held out her hand to him. He took it and followed her to the bedroom. He shrugged his shirt off and kicked off his shorts before climbing onto the bed next to her. She cuddled up to him, burying her head in his chest. "I'm going to miss this." She pouted.

"It's two weeks babe and then I will be back here with you." He ran his fingers gently up and down her arm.

"Promise?"

"Of course. I'm only going to make my boss happy and get him off my back." He smiled down at her.

"You won't find some hot American surfer girl or actress and forget about me?"

"In two weeks? When I'm going to be working most of the time. And I don't think there is a girl or woman out there who could make me forget about you." He looked into her eyes and brushed her hair off her face. "Your heart is my home, Lia. *You* are my home. Wherever you are, that is where I want to be." She blinked back tears and smiled at him as he bent down to kiss her.

"I honestly don't deserve you." She sighed as she smiled up at him.

"I agree." He grinned down at her.

"Jerk." She glared at him as he laughed.

He kissed her before sighing. "You're wearing too many clothes again." He shook his head in disappointment. She giggled and pulled her shirt over her head and threw it on the floor.

"Better?" She asked smugly.

"Almost." He whispered as he trailed kisses down her neck to her stomach to the top of her sleeping shorts.

"That was just what I needed." Angelia sighed contentedly as she ran her fingers lightly over Kyle's chest which was still moving up and down rapidly.

"Me too. The next two weeks without you is going to be hell." He grumbled.

"I know, I am so spoilt now, love and cuddles in bed every night for the last six months. I'll have to find a temporary replacement while you're gone, otherwise I will never get any sleep."

"Don't you dare." He growled as he pulled her closer to him.

She smiled sleepily. "No one gives better night cuddles than you." She mumbled as she drifted off to sleep.

Angelia stretched and reached out for Kyle, she frowned as she looked up and realised he wasn't there. She got up and wandered through to the lounge.

"Babe?" She called out to the empty apartment. She spotted a note on the table. She picked it up to read as she walked to the kitchen.

Hey baby

You looked so peaceful, so I let you sleep in.

I have to run some errands and get a few last-minute things before I fly out to NY tonight.

I'll pick up some lunch for us.

Love you

Kyle

She opened the fridge, sniffed the milk and pulled a face.

"May as well get some groceries while he's out." She grumbled to herself as she went to get dressed. She flicked her hair up into a messy bun before slipping her phone and keys into her pocket and grabbing her shopping list as she headed out the door.

Milk, eggs, cheese, pasta, rice, bread, cereal, tomatoes, potatoes, onions and lettuce. Angelia read through her shopping list as she walked out of her apartment building towards the small shopping centre down the road.

"He clearly wants me to cook while he's away." She chuckled as she slipped her list into her pocket and pulled her phone out.

'Where's my sexy man?'

'Buying some pants and shirts.'

'You going to model them for me when you get home?'

'Only if you model the sexy lingerie I'm going to get you.'

'Oooh, get yourself one of those sexy leopard print thongs babe.'

'Hells no. You are so bad. I need to concentrate. See you just now. Love you.'

Love you too.

She glanced at her favourite coffee shop. "I need my caffeine fix first." She stepped in the doorway and froze. Kyle and Kendra were sitting close together at a table having coffee and laughing. Angelia stared at them for just a moment, fury and jealousy building up inside her. Kyle glanced up and his smile faded.

"Lia." He exclaimed in surprise. Kendra looked up at her wide-eyed. Angelia glared at them, spun on her heel and stormed out the door.

"Lia." Kyle ran after her and grabbed her arm. She spun around and yanked her arm away from him.

"Don't you dare touch me." She snarled at him.

"Lia, please, it's not what you think."

"Do you honestly think I would believe you?" She shouted at him. "How could you? After what you two did? I don't trust the two of you alone together!"

"Lia you're causing a scene. Can we please go back to the apartment and discuss this calmly." He pleaded. She exhaled heavily, glared at him and turned to head back to her apartment. Kyle glanced over his shoulder at Kendra who was watching them worriedly from the doorway. He shook his head as he followed Angelia. He closed her apartment door quietly and headed to the lounge.

"Lia, we ran into each other and decided to have a quick cup of coffee before I headed back here." He explained calmly.

"I do not trust the two of you alone. Not after what happened."

"That was a mistake Lia, I told you that. You know you can trust me."

"If you don't understand why I am upset then you don't understand anything. You just lied to me AGAIN about Kendra. When I texted, you said you were buying shirts and pants and then I found you having a coffee date with her. How can I trust you when you lie to me? *Especially* about her."

"It was not a date Lia. It was two friends bumping into each other and having a quick coffee together."

"You lied to me Kyle. You're missing the point I'm making. How am I supposed to trust you if you lie to me? You promised to be honest and never lie to me again and you just did!"

"I didn't tell you I was having coffee with Kendra because I was trying to avoid this drama." He dropped down onto the couch and sighed. "I didn't take things further with Kendra after our hook-up because I didn't have romantic feelings for her, I never did. I only wanted to be with you. I took her out to dinner to explain it to her and I thought about you the whole time I was out with her, so you have no reason to worry about us being alone together."

"What dinner?"

Kyle closed his eyes and mentally kicked himself. "The night you called before we got back together when I said I was having dinner with a friend..." he trailed off.

"The friend was Kendra? She was in the car when I called?"

"Yes."

"Un-fucking-believable. I can't deal with this *or* you right now." She turned around and stormed into her room, slamming the door loudly behind her. Kyle sighed and rubbed his forehead in frustration.

His phone buzzed on the table, he picked it up and opened the messages app.

"Oh shit, this is Lia's phone." He mumbled to himself. "Wait." He frowned at the phone. "Who the hell is Thomas?" he clicked on the message.

Hey, my little sex goddessWhen are you coming back? I miss that sexy little ass. You said you'd be gone for a couple weeks; it's been months now. Can't wait to see you again. I sent a video so you can remember what you are missing.

T

Kyle clenched his jaw as he closed the message. The phone vibrated in his hand as another message came through, the video Thomas had promised. He glanced up the passage and hesitated briefly before clicking on the video. He watched for ten seconds before closing it, he took a deep breath and checked the date on the video clip. He felt pain and anger well up in his chest. The video had been taken less than two months after Angelia had found out about him and Kendra. He threw the phone down on the table. Angelia walked out of her room and looked at him.

"What was that?"

"I threw your phone down." He said in a calm cool voice. She looked at him, she recognised his tone.

"Why would you do that?" She asked warily.

"Watching a video of you fucking a guy I assume is Thomas is not really how I wanted to spend the rest of my morning."

Angelia's eyes widened as she stared at him. "You went through my phone?" She asked angrily.

"No. No, Lia, you don't get to take the moral high ground here. He's expecting you to return so you clearly haven't told him we're back together. Does he even know about me?" Kyle's rage was simmering. Angelia bit her lip and shook her head slightly. "This video was taken just over a month after you left, Lia. You didn't waste any time jumping into someone else's bed. You never mentioned this man to me, not *once* in the last six months."

"It wasn't like that. I was sad and hurt and confused, and Thomas was there for me."

"Oh, I bet he was." Kyle laughed sarcastically. "You told me that the whole time you were away I was all you could think about and all you wanted to do was be back in my arms. You stayed away for four months because you wanted space to think about our future and to clear your head. How is screwing someone else and recording it giving yourself space to think and clear your head?"

"Maybe I didn't want to think. Maybe I didn't want to be an ice princess anymore. Maybe I just wanted to have meaningless sex with someone."

Kyle's face paled as the realisation hit him.

"All this dirty talk you suddenly started saying and all those new little sex games and moves you've been doing with me, you learned from him."

"Kyle." She pleaded. He held up his hands.

"I can't deal with this right now. I don't...I can't even look at you. You stand here preaching to me about honesty and giving me grief about a harmless lie and all you have done since you got back is lie. I asked you about your time away Lia and not once did you ever mention this man to me.
"You are a hypocrite. You know what? I wasn't going to tell you this because I was trying to protect you from being hurt again and to save your

friendship with Kendra but I honestly don't care anymore. Kendra and I *never* slept together. She tried to seduce me, but I turned her down even in my drunk state because I was in love with *you*. She lied and I only found out after you left but even if I *had* slept with Kendra, it doesn't even come close to this, to what you've done."

"Kyle please, we can talk about this." She took a cautious step towards him.

"No. I can't get the image of you on top of him out of my mind. The first few seconds of that video keep replaying over and over in my head. I have to get out of here." He shot to his feet, picked up his laptop and headed to the door, Angelia collapsed against the wall as tears streamed down her face. He turned around to look at her one last time before slamming the door angrily behind him as she slid down to the floor and buried her face in her hands.

"Kyle, what's wrong?" Mark frowned at his brother as he pulled out his suitcase and packed more of his clothes in. "Did you and Lia get into another fight?" Kyle shook his head. "Speak to me, you're worrying me."

"I need to get out of here, I can't see her." He muttered as he zipped his suitcase up and grabbed his passport and papers.

"Kyle." Mark snapped. He looked up at his brother as angry tears formed in his eyes. He blinked them back as he collapsed down on his bed and dropped his head into his hands.

"Do you know what she was doing while she was away?" He asked as anger and pain radiated from him. "She was fucking one of the guys at the rehab centre. I was here worrying about her and missing her like crazy and wanting to find her and bring her back and a month after she left, she was having sex with some guy named Thomas. Oh, and they recorded it. I got to see it today. It gets better; he is expecting her back there. She hasn't told him she's not returning, she hasn't told him that we're back together, she hasn't told him anything and yet she gave me attitude about not telling Laura about us and for even being with Laura in the first place. For all I know, she was planning to go back to him because she didn't tell him she was staying here.

"And the best part is that she told me nothing about him but flipped out because she caught Kendra and me having coffee today. I can't do it anymore Mark. It feels like I am on a rollercoaster all the time. I'm up, I'm down, I'm happy or I'm screaming, normally at Lia and I'm emotionally exhausted. I'm tired of her jealousy, I'm tired of apologising for something I didn't even do and I'm tired of fighting. Fuck knows I love her, and I probably always will but all I can see right now is that video and I feel like I don't even know who she is anymore." He ran his hand through his hair and shook his head before looking back up at his brother.

"Can we leave now for the airport? I'd rather stop somewhere and have lunch or beer or tequila or try and catch an earlier flight, anything but being here and seeing everything that reminds me of her. I thought this was it; I thought we were finally going to get it right and now I don't know." He said sadly.

"Go to New York, get your mind off all of this and decide when you get back." Mark said gently as he gave his brother a hug. Kyle nodded and hugged him back. Mark let go and picked up Kyle's suitcase with a sad smile. "I'll load this in the car." He nodded and looked around his room. The memories made his heart ache. The nights they spent cuddled up in bed or Lia sitting on his lap while he worked looking over her shoulder. He looked up at the photo of them on the wall. He reached up and brushed his thumb over her cheek in the photograph.

"Goodbye, my Angel Lia." He whispered sadly as he turned to walk out of his room, closing the door behind him.

****

"Give me a minute." Blaine yelled as the doorbell rang for the sixth time. He wrapped his towel around his swimming shorts and swung the door open. "Lia." He said taking in her tear-soaked face.

"I need to speak to Kyle." She pushed past him and ran down the passage.

"Lia." Blaine called after her. He turned to follow, almost slipping on the wet floor. "He's not here Lia." He explained as she walked into Kyle's room. He sighed and walked in after her. She stood staring at his empty desk. She looked up at Blaine as he joined her.

"Where is he?"

"He left for the airport about an hour ago. He was trying to get an earlier flight or check in as early as possible."

She pulled her phone out of her pocket and dialled; it went straight to voicemail. "His phone is off." She said quietly. She glanced at the clock and reached for her keys. He grabbed her arms.

"Lia if his phone is off then it means he has already boarded the plane." He explained gently. She looked up at him as tears welled in her eyes.

"Or he doesn't want to speak to me." She said sadly.

"Let him go hon, give him the time and space that you needed not so long ago." He said softly as he pulled her into a hug. She sobbed quietly on his chest.

"I love him so much, Blaine."

"Oh, my Lia." He tightened his arms around her. "I know you do. *He* knows you do. Whatever has happened, you two will work it out. Ok, sweet girl?"

"I don't know if we can. I screwed up so badly this time." She whispered as she turned her head to look at the picture of her and Kyle sadly. Blaine let go of her and she sighed before collapsing onto the bed. She pulled Kyle's pillow against her chest, it smelt like his cologne. She closed her eyes as tears rolled down her cheeks.

"Lia." She heard a gentle voice. She looked up at Mark and blinked. She sat up and rubbed her eyes.

"I must have fallen asleep." She said sadly. "I've lost him, haven't I?" Mark sighed and climbed onto the bed and sat next to her. He brushed her hair off her face and smiled sadly.

"He loves you Lia as much as you love him. You needed space to heal, now he's the one who needs time and space." He said softly. She nodded dejectedly.

"Can I take you home or do you want to stay here a bit longer? I'm making dinner and I'd love for you to join us." She glanced up at the photo of her and Kyle and shook her head.

"I want to be by myself for a while." She whispered. "I drove here, I'll drive myself home."

Mark shook his head. "No, you're too upset. Blaine and I will drive you and your car home. I'm not arguing with you." He said firmly as she opened her mouth to protest. She relented and smiled. Mark stood and held out a hand to help her up. She gave Kyle's room one last sad look before walking out behind Mark.

Angelia walked into her apartment and sighed as she dropped her car keys onto the table. She walked down to the lounge and stopped short. Kendra and Kalen were sitting on the couch, looking at her. She looked down at the ground briefly before walking towards them.

"Kenz, I am so sorry for how I acted earlier."

"You have nothing to apologise for." Kendra flew to her feet and threw her arms around her friend.

"I just felt so jealous and insecure and…" she trailed off as she hugged her friend tightly. "I completely overreacted." She pulled back and looked at Kalen and then Kendra. "What are you guys doing here?"

"Blaine called me after you cried yourself to sleep on Kyle's bed. He's worried about you. We all are. I stole my key back from my brother, picked Kenz up and we have been sitting here waiting for you." Kalen got up to hug her. "I'm so sorry my Lia." She hugged him back briefly then made her way to the couch opposite them.

"It's all my fault. I ruined everything. I don't know why I didn't tell Thomas that I wasn't going to return to the rehab centre or that Kyle and I were back together. I don't know why I didn't tell Kyle about everything. I think there was a part of me that felt ashamed of what I did. I just keep seeing the look on his face. I've seen him angry; I've seen him upset, I've seen him feeling hurt, but I have never seen him the way he was today. It's the first time he has looked so disappointed in me. What am I going to do?" She looked up at them. "I think I've lost him for good this time."

"No, I don't think so Lia. I've seen Kyle with a few girls and I have never seen him look at anyone the way he looks at you. He loves you, I'm sure he's going to get to New York, calm down and realise how *much* he loves you. He'll be back in a few weeks and you guys will work it out."

"Thanks Kale." Angelia smiled at him gratefully.

"So, uh, who is Thomas? And what exactly are you ashamed of?"

"He's one of the guys from the rehab centre. We were sort of seeing each other, I was supposed to be healing, not looking for a new relationship. I didn't tell him that I wasn't going back and Kyle found out and it's just a huge, big mess."

"So, are we going out or staying in?" Kendra asked as Angelia frowned at her in confusion. "Dinner tonight? Are we going to go out and eat or should we order in and have an all-night movie marathon?" She clarified.

"I'm not great company. I just want to be on my own."

"Wrong answer. We're not leaving you on your own tonight, so your choices are go out with us or stay in with us. Either way, it's the three of us." Kalen grinned widely. "I finally get my threesome with you ladies." He ducked the cushion Angelia threw at him.

"You are such an idiot." She said with a slight smile.

"That looks much better. What's it going to be Lia?"

"Movie marathon." She replied laughing

"Yes." Kalen gave Kendra a high five as she got up to walk into the kitchen to make coffee. Angelia stood up to look out the window at the ocean before closing her eyes. Kalen reached out and pulled her close to hug her again.

"Do you know how much I love you?" She asked sadly as tears rolled down her cheeks.

"I know my Lia, I know." He whispered as he rubbed her back soothingly. Kendra walked in and watched them before setting down the coffee cups.

"Lia, I have something I need to tell you." Angelia looked at her as Kalen let her go. She wiped her cheeks with her sleeves.

"I already know." Kendra's eyes widened in surprise. "Kyle told me earlier."

"Oh," Kendra said looking down at the floor. Angelia walked up to her and reached for her hands.

"It's ok. I don't understand why you did it and I honestly don't care anymore. I was furious when he told me but I'm just tired of this whole thing, I want to put it all behind me, behind us. Ok? So, it's over. We will never bring it up again, it's all in the past now." She said sternly as Kendra nodded. "So, are we doing movies or a Pretty Little Liars or Gossip Girl binge watch?" She asked as she let go of Kendra's hands and looked at Kalen.

"Oh, Pretty Little Liars definitely. A bunch of hot girls running around while I sit with two of the hottest girls in the village." He grinned. "That's a no-brainer." Kendra gave him a soft shove. Angelia looked up as she heard a knock on the door. She glanced at her friends who both shrugged. She made her way to the door, opened it and peered out.

"Blaine." She exclaimed in surprise. "What are you doing here?"

"Checking up on my little sister." He gave her a sad smile as he hugged her. "I was worried about you. We both were." He explained looking over his shoulder at Mark.

"Come in. We're about to order food and binge-watch Pretty Little Liars."

"Do we get a vote on the Pretty Little Liars thing?" Blaine asked, raising an eyebrow.

"Maybe." She laughed as she opened the door to let them in.

"Don't close the door." She heard a voice shout. She looked up as Dylan, Robbie and Kelly walked down towards her.

Robbie bent down to kiss her cheek. "I love you, my Lia." He said quietly and walked in as Kelly Adams hugged her friend tightly before following her boyfriend inside. Dylan wrapped his arms tightly around her and kissed the top of her head.

"I love you sweet girl." He said softly before following his brother and Kelly inside. Angelia leaned against the door with her arms folded watching the elevator, she smiled as she heard the elevator ping. Christian, Ciara and Megan stepped out and looked at her in confusion.

"You're late." She smiled. "Everyone's already inside."

Chapter 5

Angelia looked at her phone and sighed. Kyle had been home for four days now and she hadn't heard from him. She set her phone down, put her head back and sighed again. Her phone buzzed and she reached out hastily and picked it up. She felt a brief flash of disappointment.

"Well, hello there, Miss Jackson. Welcome home. How was your holiday?"

"It was lame and cold. My sister was in full bitch mode and my two juvenile delinquent stepbrothers kept pelting people with snowballs and causing mayhem. I'm twenty-four, Lia I am way too old to be going on holiday with my family."

"Any chance you're being slightly dramatic Case?" Angelia smiled in amusement.

"Maybe. Bitching about my highly dysfunctional family is not the reason why I called you though."

"What's up?" Angelia stirred her orange juice with a straw absentmindedly.

"A bunch of us are going to Retro later. Why don't you join us?"

Angelia glanced at her watch. "What time are you heading out?"

"Around nine or ten. You got a shift tonight?" Angelia shook her head and then realised Casey couldn't see her. She chuckled wryly at her mistake.

"No, I took the week off. I have two exams left so I wanted to study for them."

"*Have* you been studying?" Casey inquired.

"Not so much, I've been a bit distracted." Angelia set her glass down and shifted her phone to her other ear.

"Well, Megs, Kel, Allie and I are going to Linguine's for dinner, it's right there by you if you want to join us. Bring Kenz, we'll be there around seven."

"That sounds like fun. I'll see you then." She forced herself to sound cheerful.

"Lia. If he doesn't call you, it's his issue and not yours. Don't let him ruin your weekend."

"Thanks, Case."

"Love you, gorgeous girl." Casey said laughing.

"Love you too sexy lady."

"See you shortly."

"Bye." Angelia dialled Kendra, it rang and went to voicemail. "Hey Kenz. I'm having dinner with the girls at Linguine's if you want to join us, we're going to Retro afterwards. Getting a bit worried about you, haven't spoken to you for a few days. Call me, love you. Bye." She tapped her phone with a nail as she frowned. She dialled Kalen, voicemail. "Hey, Kale. I'm starting to feel a little paranoid. I haven't heard from anyone for a few days now. Call me when you can. Love you, bye." She sighed and sat back. Her phone buzzed, she picked it up and rolled her eyes.

"Hi Jake."

"Hey Lia. I hear you joining us at Retro tonight." His voice boomed through the speakers. She winced and pulled the phone from her ear.

"You're going to Retro?" She asked, her irritation reflecting in her tone.

"Yeah, Megan's going so I'm tagging along."

"Why? Are you worried she'll figure out that she can do better than you?" She asked snarkily.

"Ouch, a little bitchy today, are we? Or are you upset because a certain someone hasn't called you?"

Angelia's heart skipped a beat.

"You've seen Kyle?" She regretted asking the question as soon as it was out of her mouth.

"Yeah, every day since he got back. We all have. Well, not *all* of us obviously." He sneered through the phone. Angelia bit back a bitchy response.

"I have to go, Jake; I'm going out in two hours and I have to get ready." She cut the call and fought back angry tears. Clearly, Kyle hadn't forgiven her yet. She dialled him but he cut her off. She frowned and opened her text app.

Hey you. I was hoping we could talk.

She pressed send and got up to walk inside. I may as well shower and get dressed while I wait for a response, she thought to herself. Her phone buzzed as she walked in the door. Her heart started racing; it was a message from Kyle. She opened it and looked at the two-word response.

We can't.

She closed her eyes briefly and shook her head. She dialled his number again, and it went straight to voicemail. She threw her phone on the table and headed for the shower.

Angelia had just pulled on her jeans and a black halter neck top when she heard a knock on her door. She swung it open and smiled.

"Chris." She exclaimed as she leapt into his arms. "This is a surprise." She said happily, but her smile faded quickly when she saw the look on his face. "What's wrong? Did something happen to Ciara? Kalen? Blaine?" She felt her panic rising.

"They're all fine hon, Ciara's parking the car, she'll be up shortly. Can I come in?" She stepped back to let him enter as Ciara stepped out of the lift and made her way up to them. She gave Angelia a quick hug before following Christian into the lounge. Angelia closed the door and followed them; she could feel her heart sinking. She took the chair opposite them and looked at them both with a frown.

"What's going on? I'm starting to panic." She was trying to keep her voice steady. Christian glanced quickly at Ciara before looking at her with a sad smile.

"Oh, my Lia." He said sadly. "I wanted to be the one who told you this because I know it's going to break your heart." Angelia glanced at Ciara, who was trying to blink back tears, she looked away from Angelia.

"What is going on, Chris? please just tell me." She begged.

"We've just come back from the airport." Angelia gave him a confused look. "We were dropping Kyle off."

"I don't understand. He just got back. I was giving him time so he would come to see me when he was ready."

"Lia, he took the job in New York. He accepted it while he was there. He came back to get some documents from work and to pack up the rest of his stuff. They want him to start immediately and they have already arranged an apartment and everything for him. It's an incredible opportunity and he is earning almost triple what he was earning here. It's an amazing step up for his career, especially being so young. He couldn't pass this up hon."

Angelia put her hands over her mouth as a tear trickled down her cheek.

"He didn't even come to see me or say goodbye." She paused and looked at them. "He's really gone?" Christian nodded as Angelia stood up. "Thank you for letting me know. I have plans for tonight. Plans with the girls and I need to finish getting ready or I'm going to be late. Fashionably late but late nonetheless." She gave them a bright smile as she flicked her hair over her shoulder. She turned to walk off as Christian stood, grabbed her arm and pulled her against him. She put her hands on his chest and tried to push him away from her.

"Don't, Lia." His voice was gruff with sadness. "Don't push me away. I'm your family. You can't pretend with me. I know you're not ok."

She bunched his shirt in her hands as she rested her head on his chest, her body shook as she sobbed in his arms. He held her tightly against him as he rubbed her back gently.

"I'm so sorry, Lia." He whispered as he kissed the top of her head gently. "Do you know how much I love you?" He asked quietly as her sobs subsided. She nodded as she pulled away from him. She smiled sadly as she wiped at the tears on her cheeks. Ciara patted the seat next to her.

"Come sit by me." She sat down and Ciara wrapped her arms around her. "Chris why don't you make some coffee?"

"No don't make coffee." Angelia stood up. "I feel drained and I just want to go to bed." The couple looked at each other quickly and Christian nodded. Ciara gave her a warm hug.

"Anytime you need me Lia, I'm a call away." She squeezed her hand. Christian put his hand on her cheek and looked down at her. She smiled sadly at him. She watched them head to the door before she walked back through to the lounge. She lay down on the couch, hugged the cushion and closed her eyes as she tried to fight back the wave of pain that flooded her body, bringing with it another round of tears.

"Lia hon." She heard a gentle voice. She looked up into a pair of concerned grey eyes.

"Blaine." She whispered tearfully.

"Yeah, my little sister." He said softly as he brushed her hair back.

"My heart hurts." She sobbed as tears streamed down her cheeks.

"I know hon." He gave her a sad smile. She sat up and wiped at her tears. He dropped down onto the couch next to her and pulled her across his lap. "I love you sweet girl." He whispered as he held her tightly.

"I love you too." She said sadly. He ran his hand gently up and down her arm.

"Do you want me to stay here with you tonight?" He mumbled into her hair.

"Please." She sniffed. "I love him so much Blaine. How could he just leave me? He was supposed to forgive me and come back to me." She asked sadly.

"I don't know hon. He's hurting, just like you were not so long ago. Give him time to heal."

"Thank you for staying with me."

"Oh, my Lia, there is nowhere I would rather be. Not when my sister needs me. I will always be there for you. You know that." He said smiling softly.

"I know. Do you know how much I love you?" She asked sadly as tears streamed down her cheeks again.

"I know sweet girl, I know." He sighed sadly as he closed his eyes and held her tighter.

****

Angelia leaned back in the lounger on her balcony and rested her feet on the low wall. She watched the waves roll, curl and break on the shore. Tears welled up in her eyes and rolled down her cheeks. She wiped them away and sighed sadly.

"My Lia." She heard a familiar voice call out. She gasped as she shot to her feet and spun around to look at the person standing in the doorway.

"JR." She ran into his arms and held him with her eyes shut tight. He looked down at her and laughed.

"What are you doing, Lia?" He asked, amused.

"I don't want to open my eyes because I'm scared that this is just a dream." Her voice broke as tears rolled down her cheeks.

"I'm here. I promise. You can open your eyes. Lia? What's wrong?" Angelia clung tightly to her brother as she sobbed into his chest. He wrapped his arms firmly around her until her crying subsided. "Come here silly girl." Jarryd Ryan sat down on the couch and pulled her down next to him. She wiped her cheeks with her sleeves before resting her head on his shoulder. He curled his arm around her shoulders and pulled her against his side.

They sat together in silence, watching the ocean. Angelia finally lifted her head and looked at her brother suspiciously.

"Why are you here?"

"To visit you, silly girl." He smiled at her; she raised an eyebrow and narrowed her eyes. "What? Now I need a reason to visit my baby sister? I mean a reason other than I love her, I miss her like crazy and I want to make sure she's doing ok."

"Jarryd Ryan." Angelia rolled her eyes. He raised his hands in surrender.

"Fine. I've been planning a trip back home to come see you and Blaine, but I hadn't settled on a date yet. Three days ago, I received a rather strange voice message from Chris saying I should book a flight back home ASAP because my sister is going to need me right now. I have lots of leave due to me, so I booked a flight and here I am."

"Chris worries too much. He shouldn't have bothered you." She sniffed and rubbed her cheeks.

"I'm so glad he did Lia. You and Blaine are all I have left in this world. I really wish you would move to London and stay with me again."

"This is my home JR, besides, you have a whole life that you set up for yourself over there; you don't want your baby sister and little brother cramping your style." She smiled and bumped him with her shoulder. He looked at her thoughtfully.

"Yeah, I guess you're right." He agreed with her. Angelia shook her head and punched him lightly in the arm.

"Jerk." She grumbled before bursting into laughter.

"Seriously though Lia. You just say the word and you're on the next flight to London, both of you."

"Can't you move back here instead?" She asked wistfully.

"I wish I could Lia, but I'll never get a job here that will pay me as well as I'm paid over there. I am coming back one day so we can open a family business together." He wrapped an arm around her shoulders. "You, Blaine and me silly girl, it's us against the world. Do you know how much I love you?" He asked as he rested his cheek on the top of her head.

"As much as I love you." She sniffed softly. "I miss you so much." She said in a teary voice.

"I miss you too, sweet girl." He kissed the top of her head gently before standing up and walking into the kitchen.

"So, tell me about him." He said as he pulled two wine glasses out of the cupboard before grabbing a bottle of red wine from the rack.

"Who?" Angelia pulled her legs up to rest her chin on her knees.

"The knucklehead with the black eye who broke my baby sister's heart." He explained as he poured the wine.

"He doesn't have a black eye."

"Not yet." Jarryd smirked as he handed her a glass of wine.

"JR! You can't go around beating people up."

"I can when they hurt you." He said with a serious look. She smiled as she took a sip of her wine.

"It's great to have my big brother home." She watched as he took a seat at the table and gestured for her to join him. She stood and took the seat across from him.

"Uhhh Lia, sweet girl, what the hell is this?" Angelia looked at her brother as she sat down.

"It's a plant. It has such pretty pink flowers." She smiled as she reached out to tap the potted plant in the middle of the table.

"Hon, this is dead." He sighed, shaking his head.

"No, the lady at the plant shop..."

"You mean the nursery?"

"Same thing." She shrugged. "She said that sometimes in Winter the plants look dead but then in Spring they come back to life. Almost like hibernating."

"Lia, nothing short of a resurrection is going to bring this plant back to life and you are aware that it's currently summer."

"I know, I'm in denial." She sighed. "And the people at the nursery won't sell me any more plants. I need to look for a new place."

"Or maybe stop buying plants or stop killing them at least."

"I don't mean to." She looked up at him with tears in her eyes. "I keep destroying everything. My plants, my life, my relationship with Kyle. What's wrong with me JR?"

"Oh, Lia. Nothing's wrong with you. Talk to me. Tell me what's going on." He said gently.

"I can't. You'll think I'm stupid and immature and your opinion means more to me than anything in this world."

"I could never think that, Angelia. I am so incredibly proud of you. When Mom and Dad died and didn't leave your money in a trust, I was worried that you would party your way through it, but you surprised me. You bought yourself a good car, put money aside to study and bought this place. You got a bar job to pay for expenses instead of dipping into your college money or savings. You turned from a hell-raising party girl into a level-headed and mature woman. There is nothing you could do that can make me stop being proud of you. Now stop dodging my question." He raised an eyebrow at her as he took a sip of his wine.

"It's a long story."

"I got time and wine." He said flashing her a grin.

"Ugh, really? Trying to rhyme? You were never good at that." She grimaced.

"You were though." He chuckled. "Now tell me everything."

"His name is Kyle. I did some really stupid things and now I've lost him forever."

"I highly doubt it." He gave her a warm smile.

"You haven't heard the whole story."

"By all means, continue." He gestured with his hand as she rolled her eyes and shook her head.

"The last few years has been backwards and forwards between us. We get together, we fight and make up. Even when we were with other people, we always ended up back together. Then something would happen, we'd fight, split up and then just repeat the cycle." She stole a glance at her brother who was listening to her intently. "He chose his one girlfriend over me because she told him she was pregnant, and I self-destructed. I was partying, dancing on bars, kissing random guys and just drinking out of control." She gave him a rueful smile. "Guess you're not too proud of your baby sister right now."

"Of course, I am. You're allowed to go wild now and then. You were betrayed by someone you love and you went off the rails. We all go through it, Lia. The important thing is that you realised how destructive it was and you stopped."

Angelia shivered. "Sometimes I think of how badly those nights could've ended. Being so wasted and going home with some strange guy."

"You had too many eyes on you for that to happen. If some random guy thought he was sneaking you out the door and into his car...let's just say he would've needed reconstructive surgery by the time Chris, Blaine, Robs, Kale, Dyl and the others were finished with them."

"They weren't even there half the time."

"Oh yes, they were." He said confidently.

"How would you even know that?" Angelia raised an eyebrow. He looked at her thoughtfully.

"I know that because I asked them to be there for you. They agreed because they love you and are protective of you. They know that I'm not there to protect you, so they've taken it upon themselves to be your brothers and one actually is your brother." He laughed. Angelia blinked back her tears.

"Are you being serious?"

"I am. The only time they let their guard down was at Jake's party. They thought you would be safe with friends." A smile played around his lips. "I hear your boy set him straight."

"Yeah, Jake needed seven stitches on his cheek." Angelia smiled wryly.

"Serves him right, I never liked the guy." Jarryd said with a smirk.

"He's Kendra's brother Jarryd, please be nice."

"I will try." He promised and nodded for her to continue.

"I won't bore you with all the details, I'll summarise it for you." She sighed. "Turns out the girlfriend wasn't pregnant which made me even angrier, so we fought all the time. We eventually called a truce and became friends. We just got back together when I found out that he slept with Kendra." Jarryd gave her a surprised look. "They didn't. Kendra lied and Kyle was too drunk to remember. But he rejected her because he loved me. Unfortunately, I only found that out after I got back. I left because I was so hurt and when I got back, we worked things out and I was so happy. We were finally in a good place. And then I went and overreacted to something so stupid and..." she trailed off and looked away. "He found out that I was...that I had..." She leaned back and sighed. "That I had sex with one of the guys at the wildlife rehab centre. He saw a video of me and Thomas..." She trailed off and looked down at her hands as her cheeks flushed a deep red.

"A video of you and Thomas doing *what* Lia?" She didn't need to look up, she could hear the anger in her brother's voice. She exhaled heavily before looking up at him and giving him a grim smile. "Oh Lia, no." He put his head in his hands. "How could you be that stupid?" He asked angrily.

"I wasn't thinking." She whispered. "I spoke to him after Kyle left for New York and asked him to delete the video. He says he has, but I have no way of knowing for sure."

"I can't say I'm not angry and disappointed Lia, but we all make mistakes and I hope you've learnt your lesson on this one." He looked at her with a small smile.

"Yes, I have." She said quietly.

"So, Kyle saw the video?" She nodded sadly.

"He saw a part of it and he was so angry and hurt, he was supposed to go to New York for a few weeks and come back, but he's gone there now for good." She looked up at him as tears ran down her cheeks. "I've lost him Jarryd, and I love him. He means everything to me."

"Oh, my Lia." He said comfortingly as he got up and went to hug her. "If he truly loves you, he will forgive you and find his way back to you. Ok? If you two are truly meant to be, then no force in this world can keep you apart." He ran his hand over her hair soothingly. She nodded and wiped the tears from her cheeks. "Do you want to give me Thomas's number so I can have a little chat with him?" She looked up at her brother and started to smile. Her smile faded when she saw the serious look on his face.

"Ok." She said nervously as she reached for her phone. A knock on the door interrupted their conversation. Angelia looked at her brother who shrugged his shoulders. She put her phone down, walked to the door and swung it open.

"Chris." Her face lit up and she threw her arms around him. He laughed and hugged her back.

"You seem a lot happier than you were last night." He said as he looked at her with a surprised smile.

"Thank you for always looking out for me and being there for me. I love you so much." She said as she hugged him tightly. He squeezed her back before letting her go and following her to the lounge.

"I love you, too Lia and I'll always protect you. You're my baby sister." He said with a smile.

"Just remember that she already has a big brother." Jarryd said from the kitchen. Christian spun around.

"JR! What? When did you get here?" Jarryd pulled Christian into a big bear hug before pulling away and patting his shoulder.

"I got here this morning. Surprise visit. I missed my baby sister and my brothers." He laughed

"Yeah, I better be one of those brothers!" Christian said with a sideways grin. Jarryd laughed as he hugged him again.

"Of course. Thank you for looking after our little sister, even when she's being impossible." He smiled at Angelia, who rolled her eyes.

"I'll always be there for her, even when she doesn't want me to be. You got any plans for tonight? We could get the whole family together?"

"Tonight, I'm spending time with Lia, thought we'd drink some wine, have a long chat and watch some movies. Quiet night in with my little sister." Jarryd put his arm around her shoulders.

"That's a great idea. Let's have a get-together at my place tomorrow afternoon then. We'll keep you being here a surprise, they can all find out then."

"That sounds perfect, we'll be there." Jarryd walked to the lounge and sat down. He indicated to the other chair and Christian smiled and sat down.

"Does Blaine know you're here?"

"No, and don't tell him. That boy cannot keep a secret to save his life." Jarryd said laughing as he shook his head. "I just think Lia and I need to spend some time together." He added quietly. Christian nodded in agreement.

"Wine or coffee Chris?" Angelia asked from the kitchen.

"Coffee, please Lia." He replied before smiling at his friend. "I can't believe you're here."

"Yeah, it's been a long time coming. I think I should try to come home more often, it's been years since my last visit. I haven't been back since…" He trailed off as he glanced in the direction of the kitchen. "Our parents' funeral." He said quietly.

"Yeah, I know." Christian smiled. "It would be great to see your ugly mug more often." He chuckled.

"My ugly mug? Have you looked in the mirror lately? Did your razor run away from you? It's the scruffiest I have ever seen you look."

"You want to see scruffy? Wait till you see Kalen." Christian laughed as Angelia handed him his cup of coffee and sat next to Jarryd.

"You are so mean to him, Chris." She gave him a stern look.

"How is my little brother doing?" Jarryd asked him as he reached over to flick Angelia's ponytail. She swatted his hand and rolled her eyes.

"Blaine's doing well. He lives with Mark and…" He trailed off as he glanced quickly at Angelia.

"Kyle." She finished his sentence quietly.

"Yeah." He said softly. Angelia turned to Jarryd.

"You'll like Mark. He's co-parent of our group with Chris." She smiled before giving a small laugh. "He's the reason I stopped partying after Kyle and I split up the first time." She admitted looking at Christian. "He drove me home, gave me a lecture and shamed me good."

"I like him already." Jarryd laughed. He looked up as Angelia's phone rang. Christian leaned over to grab it.

"It's Kendra." He said. She nodded and reached out her hand to catch it.

"Hi Kenz." She answered as she stood up and walked outside. Jarryd glanced back at her before leaning forward.

"Did she tell you why she and Kyle split up?" He asked quietly. Christian shook his head.

"No, she won't tell me why and Kyle was pretty tight-lipped about the whole thing as well."

"Apparently, our little sister participated in a sex tape," Jarryd said clenching his jaw. Christian's eyebrows shot up.

"With whom?"

"Some guy at the rehabilitation centre she volunteered at."

"Are we going on a road trip?" Christian asked, glancing at Angelia. Jarryd shook his head.

"She spoke to him, and he says he's deleted the video. I'm going to have a little chat with him myself and see what he has to say." He sighed. "I don't blame Kyle for being pissed. I was ready to kill Lia myself." He looked up as his sister walked back in.

"I told Kendra you were thinking of having a get-together at your place tomorrow afternoon and she said she will round up the hooligans."

"Great, I need to give Ciara a heads up before one of those clowns calls her. She will have my head for organising a party without letting her know." He pulled his phone out of his pocket as Angelia giggled. He looked up at her warily. "What Lia?"

"I think it's hilarious that you are terrified of her."

"Not terrified." He corrected. "It's just respectful to let your other half know when you organise for the hooligans to come over."

"He's terrified of her." Jarryd chuckled.

"Yeah, a little bit." Christian admitted smiling as he got up. "I'll leave you two alone now. Looking forward to having you spend time with all of us tomorrow." He said as he pulled Jarryd into a hug. "It has been way too long brother."

Chapter 6

Kendra bumped her hip against Angelia's and turned her head to smile at her friend.

"I'm so glad you came out tonight, Lia. I know you're sad about Kyle, but this is good for you to be around your friends. He's far away and you can move on to better things and hotter guys." Angelia wrapped her arm around her shoulders and rested her head against Kendra's. She raised her glass and clinked it against Kendra's.

"I love you, Kenz. We'll always be best friends." She said with a big smile.

"Yeah, if my kissing, trying to seduce and lying about having sex with the love of your life didn't end our friendship then there is nothing that can tear us apart." Kendra declared as she raised her glass triumphantly. Angelia looked at her for a moment before bursting into laughter and hugging her.

"You are too much. That is the first time I have laughed all week. Thank you, Kenz." Kendra laughed with her before bowing awkwardly.

"Kendra Landers, Court Jesterix at your service my Queen." She said in a terrible attempt at a posh voice.

"Jesterix? That's not a real word Kendra." Angelia laughed, shaking her head in amusement.

"You are the Queen; you could declare it a real word and they will have to put it in the dictionary and on the internet and stuff." Kendra bowed awkwardly again, almost falling over. Angelia grabbed her arm and steadied her.

"You can't bow in a tight skirt and high heels; you're going to fall over and hurt yourself." Angelia chastised her. "And besides, you're a girl, you're supposed to curtsey not bow." Kendra slapped her forehead.

"Oh yeah, I forgot. I'm not a jester I am a jestesteress." She did an awkward curtsey and almost fell over again which sent Angelia into giggles.

"Stop Kendra, you are a jesterix, you can't change it to jestesteress now."

"Yes, my Queen." Kendra started to bow, realised her mistake and tried to change it to a curtsey. She lost her balance and landed on the floor in front of Angelia, which sent them both into fits of laughter.

"That's a welcome sound." Mark smiled as he watched Angelia and Kendra in amusement.

"That is a Lia laugh." Christian chuckled. Ciara wrapped her arms around his waist.

"It's so wonderful hearing her laugh and seeing her smile again, especially after seeing her so heartbroken the other night." She glanced at Mark who nodded.

"I was worried she would go to pieces and start partying like crazy again."

"Yeah, she seems so happy." Kalen watched them, feeling confused.

"That is because she has someone special helping her through all of this." Christian smiled warmly as he watched Angelia help Kendra to her feet and hug her.

"Who is this *mysterious* someone?" Ciara asked playfully.

"That would be me." A voice said behind them. They all turned to look.

"JR." Kalen yelled as he moved to Jarryd and held out his hand. Jarryd smiled, shook his hand and pulled him into a hug. "When did you get here?"

"I arrived yesterday. You know, you get scruffier every time I see you, Kale." He laughed as he let go of him and gave him a playful punch to the shoulder. Kendra spun around to look at Jarryd before turning back to Angelia.

"JR's home?" She asked incredulously. Angelia grinned and nodded. Kendra flew across the yard and threw herself in Jarryd's arms. She wrapped her arms tightly around his waist. Jarryd laughed as he hugged her.

"There's my other little sister." He said, smiling down at her.

"I'm so glad you're home. She really needs you right now." She whispered to him.

"I know, that's why I'm here." He whispered back before moving her to arm's length. "You look so grown up my little Kenz." Angelia watched them with a contented smile on her lips.

"JR's back huh?" She turned to look at Jake and watched the blood drain from his face.

"Yeah, he's back." She gave him a bright smile. He nodded quickly.

"Tell Chris I said great party, but I had to run."

"See ya, Jake." Angelia said sweetly. Jarryd looked up, his eyes narrowed as he watched Jake make a hasty exit.

"He's my brother Jarryd." Kendra implored him.

"That fact, and that fact alone, is the *only* reason why he is still breathing." Jarryd growled as anger flickered in his green eyes. Mark glanced at Kalen who shook his head and gave him a small smile.

"Don't do anything stupid." Kendra pleaded.

"Yeah, he's not worth it." Christian placed a hand on Jarryd's shoulder and handed him a beer. Jarryd nodded and turned his attention to Angelia who had just joined them. Mark took a deep breath, stepped up to Jarryd and extended his hand.

"Hi, we haven't met. I'm Mark. Mark McAllister." Jarryd turned to look at him.

"Oh yeah. Mark. You're Kyle's brother, right?" Jarryd shook Mark's hand. "I've heard a lot about you." He placed his arm around Angelia's shoulders and pulled her against his side. "You talked my sister down from the ledge a few times and you were there when she needed you. I appreciate that.

It couldn't have been easy for you to be stuck in the middle between your brother and my sister." He said with a warm smile.

"It couldn't have been easy for you to be stuck on the other side of the world, knowing your sister is hurting. Thanks for trusting us to look out for her." Mark reached out and rubbed Angelia's arm affectionately. "I told Kyle that Lia is like a sister to me, so I can't choose sides. I'll be there for Kyle *and* I'll be there for Lia. Always."

Jarryd patted Mark on the shoulder and smiled at him.

"JR." They heard a surprised voice seconds before Blaine barrelled into Jarryd, pulling him into a hug. "It's so good to see you, big brother." He mumbled into Jarryd's shoulder.

"There's my baby brother." He laughed as he hugged him back tightly. "I really wish you and Lia would move to London and stay with me." He sighed as he reached out and pulled Angelia into their hug. Blaine smiled and wrapped an arm around her before clearing his throat and laughing.

"Our little beach bunny will die in London. Our winter is hotter than your summer." He grinned at Angelia as she rolled her eyes. "Robbie's here, he's offloading beers into the fridge. Dyl and Ant are with him. They're not going to believe you're here." Blaine said, laughing as he headed back towards the house.

"Should we go sneak up on Robs and surprise him, silly girl?" Jarryd looked down at his sister. She smiled and nodded. Jarryd flashed his friends a quick smile before walking off with his arm around Angelia's shoulders. Kendra, Christian and Ciara followed them while Kalen and Mark stood back watching.

"On a scale of 1 – 10, how relieved should I be that Kyle is in New York right now?" Mark asked quietly. Kalen crossed his arms over his chest.

"I'd say 20 possibly 30. Jarryd was always very protective of Blaine and Lia. When their parents died his protectiveness intensified. They are *literally* all he has left in this world. They have no other family. Their parents had no siblings and their grandparents died many years ago, Blaine has had nothing to do with his biological family for almost eighteen years. They are all the family they have. You have no idea how many times Chris, Dylan, Robbie and I have had to talk JR out of a flight back here. He's young and driven and doing so well at his job, he can't afford to keep running back here, but he would do it in a heartbeat for them."

"So, I should definitely be relieved that Kyle's not here." Mark stated. Kalen smirked.

"Let's put it this way. I would not want to be Jake right now and he only hurt Lia once." Kalen patted Mark on the back and walked down to join the others. Mark's phone buzzed in his pocket. He pulled it out and glanced at the screen. He looked up at everyone before moving further away to answer the call.

"Hey, Kyle."

"Hey, big brother." Kyle replied. "Where are you?"

"I'm at Chris and Ciara's. We're having a little get-together." Mark leaned back against a wall. "Lia's here."

"How is she?" Kyle sounded concerned. "I felt so guilty when I landed. I should have gone to see her or called her or something. I remember how badly she took it when I disappeared from her life before. I was so hurt and angry that I didn't consider how she would react when I disappeared again."

"She's doing great, actually."

"Really?" Kyle asked, feeling hurt.

"Yeah. JR is glued to her side. I think it's helped her a lot."

"Who's JR?"

Mark rolled his eyes at the jealousy creeping into his brother's voice. "Jarryd Ryan. Lia and Blaine's older, and I can't stress this enough to you, very, very protective brother."

"Very, very protective huh?" Kyle asked with a sigh of relief.

"Jake is trying to leave the country."

"That bad? Well, unless Jarryd is planning on travelling to New York, I think I'm safe."

"Yeah."

"What is it? I can hear you frowning over the phone."

"JR arrived the day after you left and Lia is so happy. I'm just worried about what happens when he leaves to go back home."

"She'll be fine Mark, she's stronger than you think and she has a loving, protective brother as well as an amazing group of friends who love her."

"Yeah, you're right." Mark smiled.

"I have to run; I have a lot to get done today."

"Goodbye, little brother." Mark said as Kyle ended the call.

***

Mark closed the dishwasher with a frown.

"How do two people use so many dishes?" He muttered to himself. He looked up as he heard a knock on the door. He looked through the window and groaned quietly. "This can't be good." He mumbled as he took a deep breath and reached for the door. He swung it open with a smile.

"JR, this is a surprise." He said in a friendly voice.

"Yeah, I was in the area and thought I would swing by and say hello. We didn't really have a chance to talk last night." Jarryd greeted him with a warm smile. Mark stepped aside.

"Come on in."

"Thanks, mate." Jarryd followed Mark to the lounge.

"Can I offer you anything? We have fruit juice, coffee, wine and beer."

"I'll have a beer, thanks. I love my sister but all she stocks in her fridge is wine. I don't think I could drink another glass of the stuff." He took a seat on the one-seater couch. Mark chuckled as he pulled two beers out of the fridge and headed back to Jarryd.

"I hear you. I had a girlfriend who told me that only hooligans and criminals drink beer and wine was the only acceptable alcoholic drink. She bought me a bottle of the most disgusting wine I have ever tasted and told me it cost her 200 bucks. I told her they ripped her off." He handed Jarryd one of the beers and sat on the two-seater couch opposite him.

"How did that go down?" Jarryd asked, grinning before taking a sip of his beer.

"Like a concrete parachute. That bottle of wine lasted longer than the relationship." Mark gave him a wry smile. Jarryd chuckled and Mark took a swig of his beer before clearing his throat and looking at his guest. "I highly doubt you came here to discuss my questionable taste in women. What can I do for you, JR?"

"I like you, Mark. I've heard great things about you from Lia, Blaine and my friends. The way I've heard it, you can get through to Lia when the rest of them can't." He sighed and rubbed the side of his head. "You were right last night. It is difficult being so far away from my only family." He paused. "I might be far away, but I hear about everything. I've seen Lia moon over this guy and that guy. I was there for Lia's first love and then I've seen crushes on waiters, barmen, surfers and the cute guy from the coffee shop, but I have never seen Lia love someone like she loves your brother."

"He loves her too," Mark said quietly. "In a way that I have never seen him love anyone."

"You're closer to them than most. What is your take on them?" Jarryd pulled at the label on his beer before looking up at Mark, who sighed.

"I have never seen two people so connected or so in love. They keep doing stupid things and hurting each other. I do think they will find their way back to each other, they've been doing that the last few years. They both need to figure out what they are doing and what they want so they can stop this back-and-forth situation they are currently stuck in. I think my brother going overseas is a good thing, I think they need the space. Both of them being here they keep getting back together without sorting out their problems. Lia came back from her four-month hiatus and they jumped straight back into a relationship without really discussing what happened. I'm hoping that now they have the space and time to do just that with him being in New York." Mark explained.

"Thank you for that. I'm very grateful to your brother." Jarryd chuckled. "I heard that apart from giving Jake the beating he deserved, he also picked Lia up and carried her out of the bar when she was out of control."

"Yeah, it was a sight to see." Mark laughed.

"Thank you for talking to me and giving me a bit of insight. Everyone speaks very highly of your brother, even Lia, as sad and hurt as she is. He sounds like a great guy." He sighed and shook his head. "I understand why Kyle is angry with Lia, she told me the whole story. Hell, I'm angry with her, so I can only imagine how Kyle feels." He sat back and looked at Mark. "I hope that they can work this out. I'm sorry I didn't get to meet him." Jarryd rose to his feet. "I won't take up any more of your time."

"If you don't have any plans, the game is starting in twenty minutes, Blaine and Kalen are on their way with pizza and we have plenty of beer. Why don't you stay and watch with us?" Mark offered.

"Are you sure? I don't want to impose?"

"The more the merrier."

"Thanks, you are a lifesaver. Ciara, Kendra and Lia are having a girls' pamper evening at home, and there are more of them joining. I saw nail polish, home waxing kits and some torturous-looking devices. I have a sneaking suspicion that I heard wax, hairy legs and Jarryd in one sentence, followed by a lot of evil cackling. I grabbed my keys, shouted bye and ran for my life." Jarryd explained as Mark chuckled.

"Yeah, I think you'll be safer here."

"Pizzas arrived." Kalen shouted from the door. "I brought extra pizza and beer because I picked up a stray." He walked into the lounge with Blaine and Christian trailing behind him. "JR" He exclaimed in surprise. "What are you doing here?"

"I picked up a stray too." Mark laughed as he rescued the pizza boxes from Kalen.

"I'm hiding from the women in our lives. I think they have sadistic intentions with their wax kits and nail polish." Jarryd said, shaking his head.

"Hey, remember that time when Lia was thirteen or fourteen and she decided that she was going to be a beautician and she wanted to practice on someone." Blaine dropped down on the chair opposite his brother and grinned at him as he groaned.

"She put green and silver eyeshadow all over my eyes, hooker red lipstick on my lips, mascara on my eyelashes, painted my nails hot pink and told me I looked pretty. The things I did to keep our sister happy." He said, looking at Blaine and shaking his head.

"Oh, please tell me Mom took photos."

"Not a chance, and if she did, you would never see them. No one would." Jarryd said laughing. "However, I'm pretty sure there is a picture or two of you that time that Lia decided she wanted to be a hairdresser, and she put Mom's curlers in your hair and cut you a fringe."

"Oh, shit yeah. I forgot about that. Those photos have been locked away. Do you remember when she peroxided our hair and we had platinum blonde-looking hair for ages?"

"Oh yeah." Jarryd groaned. "I think mine eventually went orange or some terrible colour."

"I thought Mom was going to kill Lia." Blaine chuckled. He shook his head and looked at Mark. "So, we lied to her and told her that we did it ourselves as a dare so that Lia wouldn't get into trouble."

"We were grounded for two weeks because of that."

"Poor Lia felt so bad that she stayed home with us the whole time."

"Didn't she try and cook for you guys as well?" Christian asked laughing.

"Lia and cooking." Blaine groaned. "That girl is a menace in the kitchen."

"Oh, she's a disaster." Jarryd chuckled.

"Anyone home?" They heard a voice call out.

"Hey, Rob, we're in the lounge. Grab a beer and come join us." Mark shouted to him.

"Hey. I'm so glad we found you guys." He looked at Jarryd. "Dyl and I swung by your place to drop Megs, Case and Kel off and the girls were trying to convince us to wax our underarms, so we ran as fast as we could. We tried Chris's place first, but no one was there so we thought we'd come hide out here." He laughed as he dropped down onto the floor and took a quick swig of his beer. "What are we talking about?" He asked as Dylan sat down next to him.

"Lia's cooking." Jarryd laughed.

"Oh no. Lia should be banned from *all* kitchens." Robbie chuckled.

"She can't be *that* bad." Mark looked at his friends. Robbie shook his head as he glanced at his brother.

"I moved in with them for about a year while our parents were getting divorced and Lia who was, what, about fourteen or fifteen at the time, tried to cheer me up by baking a cake, in the oven in a plastic container. There was just cake batter and melted plastic everywhere. Took us two hours to clean that up before Mrs. Ryan came home. We never told her what happened to her favourite container."

"Nothing can beat the time that Lia burnt her instant noodles." Christian laughed. "We had to throw that pot out; it was not salvageable." He shook his head.

"Yeah, Mom hunted for that pot for months." Jarryd laughed. "I think she had her suspicions about what happened to it but none of us had the heart to get Lia into trouble."

"The only thing worse than Lia's cooking is her driving." Blaine added as Jarryd groaned.

"She doesn't drive, she flies." He looked over at his brother. "Dad aged ten years in one car trip with Lia. I swear he had at least five hundred new grey hairs after their short trip to the mall."

"Never mind that, he refused to teach her to drive after two lessons, so he organised a driving school and they refunded Dad after one lesson and said she was unteachable, so did the next two schools after that." Blaine laughed.

"You're exaggerating, she seriously couldn't have been that bad?"

"Oh yeah. She was so upset after the third school dropped her that she refused point-blank to drive. So, one day we kidnapped her and took her down to an empty parking lot to try to teach her ourselves." Robbie smiled at the memory.

"There was one pole in the entire parking lot and Lia somehow managed to hit it and leave this huge dent in Mom's car." Blaine laughed as Jarryd shook his head.

"So, we drove the car back, parked it in the garage and swore each other to secrecy." Jarryd added chuckling. "Blaine, Robs and I were interrogated mercilessly by Dad, but we stuck to our story that we had no idea where that dent came from and it was already there when we got home."

"They eventually gave up and decided that it must have been hit while they were out at the shops, and they didn't notice." Blaine added. They all looked up when they heard someone clear their throat from the doorway.

"Lia," Jarryd said in surprise. She was leaning against the wall with her arms folded over her chest. She straightened up and glanced around at them as tears brimmed in her eyes. She brushed them away quickly with her fingers and looked back at them. "How long have you been standing there?"

"Long enough." She sniffed quietly. "I don't think any of you have an idea of how much I love you. I had such an incredible life growing up because I had the most amazing brothers and friends. There was not one day where I didn't feel protected, loved and wanted. And all the stupid things I did, you never made fun of me or made me feel bad.
"I don't know how I got so lucky, but I am beyond grateful for each one of

you. And standing here listening to all these memories just reminded me of how amazing each one of you are and that even when we were kids, your first instinct was always to protect me and shield me. When I made a mess of things someone always jumped in to help me clean it up and fix it as much as possible.

"Nothing's changed. Now, when I make a mess of things, you all fix what you can and stand by me when I honestly don't deserve it. There are not enough words to explain to you how much each of you means to me and I can say thank you a million times and it still won't be enough. I was standing here listening and trying to imagine my life without even one of you." She sniffed as tears rolled down her cheeks "and that thought just broke my heart so I want to say how sorry I am that I disappeared on you and made you worry about me for those four months because I realise now how hard that must have been. It was a selfish and stupid thing to do, and I will never do anything like that again." She wiped the tears off her cheeks. Robbie shot to his feet and pulled her into a hug.

"We know how much you love us." He said softly. "That's why we're always here for you, silly girl." She smiled up at him and nodded. Kalen patted the seat next to him.

"Come watch the game with us, Lia." He smiled at her.

"I brought some friends with me." She explained looking over her shoulder as the girls came walking in. "We thought we'd watch the game with you." She smiled as the guys all shifted around to make space. She caught Jarryd's eyes as he smiled warmly at her before looking up in surprise as Casey sat down between him and the arm of the couch.

"Hi again JR." She gave him a flirty smile.

"Hi again. Casey." He leaned over and kissed her cheek as Angelia rolled her eyes. Mark moved over and patted the space between him and Blaine. Angelia settled in between them, Blaine reached over and squeezed her hand before turning back to the game. Mark put his arm around her shoulders and smiled at her.

"I'm sorry." She leaned over to whisper to him.

"Sorry for what?"

"I'm the reason Kyle left." She said sadly. "Now your brother is far away from you and it's all my fault."

"His decision had nothing to do with you, Lia. No one is blaming you. *You* shouldn't blame yourself."

"We can make our own memories." She whispered. He looked at her in surprise. "I saw you when they were all sharing memories of the silly things I did and you looked sad. So, I think we should make our own memories." She smiled at him. "Will you teach me how to cook?" Blaine leaned over.

"Only say yes if you are happy to renovate the kitchen." He sniggered. She punched him in the shoulder.

"Don't be an ass." She glared at him. Mark pressed his lips together to stop himself from laughing.

"Maybe we should start with something a little less dangerous."

"Ice skating." She whispered, grinning evilly at him.

"Cooking lessons start at 8 am."

"I want to go ice skating." Megan piped up. "That sounds like so much fun."

"Anything but ice skating." Mark pleaded.

"How did you hear that?" Angelia looked at Megan in surprise.

"Yeah, Lia, you don't whisper as quietly as you think you do. We heard a whole lot from you and Kyle over the years that we could have done without hearing." She said smirking over her shoulder at her friend as Angelia blushed. Jarryd glanced over at her as he wrapped his arm around Casey and pulled her closer to him.

"Do I want to know?" He asked, sighing heavily.

"No, you don't." Christian shook his head. "You really don't." he added chuckling.

"Yeah, the whipped cream business is taking a bit of a hit at the moment." Robbie shot a smug smile at her over his shoulder as Kelly giggled and Christian groaned.

"Shut up and watch the game, Robs." Angelia fought a smile.

"Do I want to know the story about the whipped cream?" Jarryd asked, sighing again.

"No." Christian and Blaine answered together.

"Oh, Lia." Jarryd said, shaking his head.

"Hey, Case." Angelia smiled as she glanced at her. "There's a can of whipped cream in my fridge at home. I'm not going to be using it and I'm assuming you're staying over again tonight." She shrugged and bit her lip as Casey shot her a quick look and burst into laughter.

"Ok, someone is going to have to explain the whipped cream thing to me." Jarryd grumbled.

"I'll show you later," Casey said smiling as she kept her eyes on the television screen and snuggled up to Jarryd.

Chapter 7

"Today was just what I needed." Jarryd sighed contentedly as Casey handed him a beer and sat on his lap.

"Beach, burgers, a dip in the pool and the best company." Kalen smiled as he lay back in his lounger.

"It was a perfect day today." Angelia agreed as she dropped down in the chair next to Mark, who put his arm around her shoulders.

"Oh yeah." Jarryd pointed a finger at her. "Casey explained the whole whipped cream thing to me last night. You are *never* buying whipped cream again young lady." He said sternly. Casey turned to look at him.

"Ahhhh." She said in a disappointed tone. He looked up at her.

"I said *she* couldn't, I didn't say *we* couldn't babe." She grinned and leaned over to kiss him.

"Oh yeah, I heard Casey explain it to you a few times last night." Angelia smirked at her brother. He raised an eyebrow at her. "The bedrooms have thin walls." She said rolling her eyes.

"Ohhhhh." Casey said blushing.

"Yeah, I heard something similar to that a few times last night too." She turned to Mark. "I'm sleeping here tonight." Mark chuckled and shook his head.

"Why do the Ryan siblings feel the need to overshare?" He asked looking at Jarryd with a smirk. Jarryd wrapped his arms around Casey.

"Well since you're going to be staying here tonight, I think I'll let Casey explain the whipped cream thing again later." Jarryd grinned at his sister. "Feel like going for a swim babe?" He asked Casey as he kissed her neck. She smiled and nodded.

"No sex in the pool." Angelia gave her brother a stern look. He turned and pulled a tongue at her as they made their way into the water.

"Hey, that's my line." Mark protested.

"Ok, you tell them then." She gave him a smug smile as she inclined her head towards the couple in the pool.

"Yeah, I'm good." Mark leaned back in his chair. He glanced over at Angelia. "Should we cook dinner tonight hon?"

"Oh hell. Someone alert the fire station that they need to be on standby tonight." Robbie grinned at her as he lazily tickled Kelly's back.

"Bite me." She pulled a tongue at him.

"Don't listen to him Lia." Kelly smiled sweetly. "They'll never get here in time; we'll just organise a few extra fire extinguishers."

"Bitch." Angelia sniped at her. Kelly giggled and sat up.

"I would love to taste Mark's cooking though. He's always bragging about how he taught Kyle to cook and yet he has never cooked for us. I'm starting to doubt that he has the skills." She squinted her eyes at him.

"Oh, I have the skills missy," Mark said squinting back at her.

"Prove it."

"Alright." Mark stood up. "I'll need to go get some stuff from the shops though."

"Lia." Jarryd called out from the pool. "Go with please and take my card with you."

"That's not necessary." Mark protested.

"Why is she bad at shopping too?" Jarryd asked with a smirk.

"Now that she's good at. I meant it's not necessary for her to come with or for you to pay."

"I insist on both counts." Jarryd said heading for the pool steps. Casey wrapped her arms around his shoulders and pulled him back.

"I want to go." Angelia reached for her brother's wallet and took his card out. "We'll be back now."

"Hey, silly girl," Jarryd called her as he pulled Casey in front of him. "Won't you grab some beers and ciders as well please, and some wine or some of those disgusting vodka things you drink." She smiled and nodded as she followed Mark to the door.

"What can I help with?" Angelia asked Mark as he spread all the ingredients out on the counter.

"I would love a beer thanks, and you can bring me the cheese and the cream while you're there." He replied giving her a quick smile.

"Anything I can do to help?" Jarryd asked as he walked into the kitchen. "I feel bad that you're cooking for the hooligans and everyone is just chilling outside." He took the beer his sister handed to him. "I'm not the best cook but I have managed to not poison myself over the years." He chuckled.

"A Ryan family member who actually cooks." Mark shot him a quick smile. "Making food for nearly a dozen people is not easy so I won't say no to the help." He added gratefully. "I should have just gone for one of Kyle's simple pasta dishes." Jarryd chuckled and stepped next to him at the counter.

"Put me to work chef." Angelia leaned against the doorway and smiled contentedly as she watched Mark and Jarryd laughing and chatting as they chopped vegetables and prepared the chicken pieces. She felt a pair of arms circle her shoulders and she smiled as she reached her hands up to squeeze them gently and look up into Blaine's grey eyes. He smiled and kissed the top of her head.

"It's good to have him home." He said quietly. Angelia nodded and leaned her head back against his chest. "Kate phoned me today." Her eyebrows shot up and she turned to look at him.

"What did that bitch have to say?" Angelia asked, anger echoing through her voice.

"Rick broke his leg and can't work so she wants me to help out with money and to help her around the house since he can't do anything."

"I hope you told her to fuck right off." Jarryd looked up at him. Blaine nodded.

"I told her she chose Rick over me years ago and she needs to live with that choice. She told me that I'm her son and that we're family and I should be there to help family." He shook his head and looked at Jarryd and then Angelia. "I told her that the only family I ever had was the Ryan family and then I told her not to call me ever again. I used slightly more colourful language, but that was the general gist of it." Angelia wrapped her arms around his waist and felt their brother wrap his arms around both of them a few seconds later.

"I'm proud of you." Jarryd whispered. "Both of you. We'll *always* be a family." Mark looked up at the three hugging in the doorway. Christian walked in, glanced at them and reached into the fridge to grab a few beers.

"You're not going to ask?"

Christian shook his head. "This is normal. Been this way since we were kids. The most affectionate siblings you will ever meet. Big brother, little brother and baby sister." He smiled as they all turned to look at him. "Lia, Blaine. Rob and I are looking for two more to play pool." He shrugged his shoulders.

"Only if I can be on Lia's team." Blaine grinned. Christian rolled his eyes.

"Fine." Blaine high-fived Angelia as they followed Christian out the door. Jarryd joined Mark at the counter again and went back to chopping vegetables.

"I envy you." Mark said quietly. Jarryd glanced at him quickly.

"Yeah? Why?"

"You have this incredible family who respects you, two siblings who look up to you and from what I've heard, you had amazing parents." He said softly. Jarryd nodded.

"Losing my parents was hard. I was only twenty-one and apart from dealing with their deaths, I became an instant parent to two teenagers who were lost. One who blamed herself for what happened and the other one who lost his family for a second time." He shook his head.

"I love them both and there is nothing I won't do to protect them. Same with Chris, Robs, Dyl, Kenz and Kale. It's difficult being so far away but I know that this family protect and help each other." Jarryd stopped chopping to look at him. "Don't think for one moment that this family doesn't love and respect you, Mark. They need you. You are as much a part of this family as I am. Those two, listen to you more than you realise. You're the reason Lia stopped self-destructing, and Blaine has so much respect and love for you. I hear it in the way he talks about you. He met you and Kyle a few months after we lost our parents and Lia left to come out to me. He was lost and he met you and your brother and he was so happy that he fit right in with you guys. I am truly grateful that he has you in his life."

"They, uh, they both mean the world to me." Mark said smiling. "I must ask you something though. I asked Kendra a while back and she couldn't really give me an answer. I'm curious about something I've heard asked between certain people in our group." Mark shot him a quick look. Jarryd frowned as he scooped the chopped vegetables into a tray.

"Yeah? What would that be?" He asked leaning back against the counter with his arms folded across his chest.

"It's um 'Do you know how much I love you?' I've heard it asked between Chris, Kale, Lia and Blaine. Kendra said it's almost like some sort of code between you guys. Look, if you say it's none of my business, I am fine with that, it's always puzzled me so I had to ask." He looked at Jarryd as he smiled.

"Yeah, um…" Jarryd trailed off as he scratched his jaw. "Kendra's not entirely wrong, I suppose it is kind of a code. When we were kids, if Lia was upset or if she fell off her bike or hurt herself, I would hug her and ask, 'Do you know how much I love you?' to get her to stop crying. She would always answer, 'As much as I love you' and she would stop crying. When Chris, Kale and I became friends, they would do the same thing because, well, you know how much they love Lia. When Kale became friends with

Blaine, he didn't have a good home life and Lia would somehow sense when he was upset, and she would hug him and ask him and he would look at her and smile and nod. That's kind of how we figured out that something was happening with Blaine. From there it just sort of became our way of expressing ourselves or letting one of us know if we were sad, emotional, upset or overwhelmed. In Lia's case its sometimes after too many tequilas or when she feels happy or content. I can't really explain it, um, it's like our way of reaching out to each other. The majority of the time the response is 'As much as I love you' or 'I know' which generally makes the other person feel better or know that they've been heard. Sometimes it's just a smile or a nod. I think it's just kind of become a habit for us, almost like a reflex." He shrugged.

"Thanks, it makes a lot more sense now." Mark opened the oven and slid the two trays inside.

"There you are." Casey slipped her arms around Jarryd. He wrapped his arm around her and looked at Mark.

"Should we join the hooligans?" Mark nodded as he grabbed his beer.

"The food needs to cook for about an hour so now it's time to relax." He laughed as he followed Jarryd and Casey outside.

"I bow to the master." Kelly announced as she pushed her empty plate back. "That was the best meal I have ever had." She grinned at Mark.

"Hey, I cooked for you last night." Robbie protested.

"I stand by my statement."

"You're sleeping on the couch tonight, woman." He grumbled sulkily.

"Oh, please." She laughed. "All I have to do is smile and flutter my eyelashes and you'll forget why you're mad at me."

"Not tonight."

"I love you." She said smiling at him sweetly as she ran her fingers down his arm.

"I'm sleeping in the car." He stated, looking away from her as everyone chuckled.

"That was by far the best meal I have had in a very, very long time. Thank you, chef." Jarryd said smiling at Mark.

"You are cooking for us more often." Robbie laughed. "You made a mistake accepting Kel's challenge, we're onto you now."

Mark sat back and looked at them thoughtfully.

"So, let's do this every Sunday then. Family dinner to end the weekend with us all together, I mean you guys are here every Sunday anyway." He shrugged.

"I like that." Angelia said quietly.

"Me too," Blaine said as he flicked Angelia's ponytail. She scowled at him before punching his arm.

"I am definitely in." Megan laughed.

"We can all take turns to help Mark." Kelly suggested.

"Except Lia." Kalen added.

"I'm starting to understand how Kyle felt every time you guys mocked him about playing pool." She protested.

"Kyle sucks at pool?" Jarryd asked, raising an eyebrow.

"He did suck but your sneaky little sister taught him how to play like a pro and blindsided Kalen and me in a game one night at Connell's." Kendra explained, pointing a finger at Angelia.

"The look on your faces was so worth all the swearing I had to swallow teaching that man to play pool."

"I'm sure he thanked you plenty for it. Especially that night." Kalen wiggled his eyebrows suggestively at her.

"Get your mind out of the gutter. He thanked me by taking me out to dinner." She said haughtily.

"Uh-huh. How many cans of whipped cream did he have to buy after that dinner?" Robbie laughed.

"Robs." Jarryd shook his head at him. "I don't want to think about that."

"I'd still like to know the story about the wet bath towel in the kitchen?" Mark looked at her.

"What makes you think I was involved?" She asked innocently.

"Because my brother was looking for you and couldn't or rather *wouldn't* explain how the towel got there."

"I have no idea." She protested.

"Liar." Megan laughed. "You're blushing."

"I am not." Angelia buried her head in Blaine's shoulder.

"You know what story I want to hear?" Kendra asked. "The night you met Kyle, I heard you let him lick salt off your wrist." She looked at her friend and raised an eyebrow.

"Lies." Angelia denied it while shaking her head.

"No, that's not a lie." Robbie pointed a finger at her. "Kyle couldn't stop bragging. He called me that night to tell me all about it."

"Angelia." Christian gave her a shocked look.

"You are shocked about Kyle licking salt off her wrist when you know for a fact that he has licked whipped cream off other parts of her body." Kendra laughed. Christian turned to look at Jarryd who was pretending to examine the back of Casey's shirt.

"Aren't you going to say something to her JR?"

"Uhhh." Jarryd looked over at his sister.

"Where do you think I learned that from?" She asked smugly.

"You were not supposed to copy what my friends and I did that night." He gave her a stern look as she returned it with a smug one.

"You're supposed to lead by example, big brother." She laughed. "Do as I say, don't do as I do." He instructed.

"Double standards much?"

"You want to go for a swim young lady?" He asked sternly.

"Blaine will protect me, won't you?" She asked sweetly.

"Let's see. Protect my little sister from our big brother? Hells no, I do not want to end up in the pool with you. You're on your own little sister."

"Betrayed by my own brother." Angelia shook her head. "I am so hurt." She looked up at Jarryd. "Should I tell them about the rest of that night, big brother?"

"Angelia Ryan." He gave her a warning look. "You keep quiet."

"Or you'll what?" She challenged him as Blaine groaned.

"Now you're in trouble Lia." He chuckled as Jarryd moved Casey off his legs and stood up. Angelia shot to her feet and leaned on the table.

"You're going in the pool Lia." He said with an evil smile.

"Yeah? You have to catch me first, old man."

"Oh, you are going to regret that." He smirked. She arched an eyebrow and returned his smirk. She turned to bolt to the door but stopped short as Blaine caught her around her waist and held her back. Jarryd picked her up and threw her over his shoulder before dropping her into the deep end of the pool.

"That was not fair. Blaine helped you." She protested as she swam to the steps. Dylan chuckled as he reached out a hand to pull her up and hand her a towel.

"You know better than to challenge your brother, silly girl." He said as he made his way back to his chair. Angelia scowled at Blaine as she walked past him to go inside.

"She's going to make you pay for that little brother." Jarryd smiled at him. Blaine shook his head.

"She'll forgive me, she always does." He replied confidently.

"So, are we doing dinner at Connell's on Tuesday fam?" Jarryd asked as he put his arm around Casey and looked at his friends.

"That sounds like a definite plan." Christian leaned back and stretched.

"And maybe Vipers for drinks and pool later." Robbie added. "We're working shift on Tuesday but will definitely have a few drinks throughout the night and join you if you go to Vipers." He looked up as Angelia walked out wearing a pair of Blaine's shorts and one of his shirts. She sat down and looked at her friends.

"We're going to do Connell's for dinner and Vipers for drinks on Tuesday." Blaine explained as he put his arm around her shoulders.

"I'm in." She smiled as she rested her head on his shoulder. He kissed the top of her head quickly and smiled at Jarryd who chuckled and rolled his eyes.

"You won't believe who I ran into this morning." Kalen said as he leaned back to look at his brother. "Remember my high school girlfriend, Cathy?" He asked as he looked at his brother who nodded.

"Yeah, I do. Is she back from Greece now?"

"No, she just came back to visit her family. It was her mom's birthday so she made the trip out."

"Wasn't she the first girl you had sex with?" Jarryd asked arching an eyebrow.

"Yeah, she was. It was so weird seeing her again." He chuckled wryly

"I wouldn't like to run into my first anytime soon. She got super clingy and started planning our wedding, I was *not* getting married at seventeen." Dylan sighed as he sat back and shook his head.

"Oh yeah, she was a little bit crazy that one." Robbie chuckled.

"Oh, like your first girl was a prize." Dylan sniped at him.

"Yeah, Mel was a little bitchy." Robbie sighed.

"That's the understatement of the year." Jarryd laughed.

"Is this really what we're going to discuss tonight?" Christian sighed shaking his head.

"It's ok Chris, we all knew you were a virgin before you met Ciara." Robbie said straight-faced.

"Bite me." Christian glared at him.

"No, no, no, Robs. Ciara was his second. His right hand was his first." Jarryd laughed as he ducked Christian's fist.

"You two are just jealous because Chris stole two of your girls right from under your noses." Angelia defended Christian.

"No way." Megan arched an eyebrow.

"What can I say? The ladies find me charming." Christian smiled smugly. "I mean they used to." He amended quickly as he heard Ciara clear her throat.

"Wait, so who was Chris's first then?" Casey frowned.

"The girl he stole from me." Jarryd scowled. "Molly? Mindy?"

"Mandy." Robbie and Christian answered together.

"Right, Mandy."

"We all know far too much about each other's love lives and sex lives." Kalen chuckled.

"Except Lia's." Kendra said looking at her friend.

"We know more about Lia's sex life than we want to." Christian protested.

"Yeah, her sex life with Kyle. You've never once told me who your first was. We're supposed to be best friends." Kendra pouted as she raised her eyebrows.

"It's no one's business." Angelia said shrugging her shoulders.

"You know who my first was," Kendra stated as she sat back and crossed her arms. "What's the big secret Lia?"

"A girl's first time is personal and private. I never asked you about your first time, you chose to tell me. I'm choosing not to tell anyone." She said tensely.

"Was he that bad?"

"No! He was incredible and loving and amazing and choosing him was the best decision I ever made but it is a highly personal event and I don't want to discuss it." Angelia replied in an edgy tone as she felt her brother tighten his arm around her shoulders and pull her closer to him.

"Leave her alone Kendra." Robbie snapped at her. "If Lia doesn't want to talk about it, she doesn't have to." He glared at her as she looked at him in surprise.

"It's Lia's choice to discuss it, Kendra." Jarryd gave her a look. "You know how private she is over personal matters."

"I agree, drop the subject and the attitude. You're upsetting Lia over something that has nothing to do with you." Blaine said irritably.

"I just don't get why it's such a big secret." Kendra shook her head. "We all know about each other's first times and who it was with. Why are you so dead set on keeping it a secret?" She frowned at Angelia.

"Seriously, Kendra. Why are you pushing the issue? It's none of your business." Dylan glared at her as he reached over to take Angelia's hand, she flashed him a quick smile as she squeezed his hand gently. Kendra's eyes flicked from Dylan to Robbie to Blaine and then Jarryd.

"I expected the Ryan brothers to jump to Lia's defense and *maybe* the Carter brothers but not the Harris brothers." She looked at Angelia. "It's someone here, isn't it? Your first time was with someone in our group. Is that why it's such a big secret?"

"Kendra." Robbie gave her a warning look as she turned back to him.

"It's either you or Dylan. I know it's not Chris or Kalen and definitely not Jake or Anthony." Her eyes flicked to Blaine. "Or you?" She asked as Blaine clenched his jaw and glared at her. "You're not siblings by blood, so you're not related. It would have to be someone she loves and trusts and someone who respects and loves her enough to keep her secret." She mused as she glanced at Dylan who glared at her as he shook his head.

"Just stop." Angelia snapped at her.

"Let it go Kendra." Jarryd said tersely as he looked over at her and shook his head.

"You know who it is, don't you?"

"Kendra." He snarled at her. "This discussion is over. I mean it." He added as she opened her mouth. She huffed and sat back before shaking her head.

"Fine. I'm sorry Lia. I didn't mean to upset you." Kendra sighed. "I just don't understand why it's such a big secret. I won't bring it up again." She shook her head as she got up and made her way inside the house.

"Thank you." Angelia said quietly as she smiled at Blaine. He smiled back at her and kissed the side of her head.

"I'll always protect you sweet girl." He said softly. She nodded as she looked up into Robbie's eyes as he smiled at her. She smiled back and mouthed 'love you' to him as he nodded and mouthed 'Love you' back to her as she squeezed Dylan's hand again before turning to flash him a shy smile. He squeezed her hand gently before letting go.

"So, are we going to call it a night or is everyone still happy to stay for a while?" Jarryd asked as he gave his sister a warm smile.

"I'm not ready to go home yet." Robbie admitted looking around.

"Me neither." Megan said, leaning back in her chair.

"Why don't we move inside and watch a movie?" Mark suggested.

"I could definitely do that." Jarryd said smiling as he stood. "Everyone cleans up. Now." He ordered pointing to the table.

"That's not necessary." Mark protested.

"You cooked for the hooligans, they can clean up to say thanks." Jarryd picked up a stack of plates. Mark smiled as he watched his friends laugh and chat as they cleared the table and moved inside.

CHAPTER 8

"I can't believe how quickly these three weeks have gone." Angelia gave Blaine a sad smile.

"I know I can't believe JR goes back home tomorrow. It feels like he just got here." He groaned as he stretched. "Though my back will be grateful to sleep in my bed and not on your couch."

"It was nice having you stay with us." She said as she hugged him.

"Yeah, it kind of felt like old times."

"I already miss him," Angelia said softly as a tear trickled down her cheek.

"Me too." Blaine gave her a sad smile.

"You guys ready to go to the movies?" Jarryd asked as he shrugged into a collared shirt. "What's this?" He asked as he looked at the sad faces in front of him. Angelia smiled as she wiped her cheek.

"We're just saying how much we're going to miss you." Blaine said quietly. He pulled them both into a hug.

"I wish you two would come with me, I want my family with me. I miss you two every day. Promise me that you'll think about it." They both nodded. "No more tears Lia." He said sternly. "Today is a happy day. Ok?" She laughed and nodded. "That's better." He said as he brushed her hair back.

Jarryd pulled into a parking space at Connell's and climbed out. He looked up as Christian and Robbie pulled up in their cars and all their friends climbed out. He looked across the roof of his sister's car as his siblings climbed out and looked at him.

"So, movies are done and dusted, let's have dinner, a few drinks and maybe head to Vipers to play some pool later." He grinned at them. "I still want Chris and I to play against the two of you."

"I don't know if your ego will be able to handle the loss." Angelia gave him a smug look.

"Is that right, silly girl?"

"Yeah." Blaine agreed. "We're the Dream Team." He smirked as Angelia nodded.

"More like the Dreaming Team." Jarryd laughed as he put an arm around each of them.

"Wait, I have to take a picture of the three of you." Ciara exclaimed as she pulled out her phone. Jarryd smiled and pulled Blaine and Angelia closer to him. "That's perfect." She smiled as she looked at the photo.

"Why don't you get Lia to stand between them. You know, the quintessential rose amongst the thorns picture."

"Did you just call me a thorn, Mark?" Jarryd raised an eyebrow at him. Mark shrugged and smiled innocently at him. Angelia laughed and stepped in between her two brothers, wrapping an arm around each of their waists. Jarryd reached up to put his hand on Blaine's shoulder as Blaine put his arm across Angelia, resting his hand on Jarryd's back.

"Smile." They smiled at her as she took the picture. She looked at her phone. "I'll send you all the pictures." She promised as they started walking towards the pub.

"Blaine Matthews." They heard an angry voice shout. They all turned around to see Delta Matthews storming up to Blaine. "How dare you tell Mom that you won't help her and that you are not a part of our family." She shouted at him. Blaine opened his mouth to answer as Jarryd stepped forward to glare at her.

"He *isn't* a part of your family, Delta, he hasn't been for a very long time. He is *my* family, *my* brother so why don't you do us all a favour and go slither back under whatever rock it is you slithered out from." He snarled at her.

"Why don't you fuck off back to London, Jarryd and mind your own damn business." She snarled back at him.

"He is my business, no matter where I am. Back the hell off and tell your mother that she is *never* to contact my brother again."

"He's not your brother; he's not even related to you!"

"Family is not defined by blood." He took a step closer to her. Blaine reached out to grab his arm and hold him back.

"Jarryd's right." Blaine said to her. "Kate is *your* mother and it's *your* family Delta, not mine. *This* is my family. Stay away from me, stay away from us." He glared at her. She stepped forward and raised her hand to slap him. Jarryd tried to reach for her hand as Angelia stepped in front of Blaine and shoved Delta backwards. She stumbled and fell before getting back to her feet and glaring at Angelia.

"Try it again Delta." Angelia said in an icy voice. "Try to raise a hand to either of my brothers again and I swear it will be the last thing you ever do." She clenched her jaw as she stared her down. Delta glared at her for a few moments before looking at Blaine and shaking her head. She turned and stormed off as Angelia exhaled angrily and turned back to her friends. Jarryd smirked at her.

"What was that silly girl?" He asked with a laugh.

"No one hurts my family." She said as she walked up to them and put her arms around them burying her face in Jarryd's chest. Blaine chuckled quietly as he rubbed her back.

"Do you know how much I love you, sweet girl?" He asked as she looked up at him and smiled.

"We should sign Lia up for ladies boxing classes. I think she could have taken Delta on and kicked the living crap out of her." Robbie laughed.

"You ok, Blaine?" Jarryd asked his brother quietly.

"Yeah, it felt good to stand up to her." He grinned. Jarryd laughed and gave him a quick hug.

"So, uh, Connell's fam?" He asked, pointing to the pub.

"Yes, I need a tequila or three after that." Angelia laughed as she started to the walkway.

"With salt or without?" Robbie flashed her a quick grin as he slipped his arm around her waist and kissed her cheek.

"Shut up." She laughed as she kissed his cheek and smiled at him.

Mark shook his head and looked at Jarryd.

"I never knew Blaine's family was so toxic." He said quietly.

"Yeah, nasty pieces of work, the whole fucking lot of them." Jarryd shook his head as he watched Blaine, Christian, Ciara, Dylan and Kalen follow Robbie and Angelia into the pub. "I don't know exactly what happened the day Blaine came to live with us. They don't talk about it, but I'll never forget the look on my sister's face, the trauma in her eyes was haunting. She came walking into the house with Blaine's hand in hers, holding on like she would never let him go. My brother was wearing a vest and his shoulders and upper arms were covered in red marks and welts."

"Poor Blaine." Mark sighed heavily.

"Yeah. I listened to what Lia had to say and managed to pry Blaine away from her to take him to our parents. They took him into their room, away from Lia and me while they checked him out. It was bad, Mark. My mother walked out sobbing and my dad had tears in his eyes. They got the authorities involved and secured custody of Blaine. My dad went with him to fetch his stuff, what little he had and brought him home. I'll never forget walking through to find my dad sitting on the couch holding my brother in his arms while he cried. I had never seen my dad cry before. From bits of whispered conversations, I gathered that Blaine was starved for days on end as punishment and I only then realised how ridiculously thin he was. I swore from that day on no one would ever hurt or lay a hand on Blaine again, I would protect him with everything I had, especially against Kate, Rick and Delta. My parents never asked if we wanted Blaine to stay, it was pretty obvious he wasn't going anywhere." He chuckled and shook his head.

"He was lucky you were able to get him out of there and keep him in your family."

"Oh, luck had nothing to do with it. Dad was a lawyer. Kate had a huge legal battle ahead of her if she wanted Blaine back. To be a spiteful bitch, she did try. My dad hit back threatening her with criminal and civil charges of abuse and neglect, anything to keep Blaine away from her. After almost a year she finally gave up, but I will always remember how she turned to this terrified eight-year-old little boy and told him he wasn't worth the trouble, that he wasn't worth anything. My parents were livid, Lia even more so. Our little seven-year-old spitfire turned to Kate and oh-so-calmly told her to fuck off. My parents were torn between being proud and being pissed. They chose to be proud that time." Jarryd gave Mark a wry grin.

"Only Lia." Mark chuckled as he shook his head.

"It was good to see Blaine stand up to that toxic little bitch for a change. Normally, he just walks away."

"It's your influence." Mark smiled. "Those two are going to be so lost when you go back tomorrow."

"No, they will be sad but not lost. I've already had a few tears and upset faces this morning." He smiled at Mark. "But they will be ok because they have you, Robs and Chris and the rest of the hooligans. I hate leaving them and I wish like hell that they would come with me. I know they will one day. If Lia leaves, Blaine will follow and if Blaine leaves, Lia will follow. Neither will stay here without the other one. It sucks that I have to go back, but I don't have a choice." He sighed. "I am going to make an effort to visit more often though."

"Well, I will look after them until then."

"I know you will." Jarryd smiled warmly at Mark and patted his shoulder as they headed into the pub. "There's my sexy lady." Jarryd wrapped his arms around Casey. She turned around to kiss him. "You going to bring us a round of drinks, babe?" He asked. She nodded and gave him a sad smile. "What's wrong?" He asked giving her a look as he let go of her.

"I can't believe you're going tomorrow." She said tearfully.

"I know. I was thinking about that."

"What were you thinking?" She laughed.

"I was thinking that you look like you could do with a holiday. Maybe a month or two long. In London." He raised an eyebrow at her.

"I could do with a holiday." She grinned at him.

"So, you let me know when and I will buy you a ticket so you can bring your sexy ass to London, and I can show you around my town."

"Are you being serious?"

"Deadly." He grinned as she kissed him. "I'm still waiting for those drinks though babe." He said laughing. She punched his arm and walked off to the bar. Angelia looked at him and smirked.

"What?"

"You are so into her."

"Yeah, kinda." He sighed. "Fine, yes, I'm crazy about her."

"I love seeing you happy." She admitted as she hugged him.

"I wish you were happy Lia." He sighed heavily.

"I will be." She looked up at him. "Kyle and I, our love story, it's not over. I don't care how long it takes or how many times we have to start over, we will get it right one day. A love like ours, is strong and it's once in a lifetime and I'm not ready to give up on him. Even though he's mad at me right now, I know he loves me and I know he'll come back to me one day. When he's ready." Jarryd put his hands over her cheeks.

"I am so proud of you. I watched you go from being a little girl who innocently caused destruction and chaos wherever she went to this beautiful, compassionate, loving and fiercely protective young woman. I love you more than you know." He looked up as Blaine walked up to them. He reached out to pull him close to them. "I love you both so much. I'm going to miss you when I leave tomorrow." He blinked back tears, cleared his throat and smiled at them. "Tonight is a celebration of the amazing three weeks we have had, so happy faces you two." He looked up as Casey approached them.

"I want to come with you tomorrow." She announced.

"Really?" He asked in surprise.

"Yes, really. If you want?" She looked at him nervously.

"Yes, of course I want you to." He laughed. "Ok, let's phone the travel agency in the morning and see if we can get you onto my flight." Angelia and Blaine shared a smile.

"I'm glad you're not going to be travelling alone tomorrow." Blaine said softly. "It will make leaving us a bit easier." He reached out to squeeze his brother's shoulder gently. Jarryd shook his head.

"It will never make it easier Blaine, but it will make it a lot less lonely." He said as he stood up. "Let's play some pool while we wait for Megs, Kel and Case to finish shift."

Chapter 9

"Hi Lia." Kyle's eyes met Angelia's across the bar counter.

"Kyle." She exclaimed in surprise. She gave him a quick smile and walked off. He watched her hand drinks over to a customer and glance at him. She looked down and bit her lip to stop from smiling. She took money from the customer, flashed them a smile and walked back to the till. She looked back at Kyle and met his eyes again briefly before looking away. She shook her head, walked to the fridge, grabbed a beer from the shelf and walked to him. She placed it in front of him and turned to walk off.

"Lia." She turned around and he gave her a half smile. "No tequila?" She bit her lip before pulling the bottle of tequila from the fridge and reaching for two glasses. She poured two shots and handed him one. He clinked his glass against hers and downed it. He reached for his wallet.

"I got it." She said softly as her hand went to her neck to run her fingers gently over the angel pendant on her necklace before walking off. He watched her with a slight frown. She seemed different; the last twelve months had flown by. His new job and two apartment moves had kept him busy. He had wanted to come back after a few months but there had been no getting away from work.

He watched her move around the bar, the familiarity of her laughter, the way she used her hands to accentuate what she was explaining and the shy smile she gave customers made his heart ache. He hadn't realised until that moment exactly how much he had missed her. He looked around; the bar was reaching its normal late-night quietness. He saw Angelia reach for her phone and bag while Beth sorted through their tips. He slid off his chair and headed to the car park. Angelia walked down the ramp texting on her phone.

"Lia."

She gasped in surprise, spun around and looked up into Kyle's light brown eyes. He was leaning casually against the car next to hers.

"Kyle, you idiot, you scared me."

"Sorry." He apologised. "I didn't mean to. I was hoping we could talk."

She felt her pulse start to race. "I'm kinda tired, I just want to go home. Can we do this another night?"

"Do what, Lia? I just want to talk to you."

"Not tonight, Kyle, please." She pleaded.

"What's wrong, Lia? You're not yourself. Something's not right."

She eyed him warily. "How would you know?"

"I know you. Something is making you unhappy. Tell me what's wrong baby." He brushed his fingers gently along her cheek. She caught her breath and closed her eyes briefly.

"Kyle please, I can't do this now." She grasped the handle behind her and opened her door, he reached across and pushed it closed. His body was close to hers; he could smell her perfume. She leaned back against the car.

"Lia." He sighed her name as he inched closer to her.

"Kyle." She protested weakly as she placed her hands on his chest to push him away. She hesitated before bunching his shirt in her hands and pulling him against her. He caught her wrists and drew her arms over his shoulders and around his neck. He wrapped his arms around her waist and pressed his body against hers. She buried her face against his chest, he lowered his head and rested it on top of hers. He breathed in and smelled lavender, her favourite shampoo, he loved the familiarity of that scent.

"My angel Lia." He whispered into her hair, just above her ear. She raised her face to look at him, tears glistened in her eyes. He let go of her waist and cupped her face in his hands, she lowered her hands to cover his. He brushed his lips softly across hers and hesitated for a moment before pressing his lips gently but firmly against hers, he felt her lips soften and yield to his pressing back gently. He moved his hands to her neck, holding her as they kissed. She pulled back for a second to look at him before running her fingers along his cheek. He lowered his arm and wrapped it around her waist holding her close to him. He ran his other hand across her cheek before resting it on the back of her neck. He heard her sigh and looked down to meet her eyes.

"I have missed you so much." She whispered. He could hear the tears in her voice.

"I missed you too, baby." He bent down to kiss her again. They shared a long, slow, lingering kiss as she ran her hands up and down his back, slowly at first and then faster.

He ran his thumb along her jaw as their kisses became deeper and more passionate. He pulled away slightly to look at her. They didn't need words; she knew what he was asking. She nodded slightly, not trusting herself to speak.

He retrieved his car keys from his pocket, his one arm still firmly wrapped around her waist. His car was next to hers. She watched him while he tried to find the unlock button in the dark. She felt a familiar ache in her heart, their time apart hadn't dulled her feelings, she still loved him. She smiled as he finally found the correct button and unlocked the car, opening the door for her to climb in before getting into the driver's side. She reached over to run her fingers through his hair, he caught her hand and kissed it before lacing his fingers through hers and putting it on the gearstick. He started the car and pulled out of the parking lot as she turned to look at him. He glanced at her quickly and smiled before turning his attention back to the road.

He pulled into his driveway a few minutes later. She made her way to the house and waited for him as he stood beside the car watching her. She turned to see what was taking him so long and met his eyes. He smiled and she gave him her familiar shy smile in return. He walked up and reached past her to unlock the door. He watched her as she looked inside but didn't move. He hesitated, she was unreadable, he had no idea what she was thinking. She turned around, reached up and rested her hand on his cheek as she gave him a half smile.

"Damn I left the can of whipped cream at home." She laughed quietly.

He shook his head smiling before reaching up to put his hand over hers. He turned his head to softly kiss her palm and he heard her catch her breath. He leaned down to kiss her before bending down to put his hands at the back of her legs, picking her up and wrapping her legs around his waist. She wrapped her arms around his shoulders and trailed soft kisses up his neck to his ear. He walked in, kicking the door closed behind him and carried her up the dark passageway to his room. He lowered her to the bed and ran his hands down her legs to her feet, he took her shoes off and threw them over his shoulder as he heard her giggle.

"You are such an idiot." He kicked off his shoes and pulled his shirt over his head. "You got a tattoo?" She looked at him in surprise.

"Yeah." He looked down at his arm. "Do you like it?" He gave her a shy smile.

"I love it." She said as she bit the side of her lower lip and looked up at him. "It makes you look even sexier." She said, smiling up at him. He smiled back and climbed onto the bed, hovering over her. She reached up to hold the silver pendant and chain that hung down between them. She ran her finger over the engraving on the back, she knew the words by heart. "You still wear it?"

"I never take it off. It was a gift from the woman I love more than anything in this world." He whispered. She looked at him and felt tears well up in her eyes.

"I love you, Kyle." She whispered.

"I love you, Lia. I never stopped loving you."

She reached up to run her fingers through his hair and pulled his face down to hers. She kissed him with a passion that surprised him as she wrapped her legs around his.

"I dreamt about doing this for so long." She said quietly. He sat back and unzipped her skirt, pulling it down slowly before running his hands up her legs. She moaned and reached for him as he bent down to kiss her.

***

Kyle woke to warm sunlight on his face, he squinted before closing his eyes again, he had forgotten to close the curtains. He smiled as the night before played in his mind. He reached out for Angelia but found only an empty space. He frowned and sat up. He heard voices and cups clinking.

"Maybe she's making coffee." He mumbled hopefully as he pulled on a pair of shorts from his suitcase.

"Hey guys." He peered into the kitchen at his brother and Jake.

"Hey Kyle." Jake greeted back.

"How long have you guys been here?" He asked as he reached for the coffee pot.

"Since 6 am."

"I ran Lia down to her car."

Kyle sipped his coffee as he avoided his brother's disapproving look. "So, she's not here?" He asked innocently.

Mark looked at him for a short while before shaking his head. "No, she's probably at home."

"So? You and Lia huh?" Jake smiled smugly. Kyle shot him a filthy look.

"It's not like that."

"Uh-huh."

"Leave her alone Jake, I'm warning you." Kyle glared at him.

Jake rubbed his cheek and returned Kyle's glare. "Don't worry, I keep my distance from Angelia" He snapped.

"Yeah, he does." Blaine laughed as he walked into the kitchen. "JR sat Jake down for a heart-to-heart before he left to go back to London." Jake shot him a dirty look and shook his head as Mark tried to hide a smile.

"I'm having an end-of-summer party at the house this afternoon. Kendra said Lia would be stopping by. Why don't you join us?" Jake gave him an innocent smile.

Kyle eyed him suspiciously. "Yeah ok, that sounds good." He mumbled.

"I don't think that's such a good idea." Mark butted in from the other side of the kitchen. Jake shot him a look.

"We need to go get supplies and we need to leave. Now." He said to Blaine and Mark.

"I'll be there shortly; I need to speak to Kyle. We haven't had a chance to talk."

"We're late, there's no time." Jake snapped while Mark looked at his brother.

"Go, it's fine. I'll catch up with you later, I need to shower and get some work stuff done anyway." Kyle gave his brother a reassuring smile. Mark shot him one last look before following Blaine and Jake out the door.

Kyle shrugged and poured himself more coffee. A few minutes later, he was relaxing on the couch with a cup of coffee and the toasted sandwich his brother had been attempting to make. He flicked through the channels, but nothing caught his interest. He sighed and dropped the remote on the couch next to him.

He reached for his phone and groaned; he hadn't had a chance to arrange a local number. His eyes fell on the portable house phone. He picked it up and dialled. The phone rang for a while before clicking over to voicemail.

"Hey, it's Lia. Leave your message at the tone." Her cheerful voice echoed through the phone.

"Hey, Lia." He said in a husky voice. "I missed my sexy girl this morning. Give me a call on the house phone. I have plans for this afternoon, but if you want to hang out, I can cancel them. We need to talk. I've missed you. Call me." He hung up and dropped the phone next to the remote. He sighed and got up to head to his room.

Kyle was busy drying off from his shower when the phone rang. He charged through the house, almost taking out one of the ridiculously big houseplants their mother had insisted on giving them. Cursing at the pain from his stubbed toe, he grabbed the phone and pressed answer.

"Hey sexy, I was wondering when you were going to call." He smiled into the phone.

"Oh, Kyle, I didn't know you thought that way about me and that you were waiting by the phone for my call. That is so sweet."

He rolled his eyes as he dropped down onto the couch. "Oh, hey Kalen. Sorry, I was expecting a call."

"I won't take your disappointment personally. I ran into Jake. He told me you were home. Thought I was your best friend and I find out you're back here from Jake of all people. Nice one, Kyle." Kalen sounded irritated.

"It was a surprise visit, no one knew. Jake only found out because he was here this morning. It's just for a couple of days anyway, I need to collect some documents from work because the New York office needs the originals and I have to sort something out for my work visa."

"Clearly, someone knew you were here or you wouldn't be waiting for a call from sexy." Kalen laughed.

"Funny. You going to Jake's later?" Kyle asked as he rubbed his sore toe.

"Yeah, I am, see you there."

"Sounds good."

He sighed as he hung up. He eyed the clock. It's been nearly two hours. He pressed redial. He frowned when he went through to Lia's voicemail.

"Lia, it's me. Again. I'd really like to talk to you. Please call me back." He placed the phone back on its base. "Well done McAllister, you didn't sound desperate at all." He grumbled to himself before huffing in frustration.

Chapter 10

"Kyle, you made it." Jake announced loudly as he slapped him on the back.

"Umm, yeah." He mumbled in reply, his attention focused on a pair of green eyes that watched him intently.

"Lia, I've been trying to get hold of you all day." He fought to keep the irritation out of his voice. She glanced briefly over her shoulder, before looking back uncomfortably at him.

"It's nice to see you, Kyle." She mumbled as Jake sniggered.

"I'm sure you two lovebirds have a lot to talk about." He said with a smirk. Angelia shot him a dirty look and drifted over to the table holding ice and glasses. Kyle followed her and placed a hand on her shoulder, she stiffened and he dropped his hand to his side.

"Lia, what's going on with you?" He asked concerned.

"What are you doing here Kyle?" He could hear the desperation in her voice.

"These are my friends too, I came to see them. More importantly, I came to see you." He gave her an injured look.

"You can't be here." She mumbled.

"What is that supposed to mean?"

"Nothing. Kyle, things are…complicated."

"Lia we were together last night and it was incredible. I've missed you so much. Please, can we go somewhere and talk."

"Can we do this later? Please just leave" She hissed at him, panic evident on her face. She paled as she glanced over his shoulder. "Oh no." She whispered in horror.

"What? What is it, Lia? What is going on with you?".

"Kyle." Jake's voice boomed out. Irritation flashed across Kyle's face.

"What Jake?" He snarled as Jake and a tall dark-haired man joined them.

"There's someone you *want* to meet." He gave him a false smile. Kyle glanced briefly at the man and gave him a tight-lipped smile.

"Hi." He greeted him politely before turning back to Angelia.

"This is Nick." Jake persisted. Kyle gave him an exasperated look and turned back to the man.

"Hi. Nick." He said, shooting a venomous look at Jake.

"Lia's *fiancé*." Jake added smugly. Kyle stared at him speechlessly as the information registered.

"Fiancé?" Kyle asked blankly as Jake's smile widened.

"I told you that you'd want to meet him." He sneered at him. Nick looked perplexed as he searched the three faces in front of him for answers.

"Angelia, what is going on?" He looked at her with a frown. Angelia stared at the melting ice blocks in her glass and looked like she wished she could be anywhere but there.

"Nothing. Jake's just being an ass. As usual." She snapped before downing her drink. Jake glared at her for a moment.

"Nick, this is Kyle. Lia's…"

"Friend." Kyle cut Jake off. "I've been in the States for just over a year. I got back last night and I was trying to catch up with Lia, I'm only here for a couple of days." He gave her a forced smile. "We can do it another time. *Angelia*." He said through gritted teeth. He turned to Nick who held out a hand to him.

"It's nice to meet you, Kyle." He glanced quickly at his fiancée who was studying her glass. Kyle smiled politely and shook his hand. He sighed in relief as he spotted Kalen. He raised a hand to flag him down. Kalen waved back, his smile faded slightly when he saw that Kyle was standing with

Angelia and Nick. Kyle turned his attention back to the group in front of him.

"Guys." He nodded to Jake and Nick. "Angelia." He said looking briefly into her eyes, his pain transparent. He shoved his hands into his pockets and stalked to Kalen.

"Hey, brother." Kalen greeted him. "Is sexy here?" He asked with a mischievous smile.

"Yeah, she is. Her *and* her fiancé." Kyle said quietly. Kalen looked up and caught Angelia's eyes.

"Oh man, Kyle. Lia and Nick have been together for about eight months now. He proposed about a week ago. I had no idea it was her call you were waiting for."

"Yeah, *her* call I was waiting for because she was naked in *my* bed last night." Kyle explained in a low voice.

"WHAT?" Kalen's voice came out louder than he meant it to.

"Shh. No one knows." Kyle grimaced slightly. "Well, almost no one. Why didn't anyone tell me she was seeing someone? That she was engaged?" He asked angrily. Kalen shook his head.

"I wanted to, so many times. Mark asked all of us not to discuss Lia with you. He wanted you to focus on adjusting to living in a new country and settling in at work. He didn't want you to have a reason to drop everything and come back here."

"I wouldn't have done that." Kyle protested. Kalen looked at him and sighed.

"When it comes to Lia, you're not exactly rational. We all thought that it would be a good thing for the two of you to finally move on from each other."

"Since when does the group make decisions about me and Lia?" His anger started to build again.

"You were both hurting each other and hurting all of us in the process. We love both of you but every time you guys get close there is a meltdown down and we're tired of waiting for the next explosion. No one denies that you two love each other, we're just concerned about the both of you." Kalen explained gently. Kyle sighed and rubbed his head.

"I need to get out of here, I know you just got here but would you mind if we left?"

"Not at all. I caught a lift with Chris and Ciara so we can go in your car."

Kyle nodded as he pulled his keys out and turned to walk down the pathway to the driveway.

"Kyle." He heard Angelia call his name softly. He turned back to face her.

"Angelia." He said in an icy tone.

"You're angry, I get it. I'm sorry, I should have told you." She said apologetically.

"Yeah, you should've."

"There was no time."

"Yeah, I can see that. Between kissing me in the car park, having sex with me, sneaking off in the dead of night and ignoring my calls you were pretty damn busy." He retorted.

"Lower your voice." She snapped angrily, glaring at him. He returned her glare.

"Don't worry, I won't tell your precious fiancé where you were last night." He said in a lower voice. Her expression softened.

"Thank you. For not saying anything back there."

"When were you going to tell me that you got engaged?"

"I, I don't know." She stammered.

"You don't know? Why didn't you tell me when you started seeing him or when he proposed? You had my number, my email; you could have contacted me." He looked at her with a hurt expression.

"It was none of your business, Kyle." She snapped at him. He stared at her incredulously as anger flashed through his body.

"None of my business? *NONE* of my business?" He stepped closer to her, raising his voice. "What the hell is that supposed to mean Lia?"

"You left." She shouted at him. "You just packed up your stuff and left." Tears streamed down her cheeks. "You didn't even say goodbye. After all we had been through and what I thought we had, you just left.
"You were supposed to forgive me, you were supposed to come back to me, you were supposed to love me again. My heart is your home. That's what you said to me and then you just walked out on me. You walked out of my life. AGAIN. What did you think? Was I just going to wait around for you? Till you forgave me? Till you decided to let me back into your life? Forever?" Her voice was shaking from tears and rage. "Chris had to tell me that you left, how do you think that made me feel?"

"Did it ever occur to you for even one moment that maybe the reason I left without saying goodbye is because you were the *one* person I couldn't say goodbye to?" He shouted back at her. He took another step closer to her so they were almost touching. "Did you ever stop to think that maybe, just maybe, seeing your eyes, hearing your voice, touching you would have made me doubt my decision?" His voice dropped down to a huskier tone as he reached out to wipe the tears from her cheeks and brush her hair off her face. "But most importantly my angel Lia, did you ever think that if I had to see you cry that I wouldn't have been able to leave your side, that I wouldn't have climbed on that plane?" The emotion in his voice stunned Angelia momentarily. She fought to regain her composure.

"But you *did* get on that plane, Kyle and you left me behind. You disappeared out of my life with no goodbye or explanation." She said sadly.

"I was so hurt and angry and I was scared that I would say things to hurt you and push you away forever. I thought I would go for a few months and come back for you but when I looked again, it was eleven months later. All

I thought about was you, I didn't want anyone else and it took moving away for me to realise how much I want you. How much I need you. You are the single most important thing in my life, Lia. I love you. I thought I didn't anymore but leaving made me realise how *much* I love you, how much you mean to me." His pain echoed through his words. She reached out and gently ran her fingers down his cheek and smiled sadly up at him.

"We live in two different worlds now, Kyle. I was so broken and lost when you left and then again when JR left. I built this whole other life without you. Seeing you last night, everything I ever felt for you came rushing back to me." He held her cheeks in his hands, she put her hands over his. "Last night was a moment of weakness. We can't keep doing this Kyle, we can't keep hurting each other. We both need to let go and move on for good."

"Is that what you really want?"

"No, but it's what we need to do." She put her hand on his chest over his heart. "Your heart is my home, Kyle. Maybe one day we'll find our way back to each other." She gave him a sad smile.

"Do I get a say in this?"

"No, I've made my decision." She said quietly, blinking back tears. He nodded sadly.

"I'll respect your decision then." He leaned down to gently brush his lips across hers. He groaned as he looked up. Everyone from the party was standing and watching them. "We're causing a scene." He said in a low voice. "I'm going to go. I'll never stop loving you, Lia." He ran his thumb along her cheek to catch the tear that trickled down it. He turned and walked down the pathway. Kalen gave her a sad smile before turning to follow Kyle. He climbed into the car and looked at his friend.

"Where are we going?" He asked as Kyle started the car. He glanced at Kalen and realised that he hadn't heard him get in.

"I'm going down to the beach."

"Sounds good. Do you want to talk?"

"No." Kyle answered flatly.

"Ok, then I'm going to talk." Kalen announced, Kyle gave him a pained look and then shrugged. "What were you expecting Kyle? She is an amazing woman and she was crazy about you."

"Was?" Kyle interrupted.

"Maybe she still is. I don't know. What I do know is that she went to pieces after you left. Just about broke her heart. I know you were mad at her, but you could've seen her or called her or done something. Jarryd's visit helped her but when he left, she was heartbroken again. She picked herself up and met Nick a few months later. He's been really good for her. She's happy now, don't ruin this for her Kyle."

"She's not happy," Kyle stated.

"What makes you say that?" Kalen asked frowning.

"Last night at the bar. I was watching her. She was smiling and laughing and putting up a front but something was missing. Her sparkle, her…" He sighed, "I can't explain it. She wasn't Lia." He finished lamely. "I love her Kalen."

"If you really love her, Kyle, let her go."

"What if I can't?"

"You have to. You guys keep hurting each other, it's not healthy. The rest of us feel like we are always caught in the middle." Kalen shook his head as Kyle sighed and headed towards the beach.

"Angelia?"

She looked up startled, into Nick's pale blue eyes. He was seething as he threw her bag at her and headed towards his car. She clutched her bag tightly as she reluctantly followed him. She climbed into the passenger seat and stared straight ahead.

"Are you going to explain to me what the fuck just happened?" He glared at her. She looked down at her hands.

"There's nothing to explain." She replied weakly.

"Of course not, you cause dramatic movie-worthy scenes with your friends all the time. Every week for the last eight months I have been left standing on the side-lines watching you shout hysterically at one of your friends while crying. You were passionate, fuming, and heartbroken. I have *never* seen you like that before. I've seen you cuddle, embrace, and kiss your guy friends and it has never bothered me. What I just witnessed was intimate and emotional. The way he looks at you, touches you and the way you look at and touch him. He's not just another friend, is he?" Nick's voice was shaking with fury.

"No." She whispered. "He's just a friend."

"Really? Because the intimacy and love I just saw was way more than friendship."

"Kyle and I have a complicated history. Our relationship is …different."

"Relationship? Don't you mean friendship?"

"Kyle is… We are… It's just too complicated to explain."

"Try." He snapped at her.

"He's the one person in the world who can look into my eyes and know something is bothering me when no one else can. He knows me better than I know myself sometimes." She said with a wistful smile. "He's my soulmate."

"Your soulmate? So, what does that make me?"

"You're my fiancé." She looked at him.

"Somehow, a soulmate seems more significant. Kyle's always going to be there in the shadows, isn't he?"

"You are my fiancé. You're more important. My life has been so tumultuous and complicated. Right now, I just want something simple and reliable in my life." She winced as she finished. "That didn't come out quite right."

"No, I think it came out perfectly right." He was silent for a moment. "Where were you last night Angelia?" She froze and held her breath for a moment.

"I was at work, remember."

"I meant after that." His voice was stony.

"Why? What have you heard?"

"It doesn't matter what I've heard. I want to hear the truth from you. Right now."

"I was with Kyle." She whispered. "It just happened. I saw him and all those feelings came rushing back. I wasn't thinking and I am so sorry. I never meant to hurt you." She turned to him. "Do you think you could ever forgive me?"

Nick started the car and drove to Angelia's place in silence. He stopped outside and switched the car off. He drummed his fingers on the steering wheel for a moment.

"I don't think I can forgive you. We're over Angelia, the engagement and our relationship. It was so easy for you to climb into another man's bed and then lie to me about it. How do I trust you again? How can I be with someone I can't trust? How do I *marry* someone I can't trust?"

"I didn't lie, I just didn't tell you." She argued feebly. "And it was Kyle, not some random stranger."

"Do you think that makes it better?" He asked astounded. "I think it makes it even worse. If it was some random stranger, I might have been able to forgive you eventually. Maybe. But this is a man you have a history with, a man you still have deep feelings for. He is always going to be in your life and I can't spend the rest of *my* life worrying about him coming back."

"I don't still have feelings for him."

"Lie to yourself all you want Angelia but don't lie to me. I saw the love, the intimacy and the affection you still share. The way you looked at and touched each other. You both still have feelings for each other, I'm not prepared to hang around and be collateral damage when you finally admit that there is still something between you. I'll box your stuff up tonight and you can collect it whenever you want."

"I'm sorry I hurt you." She sniffled softly.

"Just get out." He snapped angrily. She nodded and slipped her ring off her finger, placing it on the console. She climbed out and closed the door as she sighed heavily.

"Did you actually love me?" Nick asked quietly. "Were you ever really happy with me?" She hadn't realised he had climbed out of the car. She looked across the roof of the car at him and frowned.

"Yes, of course I loved you."

"Are you sure about that? I just ended our relationship, and you haven't shed one tear but earlier you cried an ocean for a man you claim you don't have feelings for." He climbed in the car, slammed the door and sped off as Angelia stared after him.

Chapter 11

Kyle climbed out the car and walked towards Chris, Ciara, Mark, Blaine and Kalen.

"Wait a minute." He looked up at the pub. "Maybe we should go somewhere else."

"She's not working tonight." Ciara reassured him. "She doesn't go out much since she met Nick. He doesn't really drink and he hates playing pool." She shrugged as Kyle nodded and leaned on Kalen's shoulder.

"If I kick your ass in pool tonight, you have to clean my car tomorrow." He stated. Kalen raised an eyebrow.

"Really?"

"Hey, you're the one who tracked all the beach sand into my car yesterday." He reminded him.

"No, I meant, do you really think you're going to kick my ass in pool?" Kalen said with a smug smile. Kyle laughed and opened his mouth to respond when he heard his name being called. He turned around in surprise.

"Lia." His smile faded as he took in her furious look.

"You just had to do it, didn't you?" She shouted.

"Do what?" He asked confused.

"Fuck up my life. AGAIN. I asked you to leave the party but no you wanted to stay and talk to me. Nick broke up with me. My relationship is over. Are you happy now?"

"Happy? I didn't even know you were in a relationship. You weren't wearing a ring and you were so eager to climb into my bed the other night. I'm sure you can understand my confusion." He shouted back at her.

"Would it have actually made a difference if you knew?" She asked with a sarcastic laugh.

"Of course it would have made a difference Lia. I'm not in the habit of breaking up relationships."

"Not even to get what you want?"

"No Lia. Never. How could you even think that? You know I would never do that."

"I don't know you anymore. You have been away for over a year. How would I even know who you are?"

"That's funny because I know you well enough to know that you weren't happy. Your relationship was doomed but it's easier to blame me than to admit that you were staying with someone you *didn't* love." He snapped angrily at her.

"How dare you?" She glared at him.

"How dare I what? Be right? Come on, be honest Lia, were you really happy? Because I'm betting that if you were you wouldn't have been so eager to go home with me and climb into my bed but blame me if that makes it easier for you."

"Go to hell." She shouted furiously.

"I've already been to hell and back, Lia." He snarled angrily.

"Stop it, both of you." Christian stepped between them. "Kyle, go inside. Now." He ordered as he pushed Kyle towards the pub. Kyle glared at her one last time before shaking his head and storming off. Christian turned to Angelia.
"He's not wrong, Lia. You should never have slept with him. When you did, you should have told him about Nick straight away. I'm guessing that you wanted to break things off with Nick, you just didn't have the guts to do it yourself. Maybe you didn't mean to have a huge public meltdown at Jake's but you knew it would eventually come out and that Nick would break up with you." Christian was fuming and Angelia looked away from him. "Tell me I'm wrong Lia. Please. Kyle is not the one at fault here. You are. I am so disappointed in you." She looked up at him in surprise.

"I'm sorry, Chris."

"I'm not the one you should be apologising to." She nodded and took a step towards the pub.

"Not a chance, you are going home. I do not need another scene tonight."

"But Chris." She protested.

"But nothing Lia. Go home, now."

***

Angelia sighed as she pulled into Kyle's driveway. She got out and slowly walked to the door. She was surprised to find it open. She gave a quick knock and went inside.

"Hello." She called out as she followed voices to the kitchen.

"Casey." She exclaimed in surprise as she walked in to find Blaine, Kyle and Casey in the kitchen laughing and talking. They all turned to look at her. Angelia looked at Casey and recognised the shirt she was wearing. She glared at Kyle. "Are you serious?"

"Casey was with Mark." He explained quickly. Casey glanced at him before looking back at her.

"Umm, yeah, I hooked up with Mark last night. He's still sleeping." She added. Angelia's eyes narrowed in suspicion. She looked at the doorway as Mark walked in stretching.

"Morning." He mumbled as he reached for a coffee cup before looking at Casey. "Hi Case. When did you get here?" He asked confused. Kyle groaned and Casey closed her eyes.

"You lied to me again. Why would you lie to me, Kyle?"

"I don't know Lia. Maybe to avoid these charming little fights we seem to keep having. I can't keep watching what I say because I'm worried about setting you off. I can have sex with whoever I want, whenever I want. We are not together anymore and as you made it abundantly clear yesterday, you want me to stay out of your life. I am a little confused as to what you are even doing here." He shook his head as she spun around and stormed out the door. "Dammit." He threw his teaspoon down on the table. "How is she able to infuriate me so fucking easily?"

"I honestly don't know, Kyle. But could you please stop lying to her. Honestly, I think it just makes everything worse." Mark replied while Casey wrapped her arms around herself self-consciously.

"I'm sorry Case, I shouldn't have put you on the spot like that." Kyle apologised. Casey shrugged her shoulders.

"Why did you tell her we had sex? We didn't, so why tell her we did? I don't want to be another speed bump on the Lia and Kyle freeway." She added.

"Casey." Blaine snapped as Kyle looked at her.

"I'm sorry, what?" She rolled her eyes and sighed dramatically.

"It's something we came up with a while ago. Every person who gets hurt or is in the way of the two of you is referred to as a speed bump. You two need to get your shit sorted out." Casey poured herself another cup of coffee and looked at him. Kyle shook his head, picked up his coffee and walked outside.

***

Angelia walked up to the table where Kyle was reading the newspaper. He looked up at her, sighed and folded his paper, dropping it to the table. She bit the side of her bottom lip and looked down at her sandals.

"Ok. Fine. I'm sorry." She blurted out. Kyle looked up at her with a slight smirk and arched his eyebrow. She breathed out impatiently.

"I never say I'm sorry so don't get used to it." She said with a small smile.

"Well, I guess that answers my question."

She looked at him in confusion. "What question?"

"Whether you were coming in peace or looking to start another fight."

"Funny." She huffed impatiently.

"Do you want to sit?" He gestured to the seat opposite him.

"Umm, no, I should go. I uh, have things to do." She said, looking down at the table.

"Can we fix this?" She looked up at him and met his eyes.

"What do you mean?"

"This? Us?" He gestured impatiently. "We can barely have a conversation without starting a fight."

"And whose fault is that?" She snapped.

"Are you implying that it's my fault?"

"I'm not implying."

"So, it is my fault?" She clenched her jaw and shook her head. "I like that colour green on you. It brings out your eyes, makes them greener." He gave her a half smile. She scowled at him before turning to walk off. "Wait. Please. Don't go." He pleaded, half rising to his feet. "I don't want to fight with you, Lia. I just want to have a drink or lunch or something. I want to talk to you and maybe get things back to the way they were in the beginning. I miss you, Lia." He watched her as she turned to face him and gave him a half smile.

"I miss you too, Kyle."

He smiled back and held his hand out to her. She placed her hand in his and he pulled her into his arms as he stepped out from the table. She wrapped her arms around his neck and he lifted her up off the ground. She giggled and kissed his cheek. He set her back down on the ground and took his seat, gesturing to the seat in front of him. She sat down and he reached out to put his hand over hers.

"Thank you for staying." She smiled before looking down at the menu. "Can we be friends, Lia? Please? Let's uncomplicate things between us and start over."

"I'd like that." She said quietly, blinking back tears.

"Who knows, maybe one day we can go back to being more than friends." He said rubbing the back of her hand gently. "For now, we just need to take a step back and stop letting our physical feelings cloud our judgement. We've hurt so many people as well as each other. I'm scared that if we carry on the way we have been, there may be nothing left to fight for." He gave her a sad smile.

"I know, you're right. I've never been an overly jealous person but when it comes to you…" she trailed off and sighed. "I'm borderline irrational."

"I know because I feel the same way. I've been crazy about you since the night I met you and I still kick myself for believing Jake because I think things could have been different between us. Our relationship went from sweet looks and flirting to all-out screaming matches. We started lying to each other and it really does feel like when we get back together there is a ticking time bomb that will explode any minute. We've both changed a lot in the last three years."

"I can't believe it's only been three years. It feels like a lifetime ago since we met at Vipers for a drink. So much has happened it's been crazy." She smiled up at the waitress and ordered a vodka cooler and a pasta while Kyle ordered a beer and a burger.

"Yeah, it has been crazy." He agreed.

"So, what do we do from here?"

"Well, I won't be coming out for another 8 or 9 months. So, what if we take the rest of this year to focus on ourselves and figure out what it is that we want. From our lives and from each other? Kind of like soul searching. What do you think?"

"I think it feels like I'm losing you."

"You will never lose me, Lia." He reached for her hand and rested it against his cheek. "Your heart will always be my home. I believe we'll find our way back to each other. We just need to figure out what went wrong between us and why we keep fighting all the time. We need to understand why we keep lying to each other and why we keep hiding things from each other." He smiled at her, she nodded and smiled back. "Why don't you travel overseas again? Your studies are done now so why don't you take time to travel and work? Come stay with me for a few weeks or months?"

"I'll think about it." She smiled as the waitress approached them with their food. She reached over to steal chips off his plate. He raised an eyebrow at her.

"That's my food, you should have ordered a burger if you wanted chips." He said sternly. She pulled a tongue at him and dipped the chips into the sauce oozing around her pasta.

"This sauce is so heavenly; you have to try it." she pushed her bowl towards him. He scooped up some sauce in the spoon and tasted it.

"Not bad. My pasta sauce is better though." He said smugly. She bit the side of her lower lip and looked over her shoulder. "Ummm, excuse me, missy." He said indignantly, "This is where you jump in and agree with me."

She looked at him innocently. "I thought you said we should stop lying to each other." She looked at him wide-eyed trying not to smile. He narrowed his eyes.

"That's it. You're cut off, you will never taste my culinary masterpieces again." He declared. She sighed in relief.

"Oh, thank goodness, I thought you were going to offer to cook for me again."

"Bitch." He sniped smiling down at his food.

"Man whore." She retorted. He looked up her.

"Excuse me!"

"You are sleeping your way around our group. Me, Kendra and now Casey. Who's next? Ciara? Megan? Kelly?"

"Definitely not Ciara or Kelly, I happen to be fond of breathing." He looked at her thoughtfully. "I wonder if Megs is free tonight." Angelia's jaw dropped and he burst out laughing. "I'm kidding Lia."

"You better be." She said with a laugh.

"This is how I remember us. Laughing and joking with each other." He said softly. She looked up to meet his eyes and smiled wistfully.

"Like when we were cashing up at the pub?"

"Yeah, it was the favourite part of my shift. Sitting with you trying not to laugh while watching you struggle with maths even though you had a calculator." He chuckled.

"I'm a bar lady, not an accountant." She moaned. "It was my favourite part of the shift too. And the early morning Saturdays when we would have coffee and breakfast together and Sundays that were so quiet that we sat together laughing and talking the whole day."

"It broke my heart when you went on study leave, I had to work with Kalen, he drove me nuts." She smiled and looked down at the table. "Lia?" He asked.

"Yesterday morning at your house…" She started.

"Yeah, I'm sorry for the way I reacted. Listen, about Casey…"

"Let me talk, please." She interrupted him.

"No, I need to tell you this." He said firmly. "I never slept with Casey. Mark went home early. Blaine, Case and I were having fun and weren't ready to call it a night, so we took the party back to our place. Blaine and I were too drunk to drive her back, so I gave her my shirt and my bed and I slept on the couch and you know that I didn't sleep with Kendra. So technically you are the *only* person in the group I slept with so you need to withdraw that man whore comment." He said arching his eyebrow.

"You didn't sleep with Casey?"

"No, Lia, I didn't."

"Then why did you say you did?"

"I don't know. I was still upset about the night before and then you came in with guns blazing in the morning, so I said I did to get back at you, because I knew it would hurt you." He sighed as he shook his head. "This is what I'm talking about, Lia, we keep hurting each other and hurting our friends and it needs to stop. I don't want to keep hurting you, baby and I don't want you to keep hurting me." He explained.

"Well, I came to your house yesterday morning to apologise." She said quietly. "You were right about everything." She looked down at her hands.

"Are you ok?"

"I am now." She whispered. "I wasn't happy, not for a long time."

"Did he hurt you?" Kyle asked as anger crept into his voice.

"No, no, it was nothing like that. Nick was a great guy in the beginning. After everything that happened with us, I just wanted something easy and simple and I settled for him. There were no sparks and no fights because I didn't love him and I wasn't really happy. It was just comfortable with us but then he started becoming controlling. He didn't like our group so we would stay home or only go out with his friends." She confessed with a shrug.

"You were going to marry him, Lia." Kyle said in surprise.

"No, Chris hit the nail on the head the other night. I didn't have the guts to break up with Nick, so I would have done something stupid to get him to do it for me."

"So, I was the something stupid?" He asked feeling hurt, she looked up at him wide-eyed.

"No, no. That's not what I'm saying. This is all coming out wrong. Let me try again." She gave a short laugh. "I didn't hesitate to go home with you because I didn't love Nick. My feelings for you never went away because I didn't feel those things for him so when you kissed me, it all came rushing back. I didn't mean to fight with you at the party. I was hurt and confused by what I felt for you when I knew that I should have been angry that you just disappeared on me and I couldn't believe how easy it was for me to go home with you. I didn't sleep with you to get Nick to break up with me but I would have ended up kissing someone or doing something worse to force him to do it. It's stupid, I know."

"It's not stupid." He said softly with a smile.

"It's going to suck when you leave tomorrow." She gave him a gloomy smile.

"I know. Are you coming with me to Chris and Ciara's?" He glanced at his watch. "I'm going to be late for my own farewell." He groaned as he signalled the waitress.

"I'll come with you. I wasn't invited to the last one."

He looked up sharply as she flashed him a teasing smile. He breathed a sigh of relief.

"I am so sorry about that, Lia. I know what I did was wrong. I was wracked with guilt when I landed because I knew how hurt you would feel. I just couldn't say goodbye to you. I needed to do this. My job is incredible and it's such a boost to my career but as angry as I was with you, I don't think I would have been able to leave if I had seen you."

"No, it's ok. I understand why you did it."

"We can Skype and FaceTime you know. If you want?"

"I'd like that." She said reaching for her purse.

"I got it." He smiled as he handed the waitress his card. Angelia trailed him to her car and reached for her keys. "Why don't you just drive with me? I'll bring you back later to your car." He offered as he opened the door for her.

"That would be great." She climbed into the passenger side. He closed her door and walked around to the driver's side.

"So, what's it like living in New York?"

"It's incredible, Lia. There's always something happening. I have this cosy little apartment close to work so I walk there and back every day. I haven't had much of a social life, most of my colleagues are married so I do get invited to their homes for dinner now and then. I have done a little bit of sightseeing and exploring but work keeps me pretty busy."

"Are you happy?"

"Yeah, I guess you could say I'm happy. It's a great opportunity and I am grateful that it was offered to me. I miss everyone. I miss you. It's not the same without the hooligans, especially my favourite one." He said with a laugh as he pulled into the driveway. He walked around and hugged her tightly as he kissed the top of her head. "This afternoon has meant the world to me. I'm really happy that you're here."

"Me too." She hugged him back. "Let's go join the hooligans," she chuckled giving him a playful push as she blinked back tears.

"There's the man of the hour." Kalen shouted as Kyle walked through the door. "Lia." He added in surprise when she walked in behind Kyle. Everyone froze and looked warily at the two of them. Angelia smiled shyly and bumped Kyle with her hip before walking up to Christian and hugging him.

"I'm sorry about the other night." She said quietly. "You were right and…" she turned to look at Kyle as he joined them, "we've had a long talk and we've worked a lot of stuff out." She said as Kyle nodded.

"Yeah, we don't want everyone getting caught in the middle of our drama anymore and we don't want to carry on hurting each other. So, we are going to be friends for now until we sort all of our issues out." Kyle stated proudly, placing his arm around Angelia's shoulders. She smiled at Christian before catching Kendra's eyes.

"I'm going to say hello to Kenz."

"How are you holding up Lia?" Kendra looked at her friend with concern.

"I'm great." She stated with a bright smile.

"You're not fooling me, Angelia Ryan." She said quietly. "You're hurting, aren't you?"

"Yeah." She said wryly. "But honestly, I'd prefer to have Kyle in my life as a friend than not have him in my life at all." She said forlornly as Kendra hugged her tightly.

"Come drink tequila and play pool with me, Megs and Kale." She said wrapping her arm around her friend's waist and pulling her towards the pool table.

***

A shrill ringing sound rang through Kyle's head. He groaned and reached for his phone.

"Hello." He mumbled.

"Kyle, where are you?" Mark sounded exasperated. Kyle squinted at his phone.

"For the love of Heaven, Mark it's 6 am." He grumbled.

"You have to be at the airport at 11 am. Kyle."

"I know Mom, I'll be home just now." He sniped at him.

"Now I know why Mom went grey so young." Mark groaned at him. "Don't be late *Kyle*."

"I won't be late, *Mark*." He huffed irritably.

"Good. Tell Lia I said good morning." Kyle could hear both the smirk and disapproval in his brother's voice. He cut the call and dropped his phone on the table. He sighed, rolled over and pulled Angelia against him.

"Good morning." He mumbled into her hair. "I think my brother knows I'm here." He added. She turned over to look at him and laughed.

"So, how's this friendship thing working out for you?" She teased him.

"This is ridiculous. We lasted how long?"

"Not even twenty-four hours."

"You give us too much credit woman, twenty-four hours wasn't even close. We didn't even make twelve hours. We have no restraint, Lia."

"It's not my fault you find me irresistible." She giggled as she rolled over to look at him.

"Excuse me? You were the one who said 'Why don't you come up for coffee?' and then fluttered those ridiculously beautiful green eyes at me. I was helpless."

"You are such a drama queen." He pulled her against his chest as she ran her fingers lightly over his chest. She looked up at him and smiled as she pushed his hair off his forehead before she rolled over onto her back. "So, starting now, we are officially back to being friends." She stated solemnly.

He looked over at her and grinned. "No not now. In twenty minutes." He rolled over onto his stomach and bent down to kiss her nose.

"Should I go get the whipped cream out of the fridge?" She wiggled her eyebrows suggestively.

"Lia." He moaned laughing before looking at her thoughtfully. "Can you get it in less than thirty seconds?"

"Time me."

He hugged her tightly at the elevator.

"I already miss you." She sniffed as tears welled in her eyes.

"Please don't cry. I'll be back in eight months, and we can chat on skype whenever you want." He sighed sadly as he pulled her close. "I'm going to miss you too." He whispered into her hair. "We're going to work on ourselves this year so when I get back, we can work things out. Ok baby?" He asked her gently. She nodded and gave him a tearful smile.

She reached up and ran her fingers through his hair. "You have whipped cream in your hair." She laughed as she wiped her hands on her shirt.

"Do you know that every time I see or hear about whipped cream, I think of you? Everyone in the office thinks I have a weird addiction because every time someone mentions it; I smile and blush." She gave him a shy smile.

"You better go. You told Mark you would be home over an hour ago. He's starting to stress." He bent down to kiss her gently. She ran her fingers down his cheek.

"Bye baby." She whispered softly.

"Bye my Lia." He stepped backwards into the elevator smiling sadly at her. Tears welled in her eyes again as the doors shut, she turned and walked dejectedly back to her apartment.

Chapter 12

Hey Mark, Blaine." Angelia greeted them cheerfully as they walked through the door.

"Hey, Lia." Blaine swung a bag off his shoulder. "Look what I found." He opened it and pulled out his guitar.

"Wow, I haven't seen that for years."

"I know, I shoved it in the back of my closet just after I moved in with Mark and Kyle." He gave her a quick glance. "Anyway, I was clearing out my cupboard and found it. I thought maybe I could play a bit after movies, I'm probably a bit rusty but I'm sure I'll still remember how to play." He laid the guitar on the chair next to her. She reached out and ran her finger along the strings.

"Blaine. You're rambling. I'm not going to fall apart because you mentioned his name." He shot her a relieved look.

"Sorry Lia, I know you two had a big fight a couple of months ago, he said you guys haven't spoken since."

"Yeah, and I'm fine." She gave him a forced smile. Ciara took a seat beside her.

"Do you want to talk about it?"

"How is it possible to be completely in love with someone while wanting to kill them at the same time?" She asked exasperatedly as she shook her head.

"Oh, it's very possible." Ciara laughed. "I love Chris more than I have ever loved anyone but there are days where I just want to hit him over the head with a frying pan or drown him in the pool. But then he looks at me with those puppy dog eyes and my heart just melts." She reached over and squeezed Angelia's hand as she chuckled.

"Well, I'm glad it's not just me." Her head shot up as Megan walked in and slammed the games room door loudly behind her before she stormed up to them.

"I swear I'm going to punch that bitch." She snapped, fuming.

"Let me guess who." Angelia gave her a wry smile.

"I was with Jake for like five minutes two years ago and the bitch just won't let it go. She speaks to me like I'm the world's biggest idiot but *she's* the one practically living with the jackass. I was smart enough to dump his useless ass but she carries on like I'm trying to seduce him to steal him away from her. Like he's some sort of prize. Well, all I can say is that he is all hers and I am out of here." She sniped before storming out the door.

"Yeah, she's not my biggest fan either and Jake and I have only ever been strictly platonic. I really miss Lizzie, she was the best thing that ever happened to him and the dumbass let her go." Angelia looked up as she heard loud voices approach as Aimee Allen barrelled through the door with Jake trailing after her.

"Ames, baby, she's just my sister's friend." Jake tried to placate his irate girlfriend as he glanced around quickly. "And look she's gone." She glared at him for a moment before she resumed shouting at him again.

Angelia huffed as her eyes scanned the room. Ciara had gone to join Chris who was chatting quietly with Dylan, Blaine and Mark. Kendra, Kalen, Robbie and Kelly were attempting a conversation, but Kendra kept casting concerned looks in her brother's direction.

"So much for a fun night of movies and friends." She muttered under her breath as she glided her fingers along Blaine's guitar before picking it up and holding it on her lap. She closed her eyes and gently strummed the strings. She blocked everyone out and started playing while humming softly to herself. She lost herself in the music and forgot she wasn't alone. One by one they all turned to stare at her, their eyes widening in surprise as her quiet humming gave way to words sung in a beautiful clear voice.

I'm lying here

Here on my bed

Staring at the wall

Thinking of all

 the things you said

I can hear the rain

As it beats against my window

I have to let go

But it's the hardest thing to do

Here in the night

I'm here on my own

Alone in the…

She faltered before stopping dead as she glanced up wide-eyed and realised that every eye in the room was focused on her. Her face flushed bright red as she dropped the guitar by her feet.

"Don't stop Lia, please. That was beautiful." Blaine's voice broke the silence. She shook her head and lowered her gaze to her hands that were clasped nervously in her lap. She looked up as Aimee approached her.

"Have you played guitar before Angelia?" Aimee asked curiously as Angelia nodded feeling self-conscious. Aimee's obvious dislike of Angelia was always apparent, this was the most she had ever said to her in the four months that she had been seeing Jake. "It was lovely but I didn't recognise the song. What song is that?" She looked intently at Angelia whose cheeks flushed a few shades darker.

"I uh, I kind of composed it. I wrote a uh, a..a...song and I um composed the music for the song." She stammered as Aimee reached down, picked up the guitar and handed it to her. She perched on the arm of the couch.

"That's amazing. Please play it again, with the words of course." Angelia stared at her dumbstruck for a moment as she clutched the guitar in her hands. She looked up in wide eyed panic at Blaine who nodded and smiled encouragingly at her.

"Umm ok. Sure, I, uh, I can do that." She pulled the guitar up with shaky hands and closed her eyes for a moment to compose herself. She looked down at the guitar and started playing again. She glanced back up at Blaine who smiled as she took a deep calming breath and started singing.

I'm lying here

Here on my bed

Staring at the wall

Thinking of all

the things you said

I can hear the rain

As it beats against my window

I have to let go

But it's the hardest thing to do

Here in the night

I'm here on my own

Alone in the dark

With nothing but my dreams

Life's never what it seems

Just when you think

You know just what it means

Someone changes the rules

I guess it's true what they say

That its only fools

Who always rush in

I'm watching the stars

As they sparkle up above

So far away

Yet near enough to touch

They remind me of you

Close yet so distant

I try to be there

But you push me away

I try not to show

How it hurts me inside

Nothings more foolish

Than foolish pride

Life's never what it seems

Just when you think

You know just what it means

Someone changes the rules
I guess it's true what they say
That its only fools
Who always rush in

And I'm lying here
Here on my bed
Staring at the wall
Wishing you'd call
Wondering where you've been
Were you thinking of me?
I miss you so much
When you're not here
I need your touch
And wonder if you care
How empty my world is
When you're not there

Life's never what it seems
Just when you think
You know just what it means
Someone changes the rules
I guess it's true what they say
That its only fools

Who always rush in

I'm dancing in the dark

Pretending you're there

I'm calling your name

But you can't hear

Here in the night

I'm holding you tight

Here in my dreams

Life's never what it seems

Here in the dark

I hear your voice

And you're calling me

Here in the night

Here in my dreams

Life's never what it seems.

Angelia looked up shyly at her friends. Aimee smiled at her while Kendra hugged her.

"That was stunning Lia. You miss him so much, don't you?" She whispered. Pain shimmered in Angelia's eyes as she nodded. Aimee reached out and put her hand gently on her shoulder.

"Don't give up on him honey. Fight for him if you love him. Some things, they're worth fighting for. Others, not so much." She smiled at Angelia and rose to her feet. "I'm sorry, I don't hear any clapping." She said with a stern look.

"No, please don't." Angelia looked horrified and then embarrassed as everyone started smiling and applauding. She stood and handed Blaine his guitar. Christian pulled her into a hug.

"That was incredible Lia. I didn't know you could sing or play guitar." He smiled proudly at her.

"My parents sent me for lessons, I wanted to be a musician but my singing wasn't good enough."

"Who said it wasn't good enough?" Christian asked with a frown.

"Me. There were so many other girls at school who were way better than me so I gave it up after two years. I kept cancelling auditions for plays and school concerts because I was terrified."

"Your voice is beautiful Lia." Mark gave her a broad smile as he wrapped his arms around her in a quick hug.

"Thank you."

"Lia that was stunning." Robbie hugged her. "I can't believe you wrote that. I can't believe you sing. Why have you never sung for us before?" He smiled down at her as she smiled back at him shyly.

"I told you that you had a beautiful voice. Now do you believe me?" Blaine asked with an arched eyebrow.

"Wait. You knew she could sing?" Christian asked.

"Mom sent us for guitar lessons and missy here sang at one of them. I told her she had a beautiful voice back then but she never wanted to believe me." Blaine said with a shrug.

"Grab a seat guys." Jake yelled as he waved a DVD in the air. "We're going to start the movie in a few minutes." Christian and Ciara claimed the overstuffed bean bag in the corner, Kendra and Kalen took the two single chairs and Dylan, Kelly, Mark and Robbie stretched out on the fluffy carpet as Angelia lay across the double couch. Blaine set his guitar down on the table and walked over to her.

"Shift over little sister." He commanded.

She sighed dramatically. "Serious space issues brother of mine." She rolled her eyes and lifted her legs. He flopped down on the couch and she stretched her legs across his lap as he chuckled and shook his head.

Chapter 13

"Are you going to be ok Lia?" Kendra watched her friend with concern. Angelia frowned as she looked up at her.

"Yeah. Why?"

"Kyle's going to be here in a short while and I know you haven't spoken to each other in months. You never told me what you fought about after he left."

"It was my fault. Me and my stupid jealousy." She huffed angrily. "He cut our last Skype call short because he was going on a blind date that one of his new friends set up for him. He felt obligated to go and I completely flipped out at him. I felt embarrassed afterwards and I thought he would call me back to check up on me, but he never did."

"Have you been practicing our new song?" Blaine asked as he and Dylan joined her. He sat down on the floor opposite Angelia as Dylan took a seat next to her.

"I've changed the melody slightly." Dylan handed her a sheet of music. "I thought it would sound better here if you went slightly higher and there if you dropped your pitch slightly lower." He pointed out to her. Blaine played the chords as Angelia sang.

"That does sound better, thanks Dyl." She leaned over to kiss his cheek.

"Anything for you sweet girl." He chuckled as he wrapped an arm around her. She rested her head on his shoulder.

"From the top?" Blaine asked as he strummed the strings on his guitar. She opened her mouth to respond when she heard Jake's voice booming across the room.

"Kyle, good to see you. How was the flight?"

"Very long and extremely tiring but it's good to be home for a bit."

"Hey Lia." Blaine waved his hand in front of her face. "Distracted much?"

"Listen brother of mine, you're starting to make Hitler look like a slacker." She retorted. He grinned at her and she shook her head. He ran his fingers over the strings of his guitar and played a few chords.

"Let's give it a break Blaine." She pleaded; she could feel Kyle's eyes on them.

"What's up with Lia and Dylan?" Kyle asked frowning. Jake smiled smugly.

"We have a surprise for you." He said looking back at the two sitting on the floor. Kyle eyed him suspiciously.

"Something I should know about them?"

"Yeah, probably." Jake smiled secretively. Kyle suppressed the urge to punch him as he clenched his jaw. Jake eyed him warily. "Let's go say hello." He turned and headed over to them. "Look who's home." Jake announced as Kyle joined him.

"Hey, Kyle. Welcome home, you're just in time." Blaine greeted him with a grin.

"In time for what?"

"Blaine don't." Angelia pleaded.

"In time to hear our new song. We just finished it." Blaine smiled. Kyle stared at him blankly.

"Huh? What song? What are you talking about?" Kyle looked at him confused as Blaine turned to Angelia in astonishment.

"Didn't you tell him?" Angelia bit her lip and shook her head.

"What is going on?" Kyle asked exasperated.

"Lia, Dylan and I have been writing songs and music. Lia has an amazing voice, you have to hear her sing." He nodded at Angelia and ran his fingers over the strings and smiled at her. She shook her head quickly. Kyle smiled at her.

"Please, Lia, I'd love to hear you sing." He said softly. She sighed and looked at Blaine.

"Fine." She said in resignation. He grinned triumphantly.

"My little sister is so modest." He laughed. Kyle sat down on the chair opposite Angelia and looked at her. Blaine started playing. Angelia looked at Kyle briefly before closing her eyes and taking a calming breath.

It's almost midnight

It's getting cold

The wind is howling

As I stare outside

It's getting late

I need to sleep

But I can't get you off my mind

I was doing well

Living life

Like a freight train

Fast paced

My life was on track

But all that ended

The day you came back

I keep thinking about you and I

How you never gave us a try

You left me alone and I

Couldn't figure out why

You just walked away

And I fell to my knees

And cried.

It's almost midnight

It's getting cold

The wind is howling

As I stare outside

It's getting late

I need to sleep

But I can't get you off my mind

I moved on

Kept my eye on the prize

Built a wall around my heart

Just one call

You shook my defences

And tore my world apart

Like no time had passed

Baby it's me and I

Am so sorry I made you cry

And said it was you and not I

The truth is that was a lie

I got scared and I

Left you behind

So now its midnight

It's getting cold

The rain is pouring

As I stare outside

It's getting late

I'm going to sleep

You're no longer on my mind

This time I

Get to leave you behind

Blaine looked up at Kyle, who glanced away and coughed to clear the lump in his throat.

"That was incredible. Wow. Lia, I had no idea you could sing like that."

"There's a lot you don't know about me." She smiled shyly.

"I'm starting to see that. Blaine," he paused, then smirked, "your guitar playing has improved a bit." Blaine stood and punched Kyle lightly in the shoulder.

"That's all you have to say?" He asked with a raised eyebrow. Kyle laughed.

"It was amazing. The song, Lia's voice, your playing. Amazing doesn't cover it. I'm blown away."

"I have to head out now, I need to pick Cara up from work." Blaine stretched and reached for his keys.

"Who is Cara?" Kyle asked, confused.

"My girlfriend. Didn't you read the message I sent last month?"

"I've been busy." Kyle gave him a sheepish grin. "Work and Charlie keep me pretty busy."

"Who's Charlie?" Blaine asked as Angelia looked down at the floor. Kyle gave her a quick look. "Ahhh, I'm guessing she's the reason you two aren't speaking." Blaine glanced at Angelia, who had pulled out her phone and was busy scrolling through messages. She glanced up quickly and gave him a small smile. Blaine squeezed her shoulder before heading off to greet their friends.

"It's good to see you, Lia." Kyle said quietly once they were alone.

"Good to see you too. Welcome home." She flashed him a forced smiled as she slipped her phone into her back pocket.

"It's good to be home even if it's just for two weeks. I've really missed everyone." He looked at her intently. "Especially you Lia. I miss our chats. I miss our friendship."

"I know, I've missed you too."

"Mark and I were talking about going out for dinner and drinks tomorrow night with the whole group. You going to join us?" He asked hopefully.

"No, I can't, I've picked up some extra shifts at Con's. I managed to get an internship at a marketing company but it's unpaid, so I need to make money to pay bills." She said as she realised, she was answering a question he hadn't asked.

"Maybe we can get together during the week then?" He asked with a quick shrug.

"I'm working, sorry. My internship." She replied weakly.

"I didn't realise that you work 24/7?" He asked with a hint of sarcasm. She shook her head slightly, ignoring his tone. "Well, hopefully I'll see you before I head back. I really wanted to meet up so we can talk and catch up."

"I'm sure we will."

"I'm going to head home; I'm feeling a bit tired after that long ass flight and I desperately need to take a shower. I just wanted to drop in to say hello to everyone." He leaned forward to gently kiss her on her cheek. She looked up at him in surprise as she felt the familiar rush go through her. He bent down to whisper softly in her ear. "It was wonderful to see you Lia, you sang beautifully tonight." She bit her lip as she fought back tears. She looked up at him and saw sadness flicker across his face. He turned away to look across the room and waved to his brother. Mark made his way over to join them, he gave Angelia a quick hug and followed his brother out the door.

"Lia." She looked up into Ciara's concerned brown eyes. "Are you ok?"

"I'm fine." She flashed her a brave smile.

"You don't look fine." Angelia cringed as she realised that Kendra was standing next to Ciara staring at her intently.

"I am. Blaine has been pushing the late-night practices and I'm just worn down. I need a good night's sleep."

"Did Kyle say something to upset you?" Kendra scowled at her. "Do I need to kick his ass?" Angelia stared at her for a second before bursting into laughter. The mental images of petite 5ft 4 Kendra trying to beat up a man who was 6ft tall and muscular flashed through her mind.

"Oh Kenz. You would have very little effect on him." She sat down on the chair and sighed sadly. "I looked at him tonight and it feels like he's given up, like he's not even fighting for us anymore. He told me he missed our friendship. Not us. Just our friendship." She looked up at her friends with tears in her eyes. "I think I've lost him. I finally pushed him too far and now he's gone. For good. It's all my fault. I pushed him away and straight into another woman's arms."

"Oh, honey." Ciara wrapped her arms around her. "It's you and Kyle. You guys will work it out. You didn't fight tonight; that's a huge improvement. And no relationship you have with other people lasts too long. Weren't you engaged once?" She asked, raising an eyebrow. "This new girl is just a distraction for him, you'll see."

Angelia laughed as she wiped at her eyes with her sleeves.

"I honestly don't know anymore. I feel like it's two steps forward and three steps back with us. The long-distance thing never works out and I," She sighed, "I just don't know anymore Ciara. I love him, Heaven knows I do but this dance we've been doing the last few years, it needs to stop now. We need to decide, we either give it 100% and one of us moves to the other or we finally end it, stay friends and move on." She said sadly.

Ciara nodded and looked at her. "What do *you* want Lia?"

"I want him." She said sighing. "It's always been Kyle. From the first time we met, we just had this instant spark and connection and with everything that's happened, my feelings for him are still the same, if anything, they're stronger."

"You're coming with tomorrow night? Out to dinner?" Kendra asked. Angelia groaned and dropped her head in her hands.

"I gave him some stupid story about having to pull extra shifts because I have a non-paying marketing internship. What is wrong with me? The whole point of this break from each other was so that we could work on ourselves and communicate more and stop lying to each other. We had a huge fight because my communication skills with him are not great and he's just gotten back and I'm already lying to him. Seriously, what is wrong with me?"

"Come with tomorrow night. Be friendly and flirt with him. Remind him why he fell in love with you in the first place. You are Angelia freaking Ryan. The love of his life. You don't just move on from that." Kendra hugged her tightly. Angelia laughed and hugged her back.

"You are crazy."

"Wanna hear the bad news about that?" Kendra asked with a straight face. Angelia gave her a sceptical look.

"I'm not sure I want to."

"You are stuck with me for life lady. We will always be best friends…"

"I know too much." Angelia finished her sentence laughing. "That's not bad news, Kenz, that's the best news." Kendra lay her head on her friend's shoulder.

"I love you, LiLi." She said laughing.

"Keeeeeendraaaaaa. Don't call me LiLi."

Chapter 14

"Whoever is ringing the bell is a dead man." Mark muttered to himself as he stormed to the front door. He swung it open and glared at the auburn-haired woman who was reaching for the doorbell again.

"That took long enough." She snapped at him. He glared at her and opened his mouth to respond when he heard his brother walk up behind him.

"Charlie?" He asked, half asleep and confused. "What are you doing here?"

"I decided to surprise you, sweetie." She flashed him a huge smile as she pushed past Mark to hug Kyle. Mark shook his head and slammed the door. He turned around to look at a perplexed Kyle.

"Charlotte, this is my brother Mark." She turned around to smile brightly at Mark who gave her a furious look, turned around, stormed back to his room and slammed the door loudly.

"Not very friendly, is he?" She asked in a snarky tone.

"He's not a morning person. He also doesn't like the doorbell being rung a hundred times." He said, giving her a disapproving look.

"I was just so excited to see you." She beamed a huge smile at him.

"I'm still not sure what you're doing here." She wrapped her arms around him.

"I missed you and I wanted to see where you're from and meet your family and friends." She purred.

"You should have told me you were coming." He said, running his hand through his dark blonde hair. "Wait. You missed me?" He looked at her. "I literally just left; you must have caught a flight not long after mine." He frowned at her.

"I tried to invite myself so we could fly together but you clearly didn't understand what I was trying to do." She gave him a pouting look. "So, I decided to fly here by myself." She gave him a dazzling smile.

"It's too early for this. I'm going back to bed." He grumbled. She looked down at her suitcase and then at Kyle's retreating back. She sighed dramatically, grabbed the handle and pulled her suitcase down the passage.

"Charlotte is…charming." Blaine gave Kyle a sideways look

"Sarcasm?" Kyle asked as he sipped his coffee. Blaine laughed and nodded.

"Oh, she's really charming." Mark sniped from the coffee machine. "I hope she's jetlagged and not planning on coming out with us tonight.

"We're going out tonight?" A loud voice interrupted them.

"Ughh." Mark groaned as he shot his brother a look, picked up his coffee and toasted sandwich and walked out of the kitchen. Blaine looked at Kyle, then at Charlotte, grabbed his plate and coffee and followed Mark out.

"I'm starting to get the impression that they don't like me." Charlotte looked at Kyle and tapped a manicured finger on the countertop.

"We're going out with some friends tonight." He explained, ignoring her comment. "It'll be a boring get-together. Why don't you stay here and get some rest. You must be tired after your flight." He gave her a caring smile.

"I feel perfectly fine and I am *dying* to meet everyone and see where you used to party and drink with your friends." She beamed at him.

"That's just great." Kyle mumbled as he contemplated adding whiskey to his coffee.

"I need to start planning my outfit." She headed out the door.

"Charlie, it's a pub. Jeans or a skirt or something casual will be perfectly fine, no need to plan." She gave him a look over her shoulder.

"It's like you don't even know me." She said haughtily as she made her way to his room.

"Where's Little Miss Perky?" Mark asked as he walked back in the kitchen.

"Planning her outfit for tonight." Kyle shook his head. "Be grateful she's perky." He warned. "She can go from perky to super bitch in less than 5 seconds."

"Why are you with her?"

"She can be a lot of fun and we have the same taste in music and movies. We get on well and she likes to keep active so we go on lots of hikes and walks. Most of my co-workers are married so it gets a bit lonely over there, it's nice to have someone to spend time with." Kyle smiled at his brother.

"At least Lia won't be there tonight." Blaine looked at his watch. "I'm going to spend time with Cara, I'll see you later at the pub." He picked up his phone and keys and headed for the door. Mark reached for his keys and Kyle turned to look at him.

"Going somewhere?"

"We need some groceries, can't have coffee without milk. If I go without coffee…" He gave Kyle a look.

"Yeah, no one wants to see that. I thought Lia had a coffee addiction." Kyle shook his head.

"Kyyyyllllle." Charlotte whined from up the passage. He rolled his eyes and Mark picked up his phone.

"That's my cue to leave."

"Take me with you." Kyle pleaded. Mark laughed and headed quickly out the door.

***

"Hi, everyone." Kyle greeted his friends as he walked into the outside area of the pub.

"Hello." Charlotte beamed at them; Mark rolled his eyes as he walked past the couple to Blaine who whispered something to Cara as the rest of their friends stared blankly at Charlotte. Kyle cleared his throat.

"Charlie this is Kalen, Chris, Ciara, Kendra, Megan, Robbie, Kelly, Casey, Dylan and of course, you know Blaine and I assume that is Cara." Kyle gave all of them a tense smile. "Oh, and this is Charlie, um, Charlotte." He said, putting his hand on her shoulder. She wrapped her arms tightly around his waist and smiled at all of them.

"Hello. It's so nice to *finally* meet all of you." She said gleefully. "I've heard so much about you I feel like I know all of you already." Kyle flagged a waiter down as his friends exchanged confused looks before turning to Mark who rolled his eyes and shook his head.

"Does anyone need a drink?" Kyle asked, removing Charlotte's arms from his waist as the waiter finally made his way to them. His friends all shook their heads in silence. Mark made his way over to him. Charlotte perched on a barstool and looked at Mark.

"The waiter is taking too long." She whined before snapping her fingers in front of Mark's face. "Why don't you go fetch us drinks from the bar. It will probably be quicker." Mark's eyebrows shot up in surprise. He opened his mouth to respond but Kyle shook his head so he clenched his jaw instead.

"We've only just ordered the drinks Charlie, you need to be patient." He gave her a firm look.

The waiter appeared with two beers and a cocktail.

"About time." She snapped at the waiter. "Did you have to go and pick the pineapples and coconuts?" She tossed her hair over her shoulder and took a sip. "Ugh, this is bland and tasteless." She complained as Kyle rolled his eyes.

"Just drink it and order something else just now." He took a swig of his beer and avoided his brother's eyes.

"You're being so mean to me." She pouted. "I flew all the way here to see you."

"Yeah, *uninvited*." Mark sniped. She narrowed her eyes at him.

"You're right, I'm sorry." Kyle said rolling his eyes at his brother. She turned to flash a bright smile at him.

"Ummm Kyle." Mark said quietly. He looked up at his brother with a *What now?* look. "Angelia's here." Mark looked over at the entrance to the pub where she was hugging one of the waitresses. She waved at her friends, who were looking at each other in concern. She moved across to them and hugged Ciara tightly before looking up and seeing the two brothers watching her. She smiled and waved at them before hugging Kalen. Charlotte looked from Kyle to Mark to Angelia and back again.

"Who is that girl?" She asked disdainfully. Kyle shot her a cautious look.

"We're friends." Kyle said giving his brother a quick look.

"With a long, complicated history." Mark added as he took a swig of his beer to hide his smile. Kyle shot him an irritated look.

"Thanks Mark. Seriously. Your assistance is invaluable and unnecessary." He said sarcastically.

"What does he mean?" Charlotte asked glaring at Angelia.

"We were together romantically on and off for a while." Kyle explained calmly.

"And they have unresolved issues that they haven't quite worked through yet." Mark stated with an innocent look on his face.

"Seriously, Mark. Stop helping." Kyle gave him a pained look.

"I think *Charlie* should know the history between you and Lia." Mark smirked. Charlotte tuned the brothers out and watched as Angelia finished greeting her friends and made her way to the ladies' bathroom. She glanced at the brothers briefly and realised that they were so engrossed in their bickering that they weren't paying any attention to her. She slipped unnoticed off her chair and made her way into the restrooms. She admired herself in the mirror as she waited for Angelia to come out. She played with the rings on her fingers and smiled briefly when she heard a flush and the door unlatched. Angelia stepped out and gave her a friendly smile before opening the tap.

"You must be the Angelia I have heard so much about." Charlotte drawled as she looked her up and down. Angelia looked up at her startled.

"Umm ok, I am Angelia. I'm not sure what you've heard though." She dried her hands on a paper towel.

"I hear you and Kyle have had a long, complicated romantic on-again/off-again relationship."

"Sounds about right." Angelia mumbled as she threw the paper towel into the bin.

"Well, Kyle's with me now so I would say that your little relationship will be off again permanently. As in *forever*." She sneered at Angelia who looked back at her stone-faced.

"Oh, right, you must be Charlie, Kyle's American girlfriend." She said in an icy tone.

"Actually," she said smugly, holding her hand up in front of Angelia's face, "I'm Kyle's American *fiancée*." Angelia's face paled. She gave Charlotte a forced smile. "A word of advice, sweetie stay away from him. I will protect what's mine any way I need to. So, any little ideas you have of getting him back you can just forget. He told me about your pathetic juvenile relationship and how you just can't make up your mind about what you want. He doesn't want a silly, indecisive little girl anymore, especially now that he has a sophisticated woman who meets *all* of his needs." She sneered at Angelia who clenched her jaw before giving her an icy insincere smile.

"Congratulations, I'm sure you and Kyle will be very happy together." Angelia snapped as she spun on her heel and stormed out the door. She made her way out the bar and stormed past Kyle and Mark.

"Hey Lia," Kyle called out with a smile, stepping out from the small round table he was leaning on. "I'm so glad you made it."

She spun around, stepped right up to him, looked him in the eye and said, "Drop fucking dead Kyle." With as much venom as she could muster. She turned around, headed to her friends and spoke to them briefly as she grabbed her bag and headed towards the entrance. Kendra, Casey and Ciara looked up and glared at Kyle.

"What the hell is going on? Did I miss something?" Kyle looked confused for a second before storming off after Angelia. Mark glanced at Charlotte's empty seat and groaned.

"I can only guess." He muttered shaking his head.

"Lia. Wait!" Kyle shouted.

"For what Kyle? You? I don't think so." She snapped as she opened her car door. Kyle stepped towards her and slammed the door shut.

"You tell me to drop dead and storm off and now you're just going to leave?" He asked furiously.

"Yes, that's the plan."

"You're just going to run away like you always do?"

"Technically, I'm going to drive, but yeah, that's the general idea."

"You're really funny." He snapped at her.

"Oh yes, I met Charlie by the way. She's *lovely*." Angelia sneered sarcastically.

"You did?" He looked at her in surprise.

"Oh yes, she followed me into the bathroom to threaten me and tell me to stay away from you and to tell me that you belong to her. She's charming that one. A real keeper." She opened her door and he slammed it shut again as he moved closer to her. Angelia looked up and muttered. "Uh oh, now you're in trouble." Under her breath.

Kyle frowned. "What?"

"Kyle." A sharp voice called him. "Is everything ok?" Charlotte glowered at him.

"Everything is fine. Go inside." He said over his shoulder.

"I want you to come back inside with me. Now, Kyle." She demanded as she crossed her arms over her chest. He turned to scowl at her.

"Dammit Charlie. Go inside." He shouted at her. She turned on her heel and stormed back to the entrance of the pub. Kyle turned back to Angelia who was leaning against the car. She looked up at him, pain and defeat in her eyes.

"Your future is calling you and your past is finally saying goodbye." She said softly before turning around to open her car door.

"You're giving up on us?"

"I have to. I can't fight for you anymore Kyle. How do you fight for someone who doesn't want to be fought for?"

"You don't know that. Why would you think I don't want you to fight for me? To fight for us? I'm *still* fighting for us baby." He reached out to brush a tear off her cheek. She pushed his hand away.

"How are you fighting for us? I feel like such an idiot. How do I compete with her? You have this whole life in New York with her, how do I compete with that? Just go Kyle. Leave me alone. Stay out of my life and stay away from me." She said pushing him back. He shook his head and turned to walk off. She started to climb into the car and hesitated. "Congratulations, by the way." She snapped at him. He spun around to look at her.

"Congratulations for what Lia?" He snapped back at her. She shook her head as tears welled in her eyes.

"On your engagement. When were you planning on telling me? Before the ceremony? After your honeymoon? During your divorce? Were you ever planning on telling me? You know what? I don't care anymore Kyle. I wish you all the happiness in the world. You and Charlie deserve each other." Tears streamed down her cheeks as she climbed into her car and sped off. Kyle stared after her in stunned silence. He turned around to find Blaine, Dylan, Kalen and Robbie standing behind him. Blaine glared at him as he clenched his jaw and shook his head while Dylan, Kalen and Robbie looked down the road in the direction that Angelia had driven off in before looking back angrily at Kyle. He reached into his pocket to grab his keys. Blaine stepped forward to shove his shoulder.

"Stay away from her Kyle." He snarled before storming off with Kalen following him.

"You've hurt her for the last time." Robbie was seething.

"I just need to speak to her to clear things up." Kyle held his hands up as Robbie gripped his shirt.

"I swear Kyle if she sheds one more tear because of you, friend or not, I'll take you out myself."

Dylan grabbed his brother's arm.

"Don't Robs, let's go check on Lia." Robbie let go of Kyle and nodded at his brother before turning to walk off.

Kyle exhaled heavily as he shook his head before storming to the entrance of the pub where Charlotte was standing.

"What did you say to her, Charlotte? What did you do?" He shouted at her. She stared at him wide-eyed.

"I told her the truth Kyle. Why are you mad at me? I should be mad at you. She knew about me but I knew nothing about her. How do you think that makes me feel?" She looked up at him with tear-filled eyes. "Is that why you didn't want me to come on this trip with you? Or why you tried to talk me out of joining you tonight?" She looked up at him pouting. He breathed out heavily as he tried to control his temper.

"We're leaving. Right now." He said angrily in a low voice. "Go get in the car, Charlotte." He ran his hand over his face as she stalked off to the car. He turned around to look at his brother and shook his head. He pulled his phone out of his pocket and dialled. He sighed as the call went straight through to voicemail.

"Lia, please call me when you get this. We need to talk." He snapped his phone shut as Mark walked over to him.

"What the hell just happened?"

"Hurricane fucking Charlotte," Kyle muttered angrily looking down at his phone before looking up at his brother. "I'm taking her back to the house." He said through gritted teeth before turning to walk off.

"Kyle." He turned back to look at Mark. "Don't get blood on the carpets, it's a bitch to clean." He said with a straight face. Kyle stared at him for a moment before laughing and shaking his head.

Chapter 15

"Lia." Kyle knocked loudly on her door. "Please open the door, Lia. I need to speak to you. I'm just going to keep knocking until you let me in." The door swung open and Kyle looked at Kalen in surprise.

"Kalen. What are you doing here?"

"I may as well tell you now. Lia and I have been seeing each other for a while. We went out partying one night and we hooked up and the rest, as they say, is history." Kalen said with a small smile and a shrug. "We didn't know how to tell you." Kyle stared at him blankly. "Come in you idiot." Kalen moved aside and gestured for him to enter. Kyle took a few steps inside and stopped dead.

"Wait. What?" He looked at Kalen.

"It just kind of happened." He shrugged.

"Are you for fucking real?" Kyle was fuming. "You *are* kidding right?"

"I am, yes. Come in and sit down. Lia was in the shower; she should be out any minute."

"Kalen! What the…"

"I thought it would be funny." He shrugged and dropped down into the single chair.

"Well, it wasn't. What are you doing here anyway?"

"Blaine, Rob, Dyl and I came to check up on Lia after she drove off last night. We were worried about her so Blaine and I stayed the night." He looked up as Kyle raised an eyebrow. "I stayed in JR's room, Blaine stayed on the couch with Lia. You just missed him; he left to pick up Cara for work."

"I've been trying to call her all night, she's not answering me." He dropped down onto the chair opposite his friend and ran a hand over his face.

"Truth is brother, I have seen you guys fight a hundred times but last night was different. Last night Lia realised that she was going to lose you for good. She realised that this time goodbye really does mean forever. I saw her face as she drove off. I have never seen pain like that. You could have told her yourself man, she had to hear it from your psycho fiancée. Lia deserves better than that. You didn't even tell any of us." Kalen looked at him furiously. Kyle opened his mouth to respond when he heard his name. He looked up to see Angelia standing by the chair.

"I'm making coffee." She said softly. "Would you like some?" Kyle shot to his feet and grabbed her hands.

"Baby, please, I need to speak to you." He pleaded. Pain flashed across her face and she attempted to pull her hands away from him. "Lia, please, I need you to listen to me. I was trying to figure out why you were so mad last night and why you were saying goodbye. I know we fought about Charlotte before and I thought you were furious that I brought her with. Actually, I didn't even bring her with, she invited herself, she just pitched up on our doorstep yesterday morning. Lia, please, I need you to look at me." He put his hand under her chin and lifted her face up to his. "I am *not* engaged to Charlotte, we were barely even dating, she wanted a committed relationship and I was just looking for friendship. I had no idea what you were talking about last night. She lied Lia. She made it all up. She tried to deny it but eventually came clean about everything she said to you."

"But she had a ring?" Angelia looked at him, confused.

"She has a million rings and she normally has four or five on at any time, even when she's bloody hiking. She put one on her ring finger to make it seem real, to make you believe." Kyle brushed her hair back off her face. He saw the sadness in her eyes shift to rage.

"Where is she?" She asked in an icy voice.

"She's on a plane back to the States. I dropped her off at the airport last night and I told her that I want nothing more to do with her. Lia if I was going to make a decision like that, I would tell you first. Ok?" He pulled her into his arms. She wrapped her arms tightly around him. He bent down to kiss the top of her head and ran his fingers through her hair before leaning down to kiss her gently. She put her hands under his shirt and rested them on his chest as she kissed him back. He pulled her against him as their kisses became deeper and more passionate, she lowered her hands to his jeans and started to unbutton them.

"Umm guys. I'm still here. I love you both but I really don't want a free porno show. I mean Lia, yes anytime but Kyle I do not want to see your ugly ass naked. Again." Kalen protested from the couch. Angelia giggled and pushed Kyle away.

"Sorry Kale." She apologised.

"That coffee does sound good though." Kalen mused. Kyle gave him a look and Kalen shook his head. "Are you seriously going to kick me out so you can have sex?"

Kyle grinned and wrapped his arms around Angelia's waist pulling her back against his chest.

"Of course not, I'm going to make us all coffee and we're going to sit and have a chat."

"Really?" Kyle gave her a disappointed look.

"Yes, really. Go sit and talk to Kalen." He dropped down on the couch and looked at his friend with a smile.

"So, tell me what's been happening." Kyle leaned back and made himself comfortable.

"Well." Kalen peered into the kitchen where Angelia was busy with the coffee machine. "Kendra and I hooked up a few weeks ago. We decided to keep it on the down low until we figure out where it's going."

"Wow, that's got to be weird though, isn't she almost like a sister to you." Kyle mused.

"Thank you, Kyle, that was *very* helpful." Kalen rolled his eyes.

"I take it Lia doesn't know."

"No one knows, well now you know. You can't tell Lia either."

"My lips are sealed." Kyle promised.

"Yeah, until she offers you sexual favours for gossip again." Kalen gave him a disapproving look.

"I swear that I will not let her tempt me this time." Kyle said solemnly.

"Your coffee is served." Angelia smiled as she brought their coffee through. She curled up on the couch next to Kyle, he put his arm around her shoulders.

"Having sugar with a side of coffee there Kalen?" Kyle asked sarcastically.

"I have 3 teaspoons of sugar, that is not a lot." He protested as he stirred his coffee.

"No wonder you're always running around like a squirrel on crack. You have like ten cups of coffee a day. That's thirty teaspoons of sugar." Kyle smirked at him.

"I have four cups, don't get me confused with missy next to you there. There is no blood in those veins, only caffeine." Kalen said snidely.

"What have I done to you?" She asked wide-eyed.

"Just tell your boyfriend over there to keep his snide remarks to himself." Kalen grumbled.

"Hey, how come he belongs to me now?" Angelia protested. "I'm sure he was your friend first."

"Ouch. I thought you love me." Kyle gave her a hurt look. She shrugged her shoulders.

"I suppose I do." She sighed as she put her coffee cup down. He raised an eyebrow, pulled her legs up onto the couch and hovered over her.

"Ok. In about ten seconds you are going to be begging for mercy."

"Don't you dare tickle me." She warned him. "Kalen will protect me, won't you Kale?" She looked over at him and fluttered her eyelashes at him. He snorted into his coffee cup.

"I happen to like living thanks. I am not getting between you and Kyle. You are on your own."

"What a friend you are." She rolled her eyes. Kyle's hands moved to her sides. "Ok. I do, I love you." She laughed as he smiled at her victoriously. She bit the side of her lip and smiled as she reached up to run her fingers down his cheek. "I claim you. You belong to me." She said softly looking into his eyes.

"I've always been yours." He said, his voice dropping to a husky tone as he bent down to brush his lips against hers. She smiled up at him as he bent down to press his lips against hers as she wrapped her legs around his waist and moved her hands to the back of his neck and head.

"Seriously?" Kalen gave them a pained look. "I'm still here." Angelia laughed, pushed Kyle off her and sat up.

"Sorry." She apologised as she snuggled up against Kyle's chest and gave Kalen a smile. "What are you up to today?"

"I don't know, I was thinking of going to a movie."

"By yourself?" She looked at him with a raised eyebrow.

"Umm no, with a girl." He said, his cheeks flushing slightly.

"Oooooh, tell me more." Angelia looked at him with wide eyes. "You didn't tell me you have a girlfriend."

"We just…we um…she is uh…well we… I have to go." Kalen shot to his feet. "Bye." He shouted moving to the door as fast as he could. Angelia shook her head.

"That boy needs to get laid." She chuckled.

"Maybe he'll get lucky tonight." Kyle said shrugging. Angelia stood, collected the mugs and took them to the kitchen.

"No, Kendra's making him wait."

"What? You know about Kale and Kendra?" Kyle looked at her in surprise. She gave him an exasperated look.

"Kendra is my best friend. Of course I know. We tell each other everything."

"So, you were just torturing him now?" He asked, giving her a disapproving look before smiling. She laughed and nodded. "You are evil." He laughed as she stood in front of him and held out her hand to him. He looked up at her confused.

"You want to go somewhere?" He asked as he took her hand and stood up.

"Yeah, to my room." She said softly. "I've been waiting for you for all these months, Kyle, do you honestly think that I did that to sit here drinking coffee and discussing Kendra and Kalen's non-existent sex life?" She gave him a shy smile before turning around and leading him down the passage.

"We need to talk Lia." Kyle hugged her closer.

"Please don't ruin this, Kyle." She pleaded softly. He laughed and kissed her neck gently.

"I'm not going to ruin anything. I love you Lia, you know that. When I see my future, I see you in it. I don't want to be with anyone else. I want to be with you forever, but you won't leave here and I can't come back yet, I still have another six months left on my contract. I have to go back to New York in a couple of weeks but I would really like to spend as much time with you as I can now, preferably drama-free."

"And out of the bedroom, right?" She laughed.

"That's negotiable." He grinned.

"You're impossible."

"I missed this. I missed us." He whispered into her ear. "I dreamt about this for eight months. We have been through so much the past few years. I still remember the night I met you, it feels like it was in another lifetime." He laughed quietly. "We've hit so many roadblocks along the way."

"What roadblocks?" She asked sitting up.

"Drunken hook ups."

"Oh yeah, not quite pregnant girlfriends."

Secret boyfriends."

"Secret fiancées?"

"Yeah, so secret I didn't even know about it." He shook his head.

"Almost sleeping with my best friend."

"I think we covered that under drunken hook ups."

"True." Angelia smiled.

"I just don't want you to get hurt when I leave again." He said quietly.

"I won't. I'll miss you but it's different because I know you're going. And I know you'll come back. I haven't given up on us and I now know that you haven't given up on us either. I'm willing to try the long-distance relationship thing until you come back."

"Good, me too. I just want to rest and relax and spend time with you and the hooligans the next few weeks."

"Guess what?" She whispered into his ear.

"What?" He whispered back.

"I bought a new can of whipped cream." She looked up at him and smiled. He laughed and shook his head.

"What am I going to do with you?"

She looked at him thoughtfully. "Is that rhetorical or are you looking for suggestions?" She gave him a coy look. He laughed and pushed her over onto her back. He smiled down at her.

"I love you." He whispered.

"I love you too."

***

"So, I have a question." Robbie grinned at Kyle across the table.

"Rob if you say the words whipped cream, I am going to drown you in the pool." Christian gave him a warning look. Robbie chuckled and shook his head.

"No, my question is for both the McAllister brothers." He smirked at them as Kyle shook his head.

"What do you want to know Rob?" He asked sighing.

"I'm just wondering if you two attract crazy or if you *make* them crazy." He laughed.

"Are you calling me crazy?" Angelia glared at him.

"If the straitjacket fits Lia." Robbie grinned at her.

"Bite me." She said rolling her eyes.

"Yeah, I'll leave that for your boy to do later." He said grinning at Kyle who shook his head as he ran his fingers up and down Angelia's arm.

"Yeah, I have to apologise for Charlie. She is, uh," He shrugged.

"Batshit crazy." Kelly suggested with a giggle.

"Yeah, pretty much." He chuckled wryly. "I don't know what I was thinking." He sighed. "Charlie was the only crazy one though." He raised an eyebrow at Robbie who snorted.

"Oh yeah. What about Brianna?" He smirked

"Yeah. Ok. I'll give you that one." Kyle shook his head.

"And what about that one woman who used to stalk you at Con's?" He asked as Kyle groaned.

"Really? I never heard about this." Angelia looked up at him.

"She was scary crazy." Robbie laughed. "Like Fatal Attraction crazy. Your boy there made the mistake of smiling at her and she fell in love. She used to sit at the bar staring at him for hours on end and stalking him at the shops and gym. He tried to be nice to her but she scared the living hell out of him. Whatever happened to her anyway?" Robbie looked at Kyle.

"Her husband packed up her and all their stuff and moved far away."

"Wait. She was married?" Robbie stared at him in shock.

"Oh yeah." Kyle laughed. "Her husband came to apologise to me. Apparently, I was not her first, I was heartbroken to hear that." He shook his head as he swigged his beer.

"I totally get it." Angelia smiled at him. He looked at her with a raised eyebrow. "If you weren't mine, I would definitely stalk you."

"Is that right?" He asked as he leaned over to kiss her.

"Uh-huh." She smiled at him as she pressed her lips against his and ran her hand over his chest. She bit his lower lip gently before pressing her lips against his again. He moaned softly and pulled her closer to him.

"You two. No sex at the table." Mark sighed shaking his head. "You know, the list of places that I have to say No sex to grows longer every day." Angelia smiled and looked at him.

"We were just kissing." She protested.

"Yeah, I know where just kissing leads to young lady, I live here too, remember." He gave her a stern look as she laughed and took a sip of her cider. She looked back at him.

"Wait. Robs asked both of you that question. What's your story?" She asked looking at him.

"One was that blind date that went so well."

"Mark almost had to change his number." Blaine chuckled. "She wouldn't stop calling him for weeks." Mark shook his head.

"And then there was Lana." He sighed. "She seemed pretty cool in the beginning. Loads of fun, we got on well and then she basically moved in here the one day when I was at work. These two clowns even helped her move in." He said gesturing to Kyle and Blaine who both burst out laughing.

"How were we supposed to know?" Blaine protested. "We were trying to be helpful."

"We had been dating for a month. In what world would I ask her to move in after just one month?" Mark gave him an exasperated look. "Anyway, I got home and found I had a new roommate. I honestly didn't know what to do so I tried to make the best of the situation and then she started demanding I stay home more and not drink beer and tequila. She wanted me to change the washing powder brand we use and wash dishes by hand and a whole list of things I can't even remember anymore. She was certifiable that one." He shook his head.

"So how did you get rid of her."

"Well, I went out almost every night with the guys and she would go psycho at me when I got home. One day she came storming into the lounge while I was watching a movie and said she needed a commitment from me, I had to marry her or else." He chuckled as he took a swig of his beer.

"Or else what?"

"Well, that was the question, Kel. So, I asked her exactly that. She went psycho and said that if I didn't propose she was going to leave." He shrugged. "So, I asked her if she needed help packing or if she could manage it herself."

"What happened then?"

"We had to get a new flat screen." Blaine chuckled.

"What? Why?" Megan asked as she leaned forward with her elbows on the table.

"She decided to mark her departure by slamming a bottle of wine against our old one." Kyle shook his head. "Mark had to buy a new one."

"I was more than happy to do that." He laughed.

"Sooooo, who's cooking dinner tonight?" Kalen asked. Mark looked over at his brother.

"Did you invite this pack of wolves over for dinner and forget to tell me?" He asked raising his eyebrow.

"Not that I'm aware of." Kyle looked at Kalen.

"Earlier you said you were making dinner." Kalen grinned at him. Kyle groaned and shook his head.

"I meant for Lia, not you Kalen."

"That's not fair." Kalen grumbled. "Why only for Lia?" Kyle smiled and leaned forward.

"Because Lia does stuff for me." He smirked as he sat back and reached for Angelia's hand.

"If you want to take over from me for a while Kalen, I can explain to you exactly what Kyle likes." Angelia smiled mischievously at him as Kyle gave her a horrified look.

"Our conversations seem to deteriorate more and more." Mark sighed as he looked at his brother.

"I can make dinner if my sous chef agrees to help me." Kyle looked over at his girlfriend. She smiled and nodded.

"Yay." Kalen cheered. "I've been looking forward to having a decent meal." He grinned at Kyle who smirked at him before looking at Ciara.

"Kalen. You are now officially homeless." She glared at him. He stared at her wide-eyed.

"No, your cooking is great. That's not what I meant. I've been living on takeout and frozen meals so you know…" He trailed off as he turned to Mark.

"Can I live here?"

"No." Mark shook his head as everyone laughed. Kyle stretched and looked at Angelia.

"Should we go get the food started babe?" She nodded. He stood and pulled her to her feet before lifting her arms over his shoulders and wrapping his arms around her waist. He bent down to kiss her as she curled her fingers softly at the back of his neck. He pulled her closer to him as their kisses grew more heated.

"Seriously you two." Mark sighed. "It's like living with two horny teenagers." He shook his head as Kyle laughed and let go of Angelia.

"Let's go." He laced his fingers through hers and walked to the kitchen.

"They seem so happy and in love." Christian looked at Mark.

"They really are." Blaine smiled. "In a way, I think the whole thing that happened with Charlie was a good thing. It's almost like it made them realise how much they love each other. They've even discussed doing the whole long-distance relationship thing until he moves back here."

"He's moving back?" Mark asked. Blaine looked at him and nodded.

"Yeah. They're more in love than ever and I honestly didn't think that was possible."

"Well, they need to make it work this time. I don't know how many chances you're supposed to get but they have had a hella lot more than I think you're allowed." Kalen said shaking his head.

"Are we still doing Family dinner tomorrow night?" Robbie asked as he ran his fingers over Kelly's blonde curls gently.

"Of course. Why?" Mark asked.

"Kyle's cooking tonight." He squinted up at the window. "I hope he's cooking. It's very quiet in there."

"I'm happy to cook if everyone wants to do dinner as normal." Mark shrugged.

"It's my favourite part of the weekend." Kelly smiled. "So, we're definitely in." She smiled at Robbie who nodded.

"Favourite day of my weekend too. Just a chilled day with the fam." He grinned. "Catching up and relaxing, amazing food and a movie and popcorn with all of you. Life doesn't get any better than that." He sighed as he leaned back and put his arm around Kelly's shoulders.

"I agree." She smiled at him.

"Me too." Kendra laughed.

"Anyone need a drink?" Dylan asked as he stood up.

"May as well bring for everyone." Mark chuckled as Dylan headed inside. He came out a few minutes later and handed out drinks.

"Well, I hope no one is starving." He chuckled. Mark shot him a look.

"Why?" He asked in a pained voice.

"I've just been in the kitchen, there is no sign of the lovebirds or food, and Kyle's door is closed." He shook his head as he sat down.

"So, pizza or burgers fam?" Kalen asked dejectedly.

"Mark, have you seen my car keys?" Kyle stuck his head out the door.

"Yeah, they're in the lounge. Where are you going?" He asked looking up at him.

"Just need to get some vegetables, pasta and cream." He answered.

"Whipped or normal?" Robbie asked with a cheeky grin.

"Both." Kyle smirked.

"Where've you been?" Mark asked as he tried not to smile.

"Uhhh." Kyle looked over his shoulder and then back at his brother. "We were just getting changed quickly."

"Really? That's the same shirt you were wearing when you went in and its inside out now." He laughed as Kyle looked down and then gave him a sheepish grin.

"See you in a few minutes." He laughed as he pulled his shirt off and ducked back inside.

***

"Uggh you two are sickening." Kalen complained as Kyle kissed Angelia on the cheek and pulled her closer to him.

"No sex in the pool." Mark shouted across to them.

"You are so inappropriate." Kyle shouted back.

"You mean no sex in the pool again, right?" Angelia asked innocently looking at him over Kyle's shoulder. Christian groaned and covered his face with his hands while Mark stared at her. "What?" She shrugged.

"She's kidding." Kyle laughed.

"I'm not convinced." Mark muttered under his breath as he turned back to his game of pool with Robbie, Kelly and Megan. Angelia wrapped her arms around Kyle's neck.

"These two weeks have gone so quickly. I can't believe I have to say goodbye to you tomorrow." She pouted.

"It's not goodbye, I'll be back sooner than you think." He laughed as she wrapped her legs around his waist and sighed.

"Ok. I guess I'll miss you. For a while at least. Then I'll move on to the cute new barista at Give Me Coffee." She flashed him an evil smile. "The one who served us yesterday. Tall, dark hair, dreamy smile and musc..." her words were cut off as Kyle dunked her underwater. She came up spluttering.

"What was that for?"

"Really? Do you have my replacement picked out already? I haven't even left yet."

"A girls got needs you know." She shrugged. He laughed and pulled her back into his arms.

"Yeah, I know what needs you have and don't worry I'll make sure you are so satisfied you won't even notice how cute the new barista is." He trailed his lips down her neck and along her shoulder.

"Ummm you two. You do realise that sound travels and we can hear every word you say." Blaine looked at them as he shook his head in disapproval.

"Ooohhh." Angelia moaned as she blushed.

"You'll be saying that a few times later tonight as well." Kyle smirked as he wrapped her legs back around his waist.

"Kyle." Christian and Mark both yelled.

"Sorry." He grinned at them.

"Your little brother." Blaine sniggered at Mark.

"Your little sister." Mark reminded him. Blaine's smile faded.

"Oh yeah." He groaned as he put his hand over his eyes.

"Kind of felt like old times the last two weeks. Maybe there is hope for them after all." Christian smiled as he watched the couple share a tender kiss.

"Yeah, they do suit each other. I love seeing Lia so happy. And Kyle too obviously." Blaine smiled as he wrapped his arm around his girlfriend.

"Hey, lovebirds." Robbie called out to the couple in the pool. "You gonna get out and come partying with us? There's a hot new DJ playing at Retro tonight." He raised his eyebrows.

Kyle shook his head. "No, it's my last night before I head home tomorrow, I kind of promised Lia…"

"Yeah, we *all* heard what you promised Lia." Robbie cut him off and chuckled. Kelly wrapped her arms around his waist and kissed his cheek.

"We're going to head out now babe." She told him. She waved to the couple in the pool. "We'll see you guys tomorrow for a few drinks?" she asked. Angelia smiled and waved back.

"Yes, we haven't decided where yet, I'll text you in the morning. Try not to get too drunk Kel." Angelia laughed.

"I won't." She blew the two of them a kiss. "Love you both."

"Love you too Kel." Angelia smiled as Kyle waved at them.

"That actually sounds like fun." Mark looked at Blaine and Cara and raised his eyebrows.

"It does, I haven't gone dancing in weeks. Please honey can we go?" Cara pleaded with Blaine. He smiled at her and looked at Mark.

"I'm in."

"Us too." Kendra piped up.

"Us?" Mark asked.

"Yeah. Me." She pointed to herself. "Kalen." She pointed at him.

"Does Kalen get a vote?" He pouted.

"Not when you have a girlfriend mate." Mark said snidely. They both looked at him wide-eyed.

"Huh?" Kendra frowned.

Kalen turned to look at Kyle. "You told your brother?" He asked furiously. Kyle shook his head.

"You told Kyle?" Kendra glared at him.

"Oh please." Christian piped up. "You two are the worst kept secret ever. We *all* knew. You're not as discreet as you think you are."

"So much for being on the down low." Kyle laughed as Kendra shook her head and picked her phone and bag up.

The group waved as they left. Christian and Ciara stood up.

"We're going to see a late movie. You want to join us?" Ciara asked.

"Thanks, but we're just going to relax at home." Angelia smiled up at them.

"Yeah, I know what that means." Christian said shaking his head.

Kyle grinned. "What can I say? She can't get enough of me." He laughed, wrapping his arms around her shoulders.

"Excuse me?" She scowled, looking back at him. "I think you have it the wrong way around."

"No, I got it right." He stated confidently as Christian arched his eyebrow.

"He's not wrong." Angelia said straight faced with a shrug as Ciara laughed.

"You two are crazy. We'll see you tomorrow." Kyle watched them leave then turned Angelia around and pulled her arms over his shoulders.

"Alone again." He said wiggling his eyebrows suggestively. "What should we do?" She wrapped her legs around his waist and kissed him.

"I can think of a few things." She smiled seductively.

"Mark said no sex in the pool." He reminded her.

"Mark's not here."

"That is very true." He pulled her closer and kissed her.

"I feel like something sweet." She mused as she ran her fingers lightly up and down his back.

"Well, you are in luck then." She leaned back to look at him. "It just so happens that I'm sweet." He grinned at her as she scrunched her nose and pulled a face at him.

"Yeah. No. I want waffles. Or ice cream. The one that's dipped in caramel or chocolate. There's a new dessert place that's opened near my apartment. Why don't we go there and then stay at my place?"

"That sounds kinda perfect."

"We can do this, right?" Angelia asked quietly as she brushed his wet hair off his forehead. "The whole long-distance thing? If anyone can make it work, it's us? Right?"

"We'll *make* it work Lia. My contract ends next year so we'll need to talk and decide if I am going to move back here or sign with them again and you move to me."

"I can't leave my friends and my home." She sniffled as tears welled in her eyes. "I know it's not fair for me to ask you to move back here but…"

"You are my home, Lia." He said firmly. "I just want to be wherever you are. I don't care where we live. I want to fall asleep with you in my arms and wake up to you every morning. If this is where you want to be, we'll make it work."

"You love your job." She protested.

"I love you more my Lia." He whispered to her. "You are what matters the most to me."

She blinked back tears. "Do you really think we can get it right this time?"

"I think this is it for us babe, I don't think we're going to get any more chances." He said quietly. She lowered her face to press her lips against his. He tightened his arms around her and lowered her so they were face to face.

"We need to get out of the pool now."

"I know." He sighed as he lowered her into the water. She swam for the stairs, climbed out and started drying off. She turned around to look at him and raised an eyebrow. He smiled and swam to the steps, taking the towel she held out to him.

***

"Kyle! Lia!" Kalen pounded on the door. "Kyle! Lia!" He shouted louder as he pounded on the door again. The door swung open and a sleepy Kyle glowered at him.

"What the hell? It's almost 3 am, Kalen." He snapped angrily before he took in his friend's ashen face. "Kale, what's wrong?" Kalen shook his head as tears welled in his eyes. "You're scaring me, what the hell is going on?"

"You and Lia need to come with me. Now. To the hospital." He choked out between panicked breaths. "Rob had an accident. Crashed through a wall." He looked at Kyle. "Mark was in the car. They've all been rushed to the emergency room." He attempted to take some calming breaths while Kyle stared at him frozen in shock.

"Babe, what's going on?" Angelia appeared at the door. "Kale?" She asked confused. Kyle dragged Kalen inside and shut the door.

"We're going to get ready quickly." Kyle said to him quietly before turning to Angelia and leading her to the bedroom. "We need to get dressed and go to the hospital. Rob and Mark have been in an accident."

"Are they ok?" She asked as panic spread through her.

"I don't know. I don't think so. Kalen seems to be in shock if it was just a minor accident..." He trailed off as he realised he had put his shirt on backwards. He pulled it off and shook his head. "We just need to get there. I need to find out what's going on." He put his shirt on, then realised it was inside out. "What is wrong with this fucking shirt?" He yelled yanking it off and throwing it on the floor as he dropped down on the bed and buried his face in his hands.

"Baby, calm down." Angelia reached for the shirt, turned it the right way and handed it to him. "Everything is going to be ok." She said gently as he pulled it over his head.

"You don't know that." He looked at her as panic and fear creased his face. She put her hands on his cheeks and kissed his forehead gently.

"They have to be ok, babe. It's Mark and Robs." Tears welled in her eyes. She blinked them back. "Let's go." She said grabbing her bag and their phones. "I'll drive." She picked up Kyle's car keys, he followed her to where Kalen was sitting on the floor resting his head on his knees. "Kale, honey." She touched his shoulder gently. He looked up at her blankly. "Let's go." Kyle reached down, took his friend's hand and pulled him to his feet and then into a hug. Kalen held him tightly for a moment before letting go and nodding at them.

Chapter 16

"Kyle, I've been trying to call you and Lia." Blaine walked up to Kyle and pulled his friend into a hug, he hugged him briefly before stepping back.

"We switched our phones off last night so we wouldn't be disturbed. What's going on? Has there been any news?" He asked as he looked at Kendra's tear-soaked face. Angelia ran up to her friend and hugged her tightly.

"We're waiting for an update on Robs. They won't tell us anything about Mark because we're not family but we know he's in surgery. Rob's parents are here." he nodded at a couple sitting down the passage, holding hands. "Megan's parents are with her. She's got a couple of bruised ribs, a fractured arm and some bumps and bruises but she's going to be fine. Robs was speeding, swerved to miss a cat, slammed into a light pole, spun out, went down a bank and through a wall. From what I understand Mark, um, realised what was happening and shielded Megs with his body. That's why she's not as badly injured as the others." Kyle gave him a sad smile and nodded before looking around.

"Where's Kelly?" He asked confused. Blaine looked down at his hands and tried to compose himself.

"She, uh, she didn't make it Kyle." His voice broke over his words as tears rolled down his cheeks. "She died on impact."

"No." Kyle collapsed down into one of the chairs. Angelia dropped to her knees in front of him, holding his arms tightly with her hands as her tears flowed.

"Kelly." He said looking at her, pain creasing his handsome features.

"I know." She said quietly. They all looked up as Christian and Ciara came running down the passageway. Ciara hugged Kendra while Christian pulled Blaine and Kalen to him, holding them tightly.

"Do we know anything?" Christian asked as he finally let go of them.

"Rob and Mark are both in surgery. Megs is going to be fine, she's a bit banged up and needs to be monitored but no serious injuries and Kelly, um, she didn't, she, uh…" Kalen started crying and Christian pulled him into his arms.

"Oh man." Christian said as he hugged his brother tightly. "I'm so sorry Kale." Kyle stood and wrapped his arms around both of them. Christian placed an arm around him. Angelia hugged Blaine tightly as Ciara held onto Kendra. Christian let go of Kyle and Kalen and looked at them sadly.

"Where are Kel's parents?" He asked. Kalen started to respond but was interrupted by a blood-chilling scream from down the passage. They all turned to watch as Robbie's mom fell sobbing into her ex-husband's arms. The group watched in stunned silence, frozen in place by their collective grief.

"Rob. No, he can't be gone." Kyle whispered as his hands shot up to his face. "Please fight Mark, we can't lose you too." Christian grabbed him and held him tightly.

"Your brother is a fighter, Kyle. You hear me?" He put his hands on Kyle's face and looked him in the eye. "He will not give up; he will fight with everything he has. He will fight to stay here with you." He fought back his tears as he pulled Kyle close again. "Your brother is my co-parent of this bunch of hooligans we call a family. He's not going to leave me to look after all of you on my own." Kyle smiled at him through his tears and nodded. Christian looked up as a doctor approached them. Blaine had his arms wrapped tightly around his sister as she sobbed into his chest while he held back his own tears. He watched as the doctor stopped in front of their group.

"I am looking for Kyle McAllister." The doctor said looking around. Kyle wiped his cheeks and stepped forward.

"I'm Kyle McAllister." He answered in a shaky voice.

"May we speak in private?"

Angelia reached for Blaine's hand, holding it tightly as she stepped forward and slipped her other hand into Kyle's, who shook his head and glanced at his friends.

"This is my family, Mark's family. Whatever it is, you can tell all of us." Kyle's fear echoed in his voice. Christian stepped to the other side of him and put his arm around his shoulders. Kyle shot him a quick grateful look and squeezed Angelia's hand.

"Your brother has a broken leg, a broken arm, a few fractured ribs and a severe head injury. He also had massive internal bleeding. We have done everything we can for now. He is currently in a coma so we don't know the full extent of the brain injury as yet. We will only be able to assess him if he wakes up." The doctor explained gently.

"*If* he wakes up?" Kyle gasped as Angelia squeezed his hand.

"There is no guarantee he will wake up and if he does, he may not be himself. We have you listed as the next of kin. Are you able to contact your parents?" The doctor frowned as he looked down at the clipboard in his hand.

"No, I can't. They are on a month-long retreat; no electronic devices are allowed." Kyle explained quietly. The doctor sighed deeply and Kyle frowned at him.

"Then you may have a very difficult decision to make. Your brother is currently breathing on his own. But if his brain function deteriorates and he is no longer able to and he has to go onto a ventilator you may have to decide whether or not to have the machine's switched off." He said gently.

"You may ask me to make a decision to end my brother's life?" Kyle asked, his voice shaking.

"We are hoping that it won't come to that, but yes you may have to make that decision." The doctor explained with a sympathetic look before walking off. Kyle collapsed into one of the chairs and dropped his head in his hands. Angelia took a seat next to him with her hand on his back. Blaine took the chair on the other side of Kyle and placed his hand on his shoulder. Angelia looked up at Christian with a heartbroken look. He walked a short distance away to where the rest of their group had gathered.

"We've lost two of our family tonight." Kendra said despondently. "We can't lose Mark too." She leaned against her brother who wrapped his arm around her shoulders. They all watched Kyle as he stood up and walked over to them.

"You may as well all go home. We don't know how long he will be…" he fought back tears. "There's no point in everyone staying here."

"We're not going anywhere." Christian replied firmly. "We're family, we stick together. We lost Rob and Kelly tonight, we're all hurting and I don't think we should all be apart right now. We need to be here for each other and for Mark and for you Kyle." He stepped forward to hug Kyle who hugged him back tightly.

"Thank you." He whispered gratefully.

"I'm going to do a coffee run quickly." Jake stated. Kyle started to protest. "You need something to keep you going, we all do."

"I'll come with you." Blaine offered as he joined them. Jake nodded and the two walked down the passage as a nurse approached the rest of the friends.

She pointed to a door. "There are more comfortable chairs in there. I will let you know when you can see your brother." She gave Kyle a sympathetic smile. He nodded gratefully and followed his friends into the room.

"Mr. McAllister." Kyle heard a voice as someone gently shook his shoulder. He looked up sleepy and confused into the face of the nurse from earlier. He sat up straight, waking Angelia. "You can go through to see your brother now." He stood and held out his hand to Angelia to help her to her feet.

"Only family allowed for now."

"Lia *is* family." He said softly but firmly. The nurse nodded and motioned for them to follow her. He looked back at his friends briefly before following her. The nurse led them to a door and pushed it open. They walked through, Kyle gasped and stopped in his tracks. His brother was lying in a bed with his head bandaged. He had numerous bruises and cuts all over his face, chest and arms. Kyle made his way over to him and took his hand.

"Hey there big brother. I don't know if you can hear me. If you can, please fight. Please don't give up, I need my big brother." His voice broke and he looked down at Mark's arm as he tried to regain his composure. He took a deep breath. "This may be the wrong time to bring this up, but at the moment I am *definitely* the better-looking brother." He smiled and squeezed his brother's hand. Angelia giggled before slapping her hand over her mouth and looking at him wide eyed.

"It's ok to laugh Lia." He reached out to touch his brother's cheek. "Mark always used to tell me that if you could find the humour in the darkest situation then everything would be ok. If you can laugh when things are really bad it shows strength, courage and a fighting spirit." He said quietly. "You asked me before about my family. I never talk about them because as far as I am concerned, Mark is my only family, my only parent. Did he ever tell you about our home life?" He asked looking up at her briefly.

"No he didn't."

Kyle looked down at his brother and took a deep breath. "Our parents weren't, um, what you would call loving, hands-on parents, they were never there for us when we were growing up. They faced some pretty hard times and turned to alcohol just before we reached our teens. They were always drunk and Mark always protected me." He looked up at her quickly. "My parents never hurt us or abused us." He clarified. "But they would forget to fetch us from school or buy food or cook for us. They never supported us in anything and they would get into really bad fights. Mark found out that one of our neighbours who would always bring us food was a chef, he really cared about us. Mark got him to teach him how to cook and then he taught me. We don't really talk about the past because we don't want people to feel sorry for us, it made us stronger and brought us closer. You couldn't ask for a better brother." His voice broke and tears ran down his cheeks.
"He eventually convinced my parents to sober up and they went to the

other extreme. They became so health conscious they started going on week-long and month-long retreats, hikes and camps and opened their own wellness centre. They left us to fend for ourselves again. They always made sure that we had money and food but what we really needed were stable parents and a loving home." He shook his head sadly. "When Mark's company offered to recommend him for a position down here, he took it and I hesitated all of ten seconds before deciding to follow him. I realised afterwards that I didn't need to decide, he had no intention of leaving me behind." He looked up at Lia and shook his head. "I can't lose him Lia. He's all I have." She looked at him sadly as tears rolled down her cheeks. She walked over to him and wrapped her arms around him.

"Whatever happens Kyle. You are *never* alone. You have a family here who love you." She laughed softly. "You know they love you because they are camped out in that room and they have no intentions of leaving. And I love you." He hugged her back before moving a chair and sitting next to his brother's bed. She rested her hand on his shoulder. "I'm going to go back to the others and send Chris through. I know he would like to see Mark."

He squeezed her hand before turning back to his brother. Angelia walked out the room, leaned against the wall, slid down to the floor and sobbed quietly into her hands.

"Lia." She looked up into Christian's concerned blue eyes. "Get up off the floor, hon." He gripped her hands and helped her to her feet.

"Has something changed with Mark?" Kalen gave her a panicked look. She shook her head quickly.

"No. There's no change. I told Kyle I was going to send Chris in to see Mark now." She explained. Kalen breathed a sigh of relief, picked up the tray of coffees he had set down on the chair and headed to their friends. "Did you know?" She asked Christian quietly. He gave her a questioning look. "About their parents? Their childhood?"

"Yeah, Mark told me a few years back. It's not something he likes to talk about it." She smiled and stepped aside so he could go through the door. She took a deep breath before walking back in to join her friends. Blaine looked up at her and moved over on his chair. She squeezed in next to him and laid her head on his chest. He embraced her tightly as she closed her eyes. Christian returned a while later and sent Kalen in to see Mark. Angelia watched Kalen leave then sat up and looked at Blaine. He gave her a sad smile as she placed a hand on his cheek.

"Robs." She whispered tearfully.

"I know, I can't wrap my head around this. It doesn't seem real that we're never going to see him again or hear his laugh or…" He trailed off and shook his head. "We're not going to see him or Kelly again, it's not fair Lia."

"I know, hon."

"Blaine." Christian interrupted them quietly. "Kalen's back, do you want to go in and see Mark now?" Blaine nodded and stood up to head out the door.

One by one the friends went through to see Mark. Angelia curled up on a chair staring out the window at the cars driving by. She felt a gentle hand on her shoulder and looked up into Ciara's concerned brown eyes.

"How are you holding up Lia?" She asked concerned. Angelia blinked back tears and shook her head.

"I keep playing last night over and over in my head when Robs asked us to join them and we said no because we wanted to stay in. I remember thinking I'd have so many free nights to spend with him when Kyle flies back to New York and now I don't. He's just gone and Kelly too. They say every tragedy has a lesson. What's the lesson here? The world lost two beautiful souls whose lives were just starting. It's not right." She said sadly. "I just keep thinking what if I had gone with last night? Maybe we would have left later or earlier or stopped Robs from driving. Something, anything, that could have prevented this." A tear trickled down her cheek.

"Oh Lia. Rob knew you loved him and you meant so much to him. It was an accident; a horrible tragic accident and I don't think you going with would have changed anything. What if you had gone with? And Mark decided to ride with you and Kyle? We would have lost three of them. We still have Megs because Mark was in that car. You can't change the past Lia. All we can do is honour Kelly and Robbie in how we live our lives and hold them in our hearts and memories. Ok?" She hugged Angelia tightly. They both looked up as Blaine made his way to them.

"We've all been through to see Mark. Why don't you go back to Kyle. He needs you." She nodded, stretched, and stood up.

"Is everyone heading home now?" They all exchanged quick glances.

"No, we're staying." Christian said quietly. "Thankfully it's the weekend and none of us want to be anywhere else. What we are going to do is take turns heading home to shower, change and have something to eat. Do you want to go home first quickly? I can drive you."

"No, I'm not going to leave them." She looked up as Jake walked in the room and said something to Kalen who nodded then followed him to Angelia.

"I spoke to the nurses and explained that Kyle and Lia are going to stay with Mark and I asked if we could move the double couch from here to the ward so you guys will have something more comfortable to sit on and they agreed." Jake explained to her. "Their only condition is that we move it there and we move it back when…" He trailed off as Angelia smiled at him gratefully.

"Thank you, Jake." She whispered. He smiled and nodded before walking over to help Blaine and Kalen.

Kyle looked up in surprise as his friends walked through the door with the chair.

"Uhhh, do the nurses know that you are rearranging their furniture?" He asked with concern.

"Yep." Jake replied as they set it down close to the bed. "They said we should make you comfortable." Kyle smiled at his friends gratefully as they turned to leave.

"I'm just going to the bathroom quickly." He said to Angelia as he gave her arm a gentle squeeze. She made her way to the bed and held Mark's hand in both of hers as tears rolled down her cheeks. She turned to look at his face and ran her fingers lightly down his cheek.

"Hey hon, I hope you can hear me. We need you to come back to us. We need you Mark, your brother needs you. Our family is broken and hurting so badly right now and we can't lose you too. We need you here with us." She lifted his hand and rested it against her cheek. "Do you have any idea how much I love you?" She asked through her tears. "I owe you so much and I need you to wake up so I can say thank you for everything you've done for me. So I can tell you what an incredible man you are and to tell you all the things I should have said to you. Please don't leave us. Please don't leave Kyle." She pleaded softly.

"Lia." Kyle whispered as he reached out for her. She placed Mark's hand back down on the bed, wrapped her arms around Kyle's waist and buried her face in his chest. He held her tightly before taking a seat on the chair and motioned for her to join him. She sat down and he placed his arm around her shoulders and drew her against him. "How are you holding up baby?" He asked quietly as he ran his hand soothingly over her hair.

"I'm ok." She whispered. He put his hand under her chin and lifted her face up to his.

"Lia, you just lost a friend and a man who is like a brother to you, someone you have known and loved your entire life. You're not ok." He said looking at her in concern.

"I'm trying not to think about that. If I do, I'll fall apart and right now I need to be strong for you and Mark."

"We can be strong for each other Lia. You need to grieve, don't keep it in." He pulled her into his arms and held her against him. She shook her head as tears welled in her eyes.

"I saw Kelly's parents earlier. I was checking in on Megs and they came by to see her. I just wanted to cry. They were so devastated and heartbroken. I still can't believe she's gone. I'm never going to see Kel's blonde curls bouncing as she dances around the pool table or hear that infectious giggle of hers. I'm never going to hear Robs tease me or tell me that he loves me. I'm never going to be able to hug him again." Kyle rubbed her back gently as she sobbed quietly into his chest. She sat up as her phone buzzed on the chair next to her. "It's my brother. Hi JR."

"My Lia." She could hear the raw emotion in her brother's voice. "I spoke to Chris, he told me about Robs and Kelly. I'm about to board my flight, I'm on my way home. I'll see you and Blaine tomorrow. I love you both so much."

"I love you too." She started crying and Kyle pulled her closer to him. "I'll see you tomorrow." She ended the call, buried her face in Kyle's chest and sobbed sadly. He took her phone from her and hugged her tightly, smoothing her hair and kissing the top of her head softly. Her sobs subsided and she sat up and wiped at her cheeks. "I'm such a mess."

"Yeah, but you're a beautiful mess." She gave him a half smile. "I'm so glad you're here." He whispered. She gave him a quick kiss on the cheek, laid her head on his shoulder and watched Mark. She giggled before sitting up and turning to Kyle. He looked at her in surprise.

"I was thinking about the first time I met Mark. Do you remember?"

"How could I forget? You called him my younger and hotter brother." He looked at her with a raised eyebrow as she laughed.

"I did."

"Do you know that he walked around like a proud peacock for days after that, rubbing it in my face. He adored you from the moment he met you." He chuckled.

"He's the reason I stopped drinking so much and partying all the time. He drove me home and gave me the 'You're better than this Lia' speech. Kind of reminded me of my dad." She said with a wistful smile. "My parents would have loved him." She looked up at him. "They would have loved you too." He smiled and brushed her hair back off her face.

"If you weren't here, I would be going out of my mind. Thank you for staying with me." He whispered. She smiled and leaned forward to kiss him tenderly before resting her forehead against his.

"I can't believe I have to say this, but no sex in my hospital room." Kyle gave Angelia a startled look before turning towards his brother. Mark was watching them with a pained expression on his face. Kyle froze for a second before shooting to his feet and grabbing his brother's hand.

"You're awake!" Tears of relief filled his eyes.

"Kind of impossible to get any sleep with the two of you around." He smiled weakly at them.

"Do you remember what happened?" Kyle probed gently as Mark frowned.

"We had an accident. I tried to protect Megan." He winced in pain. "How is everyone?" Kyle looked at Angelia and she shook her head quickly.

"Megan is recovering. You shielded her so the doctor said she had minimal damage compared to what she could have had." He smiled proudly at his brother.

"Kelly? Robbie?" Mark asked as he looked intently at his brother. "I kept calling them before I lost consciousness. Robbie answered me but Kelly never did. How is she?" Mark asked, concerned. Kyle swallowed hard and looked down at his brother's hand that he was holding in both of his.

"Lia." He said finally looking up. "Go tell the others that Mark's awake." He turned back to his brother. "They refused to leave. They've taken over some sort of lounge. They've been so worried about you." Kyle gave him a forced bright smile.

"Only me?" Mark asked quietly.

"Don't talk too much. You took quite a beating, you need to rest and recover."

"Where are Kelly and Robbie?" Mark asked him again. He looked up as his friends came bursting through the door with a harassed-looking nurse running after them. She stood in the doorway glaring at them before throwing her hands up in the air and stomping away.

"They didn't make it, did they?" Mark asked quietly as tears welled up in his eyes. "Kelly wasn't responding and Robbie sounded so weak." He looked at Christian who looked down and shook his head sadly.

"Sorry brother. Kelly died on impact with the wall and Robbie fought but he didn't make it." Christian explained gently.

Mark put his head back in the pillows as tears streamed down his cheeks.

"I'm alive because of you." He heard a quiet voice say. He looked up to see Megan standing at the bottom of his bed, one of her parents on either side of her. "You saved my life, without even hesitating." She walked over and gently kissed his cheek. "Thank you." She whispered as she reached out and placed her hand over his and smiled at him.

"I need everybody out now." The doctor ordered as he walked in and saw the group. "My patient needs to be examined and he needs some rest. Visiting hours are over. You all need to go home and come back for the next visiting hours." They all made their way slowly to the door. Kyle squeezed Mark's hand reassuringly.

"I'll be back just now." He whispered to him.

"Can I stay?" Megan asked the doctor. "I'm a patient here as well." She said pointing to her hospital gown.

"If its ok with my patient, its ok with me." The doctor sighed. Mark smiled and nodded. Megan took a seat on the chair next to his bed and reached out for his hand again. She smiled at him as tears welled in her eyes. He squeezed her hand gently.

"I can't believe they're really gone." She said sadly. He nodded as he blinked back tears.

"I'm glad you're ok Megs."

"Thanks to you." She smiled gratefully before shaking her head. "What am I going to do without Kelly? She's my best friend." She asked as tears filled her eyes. "And now she's gone. I don't know what I'm going to do without her." She looked up at Mark who shook his head sadly and shifted over slightly on the bed.

"Come lie here by me." He patted the space next to him. She climbed carefully on the bed and lay against his side, resting her injured arm on his chest. He wrapped his good arm around her as she chuckled.

"Climbing up here should hurt like hell, they must have given me some really strong pain meds."

"You're lucky." He groaned. "My ribs are killing me."

"I'm so sorry." She apologised as she attempted to move away from him. He tugged her back into his side.

"You're fine, it's my ribs on the other side. I think I got thrown against the door or something. Everything hurts on my right side." He explained quickly. She rested her head on his shoulder.

"Robbie was going to propose to her."

"He was?"

"Yeah, I went shopping with him. He chose a gorgeous ring; she would have loved it." She blinked back tears. "I was so worried that I was going to slip up and tell her that I avoided her for most of the week. I wish I hadn't done that. If I had known…" her voice broke as she started sobbing Mark rubbed her arm gently.

"I don't know what to say here Megs. I wish I had some magical words that would make you feel better or make sense of this but I don't. We lost two of our family and its hurting like hell and it's just…I don't…it's not fair." He ended dejectedly.

"I felt so guilty that I was able to sit with my family and be fine while Kelly's parents had to…" she trailed off, "and you and Rob were both in surgery fighting for your lives. When I heard Mrs. Harris scream, I knew Rob had lost the fight. I got to the door and I saw your brother's face as the doctor was speaking to him, I thought we had lost you too. When I heard that you were in a coma with a brain injury, I just kept thinking how brave and selfless you were." She sniffled. Mark started to laugh and winced in pain.

"It wasn't brave or selfless, it was a reaction. When I realised we were going to hit the wall, I just pulled you away from where it would impact."

"And then wrapped your body around mine and held me tightly while the impact sent you flying against the door." She reminded him.

"Yeah, all of that is a bit fuzzy." He confessed. "I was just trying to protect you, I knew you weren't wearing a seatbelt." He closed his eyes and sighed.

"I'm grateful you did. I keep thinking about how Robbie's mom screamed. It was such a haunting sound. I kept hearing it over and over in my head while I was lying there waiting for news about you. I don't know if I'll ever get that out of my head." She wiped her tears, Mark tugged her closer and gently kissed the top of her head.

"Try to remember all the good times you had with Rob and Kel. All the nights at the bar, playing pool, going to the beach, movies. You have so many good memories of them. Don't let this be what you remember." He said gently to her.

"Kelly and I always talk about that night at the bar with those four creeps. Remember, two of them followed Lia out to the car park and two stayed with me and Kel. We felt so uncomfortable and then we suddenly had all four of them around us. You and Blaine got us out of there. That night really stood out for us, it's the night we felt like part of your family. We never really felt like we were a part of your group until that night, we realised then that you all cared about us as much you cared about each other."

"Really? We always thought of you both as part of our family. I know you and Lia butted heads in the beginning but that changed quickly. Lia's the one who told us that you two were inside and that we had to go get you." Mark smiled as he rubbed Megan's back gently.

"I never knew that. Did you hear about our trip to the tattoo parlour?" She asked with a wry smile.

"You got a tattoo?" He gave her a questioning look. She burst out laughing.

"No, none of us did. We were so brave and determined until we got to the tattoo parlour. We started looking at different designs and there was someone having a tattoo done. Rob went as white as a sheet and nearly passed out. We all bolted out of there so quickly. I don't know who was more scared out of the three of us. We haven't been back there since." She confessed as Mark chuckled.

"Yeah, I'm with you on that one. I'm not a fan of needles." She looked up at him.

"Really? Kyle has that gorgeous cross on his arm, I just thought you would have had one somewhere as well."

"You've seen me shirtless, right?"

"Yes. I just thought that maybe you might have it somewhere more, you know, more private." She said blushing as he raised an eyebrow.

"Uh-huh. Firstly, no man or woman for that matter will be going anywhere near my private regions with a needle. Secondly, why are you wondering about whether I have tattoos in places no one can see?"

"Oh, um, no, I wasn't." Her cheeks flushed a deep red. She heard him chuckle and then groan.

"Megs you are not good for my pain threshold. It hurts when I laugh." He grumbled.

"I'm sorry." She said looking up at him with an innocent smile. She laid her head back on his shoulder. "I'm glad you told me to think of the good times I had with Kel and Rob, thank you." She whispered.

He smiled and closed his eyes. "I'm feeling very tired."

"Me too." She sighed sleepily. "Can I stay here with you? I don't want to be alone right now."

"Of course, you can." He moved her a little closer to him and pulled the covers over her.

"Thank you. I feel safe with you." She mumbled as she drifted off to sleep. He rested his chin on the top of her head and closed his eyes.

Chapter 17

Mark groaned softly in pain as the dull throbbing in his ribs woke him up.

"Are you Ok? Do you need me to call the nurse?" A concerned voice asked quietly from the side of his bed. He turned his head to look as the person rose to their feet.

"JR." He exclaimed in surprise. "What are you doing here?"

"I flew home to be here for my family and Rob's family."

"Of course. I'm so sorry about Rob. I know he was very close to you."

Jarryd nodded sadly. "And I'm sorry about Kelly. I only knew her the three short weeks I was here but she made Robs happy. She was so funny and such a sweet kid. This is just…" He paused as he shook his head. "It's just tragic, there are no other words for it. I'm glad you're ok though." He gave him a quick smile. "I hear you gave everyone quite a scare." He glanced up at the door as he heard voices approaching and watched two nurses walk past chatting.

"It's so surreal…" Mark trailed off as he shook his head. "One minute we were singing, laughing and joking in the car and now we're going to be attending their memorial and funerals. It just seems like a really bad dream that I can't wake from. How are Lia and Blaine doing? They were so close to Rob."

"I haven't been to see them yet." Jarryd confessed as he exhaled heavily. "I don't know what to say to them. It's like reliving our parents' accident all over again. I know they're going to look to me for answers and I just don't have them. I mean, how do you make sense of losing two amazing young people so tragically. I landed at the airport and came straight here to check up on you. I needed to make sure that you were ok."

"They need you JR. They need their big brother, not answers." Mark said quietly.

"Those two, they've been through so much already, it's not fair." He sighed deeply as he sat back down.

"You've been through it too. They're stronger than you think they are, they try to be like you. They're hurting right now and they need their big brother to be there for them." Mark gave him a sad smile.

Jarryd looked up at him as tears glimmered in his eyes. "I'm twenty-seven years old and I have to help bury one of my closest friends, my brother, this week. I was supposed to attend his wedding, be godfather and uncle to his kids. He was supposed to have this incredible life with the woman of his dreams by his side and now it's all just gone. I can't make sense of it." He shook his head as he stood up. "I'm going to go find Lia and Blaine now. We'll be back to see you tonight, during visiting hours."

"How did you get in here if it's not visiting hours?" Mark asked looking at him in surprise.

Jarryd grinned. "I flirted with the nurse."

Mark chuckled before wincing in pain. "They're at my house, by the way. With my brother." He smiled weakly.

"So, I finally get to meet the infamous Kyle McAllister."

"Yeah, him and Lia, they've worked things out. They're finally in a good place."

Jarryd reached out and squeezed his shoulder lightly. "Happy to hear that. I'm glad that you're ok brother. I couldn't imagine us losing you as well. Let me know if you need us to bring anything tonight."

"A burger." Mark laughed. "The food here is inedible."

Jarryd chuckled. "I'll see what I can do." He promised as he headed out the door.

***

Kyle walked into the lounge with three cups of coffee in his hands. He looked worriedly at Angelia and Blaine who were seated on the double couch. Blaine had his arm resting over Angelia's shoulders while she sat with her legs up resting her chin on her knees. She looked up at Kyle blankly before giving him a tense smile.

"I made coffee." He set the cups down on the table in front of them.

Blaine gave him a sad smile. "Thanks."

"Can I make you guys something to eat?"

Angelia shook her head. "I'm not hungry. I just keep thinking about Robs and…" She trailed off as she started crying again. Blaine wrapped his other arm around her and pulled her closer to him as she buried her face in his chest. Kyle watched them as he fought back his tears.

"There they are." He heard a gentle voice say. He looked up in surprise at the person smiling sadly at Angelia and Blaine. They both looked up at him as he held out his hands to them. "Come here you two." He said softly as they flew up from the chair and into his arms. He held them both tightly as he rested his forehead against Blaine's.
"Do you know how much I love you? Both of you?" He asked, his voice raw with emotion. They both nodded as they clung to him, crying quietly. "If anything had happened to either of you, I would have gone out of my mind." He said softly as he let go of them. He brushed Angelia's hair off her face as he gently squeezed Blaine's shoulder. "You are my entire world." He looked up at Kyle who was standing behind his siblings watching them. He reached out a hand to him. "You must be Kyle." He gave him a warm smile. "I'm Jarryd Ryan, well everyone calls me JR." He said with a shrug.

"It's good to finally meet you JR. I'm sorry it's under such horrible circumstances."

"It's good to finally meet you too. I've heard great things about you." He looked back at his siblings and sighed as he ran his hand over his face, suddenly looking exhausted.

"Do you want to rest for a bit, you must have had a long flight." Kyle offered. "You can use my brother's room." Jarryd shot him a grateful look.

"Thanks, I could really do with a shower." He rubbed his forehead. "Then I have to go see Rob's parents and Dyl." He looked at Angelia and Blaine as he shook his head. "I don't know what to say here. I can't make sense of this and I wish I could say or do something to take the pain away. I'm supposed to protect you and shield you and there is not a damn thing I can do to make this better for you."

"You lost him too." Angelia said quietly as she looked at him. "I want to go with you to see them. To see Rob's parents." She added.

"No." he said firmly.

"Why not?"

"Because I said so Lia." He snapped at her. "Please just for once in your life listen to me. I am barely keeping it together. I am lost and I am hurting. I am burying my best friend, my brother this week and I am trying to make sense of all of this while dealing with the guilt and shame I feel for being relieved that the two of you weren't in that car. That it's not one or both of you that I am burying as well. What does that make me?"

"It makes you human." Kyle replied. Jarryd looked over at him. "You think I haven't had those exact thoughts? My brother *was* in that car and he's still alive. What if Lia and I had decided to go with or Blaine had gotten in that car? I am heartbroken that Robbie and Kelly are gone and I haven't stopped crying and hurting over both of them, but feeling relieved. That's normal. I would be worried if you weren't relieved." Kyle pulled Angelia into his arms and held her against his chest. Blaine reached out to wrap his arms around his brother to hug him. Jarryd sighed and held him tightly.

"I'm sorry Lia. I didn't mean to snap at you." He said sadly. She looked at him and shook her head.

"You don't have to apologise. We're all hurting. Our whole family is broken and hurting. I know you are too and I just want to be there for you like you've always been there for me and Blaine." Tears welled in her eyes. He held out a hand to her.

"Oh, my Lia." He said softly. She let go of Kyle to hug her brothers. "Let me take a shower and go see Rob's parents. When I get back, we are going to have something to eat and then we will go to visit Mark. I promised him that we would see him tonight."

"You saw my brother?" Kyle looked at him in surprise. Jarryd smiled and nodded.

"Yeah, he's looking good, better than I was expecting. I really do need to go and take a shower now." He picked his suitcase up.

"I'll show you to Mark's room." Blaine volunteered as he headed out of the lounge with Jarryd following him.

Angelia sat down and looked up at Kyle. "Come sit with me." He sat next to her and reached for her hand, holding it tightly in his. "I love you." She whispered as she laid her head on his shoulder.

"I love you too." He whispered back. "I'm glad your brother's here. I think it's good for him to be around everyone right now." She smiled and nodded in agreement.

***

Angelia reached for Kyle's hand as they walked into the hospital. He laced his fingers through hers and squeezed her hand gently.

"JR." Christian said in surprise as he saw the four of them walking towards them. "I'm so glad you're here. We all really need to be together right now." His friend smiled sadly and hugged him tightly.

"I agree." Jarryd said quietly. "I went to see Mrs. Harris today. It was one of the hardest things I've had to do. She wants me to give a eulogy." He shook his head. "This feels like a seriously bad dream that I just can't wake up from. I was working on my best man speech for his wedding and now I'm going to be writing a fucking eulogy for his funeral. This just isn't right."

"Best man speech?" Christian looked at him confused.

"Yeah, he bought the ring and everything. He was waiting for family Sunday dinner and he was going to propose to Kelly there in front of all of you, the people they love. He asked me to be the best man and you know how I like to be on top of things so I started to put some ideas together and now…" He trailed off as he shook his head before frowning suddenly. "What the hell is Jake doing here?"

"He's been amazing in all of this. He insisted on staying here until Mark woke up, he organised coffee and food to keep us going. He arranged with the nurses to take a comfortable chair in for Kyle and Lia while they were sitting with Mark and apparently, he arranged for a whole lot of home-cooked frozen meals to be delivered to Rob and Kelly's families so they'll have food and not have to worry about cooking. He's been a completely different person. I've been so amazed."

"Sometimes tragedy builds character." Jarryd smiled at him ruefully. They both looked up as Angelia made her way to them.

"Kale, Case, Megs and Kyle are with Mark now. We're only allowed four people at a time." She looked at Christian. "Do you, Jake, Kendra and Ciara want to go next? Then Blaine, JR and I will go last."

"I'm fine with that." Christian smiled warmly at her. "How are you holding up Lia?"

"Better now that my big brother is here. I'm glad we're all together. Our family needs this, we need each other." She said as Jarryd smiled down at her and rubbed her back gently before heading towards the rest of their friends to greet them. Angelia smiled as she saw Kyle walk towards her.

"Chris do you and the others want to go in and see Mark so long?" Christian nodded and headed to Ciara, Jake and Kendra. Kyle pulled Angelia into his arms.

"I know I've said it before, but I am so glad that you are here." He whispered to her. She looked up at him and sighed as he leaned down to rest his forehead gently against hers. "I don't know what I did to deserve you." He whispered as she tightened her arms around his waist and leaned up to kiss him quickly. Jarryd watched them as Kalen joined him.

"Good to see you JR." He said quietly as he looked over at Angelia and Kyle. "He would have been lost without her; she keeps him calm. They've been really happy the last couple of weeks, before all of this."

"He really does love her." Jarryd remarked softly.

"It's beyond love." Kalen chuckled. "They can't stay away from each other. They've tried, it doesn't work. He's a lot like you." He looked at his friend. "His first instinct is also to protect her. As much as he wants to kill her half the time, he'll protect her every time without hesitation. I've seen it so many times."

"How are you holding up Kalen?" Jarryd levelled a serious look at him.

He shook his head. "I honestly don't know." He sighed. "I switch from sad to angry to numb and back again. I just keep asking why. Why him? Why her? Why now? Someone is a part of your life for over twenty years and suddenly they're just gone. There was no chance to say goodbye or sorry or I love you or anything. And Kel? She wasn't a part of our family as long as Rob was but we loved her just as much, she was the sweetest person. She didn't deserve this, neither of them did."

"You know where I am if you need to talk." Jarryd patted him gently on the back. He looked up as Blaine walked towards them.

"We're going in to see Mark now." He said quietly to his brother. Jarryd nodded and turned back to Kalen.

"I mean it Kale. If you need to talk, come see me." He smiled at him before turning to walk with Blaine.

"I'm starting to feel like royalty." Mark chuckled as they entered his room.

"How are you feeling hon?" Angelia squeezed his hand gently.

"Still very sore but apparently I am improving." He smiled at her. Jarryd glanced over his shoulder quickly before turning back to him with a grin.

"As promised." He said as he unfolded his jacket, pulled a brown bag out and handed it to him.

"You didn't?" Mark asked him.

"I did. Had to smuggle it in here like it was contraband narcotics." He grinned.

"You are the best."

"Did you sneak in a burger for him JR?" Angelia looked at him horrified.

"The food here is worse than yours Lia." Mark grinned at her.

"If I had known it was that bad, I would have brought you two burgers." Jarryd sniggered as his sister glared at him.

"That's why you ordered an extra burger." Blaine exclaimed shaking his head. "I thought you were just hungry."

"I promised Mark when I was here earlier."

"I owe you big." Mark smiled happily.

"Just don't get caught, no amount of flirting will get me out of trouble with the nurses. It's probably ice cold, but it will still taste better than anything you get here." Jarryd laughed.

"That's no lie." Mark sighed sadly before looking up at Blaine. "Are you doing ok?"

Blaine gave him a small smile and nodded. "I'm glad you're ok." He said quietly. "I thought we were going to lose you too."

"You're not going to be able to get rid of me that easily." Mark smiled. Blaine nodded and Jarryd put a comforting arm around his shoulders. They all looked up as the nurse appeared in the doorway to announce that visiting hours were over.

"It was good to see all of you. Thanks for the food." Mark chuckled.

"We'll see you tomorrow." Kyle squeezed his brother's hand.

"You're supposed to be back in the States." Mark realised suddenly.

"Yeah, I phoned my boss and told him what happened and he told me to stay for another three weeks." Kyle explained.

"That was kind of him." Kyle nodded and patted his hand before stepping away so Angelia could kiss his cheek.

"See you tomorrow hon. Enjoy your contraband food." She said raising an eyebrow at him.

"Oh, I will."

"See you tomorrow, brother." Jarryd patted his shoulder before he followed Angelia out the door. Mark looked up at Blaine who smiled at him.

"I can't wait for you to be back home."

"Me neither." Mark admitted. "I'm ok, Blaine. I'm not going anywhere. I would never leave you and Kyle." Blaine smiled, looked up at Kyle and gave him a quick nod.

"I know. I'll see you tomorrow. Get some rest. And don't get caught eating that burger, the nurses here are hella scary." He chuckled before heading out the door.

"What's on your mind little brother?" Mark asked raising an eyebrow as Kyle sighed and shook his head.

"I just keep thinking how everything can change in an instant. We were all together having fun and then this." Kyle said sadly. "I want to move back home. After what happened I realised life is short and I'm stuck a world away from all the people I love."

"All the people you love or Lia?"

"Everyone. I'm missing out on so much. You don't look happy about this." He looked at Mark as he sighed.

"I will be more than happy to have my brother back here with me but only if it's for the right reasons. Don't base your decision on Lia. It has to be the right decision for you. I know you desperately want things to work out for you two but what happens if you move back here and things don't work out. Think of what you're giving up, Kyle." He said firmly.

"It's not a decision I'm going to rush into but it is one I am thinking about seriously, I have been for a while now and I will take everything into consideration." He said giving his brother's shoulder a reassuring squeeze before heading out the door to join his friends.

"Why don't you stay at our place?" Kyle asked Jarryd after they had greeted their friends and watched them leave. "It makes more sense. There's plenty of space and we can all be together."

"That would be great." Jarryd smiled at him. "I could use some sleep. I'm exhausted." He confessed.

"Let's go home then." Angelia reached out to lace her fingers through Kyle's. He squeezed her hand as they walked towards the exit.

Chapter 18

"JR" Kyle exclaimed in surprise as he walked out to the back entertainment area to find Jarryd leaning against the wall staring at the empty table and chairs. He turned to look at Kyle and gave him a quick smile before shaking his head.

"It feels like just the other day that I was sitting here with everyone laughing and joking, sharing a meal and memories." He chuckled wryly. "Learning more about your and Lia's sex life than I wanted to. It was such an incredible day, it's one of my favourite memories. Robs and Kelly were so happy and content and it just seems so surreal that they're gone now." He looked up as Blaine walked towards them and handed each of them a beer. Jarryd smiled sadly at him as he took his beer and wrapped his arm around Blaine's shoulders. "How are you holding up little brother?"

Blaine shook his head. "Every time I close my eyes I see Robs' car spin out and go through the wall. I've never felt so helpless, all we could do was watch and hope. Tomorrow is going to be…" He trailed off as he looked up at his brother. "It's going to make it more real." He said sadly. Jarryd nodded as he pulled him closer to his side and rubbed his shoulder gently.

"I know." He said quietly. They all turned and watched as Angelia walked towards them. Kyle held his hand out to her, pulled her into his arms and held her tightly.

"I love you."

"I love you too." She whispered as she fought back tears. She looked at her brothers. "We have company." She looked back at the door as Christian swung it open and walked through followed by Ciara, Megan, Kalen, Kendra, Jake and Casey.

"We wanted to all be together tonight before tomorrow." Christian explained quietly.

"Why don't we all sit down." Kyle pulled one of the chairs out.

"I brought some champagne." Megan said softly. "I thought we could…" She stopped to fight back tears. Casey wrapped an arm around her waist and squeezed her gently. Megan gave her a brave smile. "I thought maybe we could celebrate their lives and their love for us and each other and maybe share some of our favourite memories of them." Tears streamed down her cheeks and Blaine reached out to hug her.

"I think that's a lovely idea, Megs." Kyle squeezed her arm softly. "We'll go fetch some glasses." He laced his fingers through Angelia's as they headed inside. They came out a few minutes later with an assortment of glasses.
"We're not really champagne or wine drinkers in this house." Kyle chuckled. "So, we had to bring whatever we could find." He explained as they set all the glasses down.

"This is perfect." Jarryd said softly as he handed one of the champagne bottles to Kyle to open and picked up the second one. They opened them and filled the glasses. Everyone picked up a glass and glanced at each other.
"Before we start with the memories of Robs and Kelly, I'd like to say a few words." Jarryd spoke softly. They all turned to look at him. "I've always believed that family is the most important thing in the world. This family of ours is so loving, incredible, and resilient and I am honoured to be a part of it. Moments like these make us realise how fragile and short life really is and that we can never take anyone or anything for granted. We are incredibly blessed to have had these two beautiful souls be a part of our family. Their loss will be felt for the rest of our lives but we will always remember the happy, loving and caring people that they were and we will always be grateful for the impact they had on us. We will carry them in our hearts and we will honour them by living our lives in the best way possible." He raised his glass. "To Robbie and Kelly." Everyone lifted their glasses.

"To Robbie and Kelly." They all chorused together before sitting down. Jarryd turned to Megan.

"Megs, would you like to go first?" He asked gently. She shook her head as tears rolled down her cheeks.

"I'll go first." Angelia volunteered as Kyle squeezed her hand gently. "My favourite memory of Kel was the first night I met her." She smiled sadly. "It was my first shift at Con's and I was so nervous because the only people I knew there were Kale and Robs and they weren't working that night. I walked in and introduced myself and this bundle of energy came flying up out of nowhere and threw her arms around me. All I saw was this big smile and blonde curls and she gave me the hugest hug and made herself my personal tour guide. The two of us laughed and giggled for most of the night and that's what I'm going to miss most. Those warm hugs and that infectious giggle of hers."

Angelia wiped her tears off her cheeks. Kyle put his arm around her shoulders and pulled her closer against him as he kissed the side of her head gently. She smiled at him and sighed. "My favourite memory of Robs is one he shared not so long ago. When his parents were getting divorced and he moved in with us for about a year. He was so upset and I wanted to cheer him up so I decided to bake him a cake." She paused and shook her head as a ripple of laughter ran through their group. "Well as you know I am a bit of a disaster in the kitchen. I mixed the batter and poured it into a plastic container and stuck it in the oven. The whole thing melted and there was such a huge mess that I started to cry. And Robs, he..." She trailed off as she started crying. Kyle rubbed her back soothingly as she wiped her cheeks. "Rob switched everything off and sat on the floor with me as we mopped up cake batter and melted plastic. I had batter everywhere, my hair, my neck, my ears, my clothes, I can only imagine what I looked like and Robs just laughed, hugged me and told me not to cry and that me trying to bake for him made him feel so special and loved. I'm going to miss him so much." She sobbed sadly in Kyle's arms.

"Kyle, would you like to go next?" Jarryd asked as he gave his sister a worried look. Kyle nodded as he took a sip of his champagne then cleared his throat.

"My favourite memory of Kelly is when we were playing pool. She and Rob played against me and Blaine." He smiled quickly at Blaine who laughed quietly. "This was before Lia taught me how to play pool so as you know; I wasn't all that good before."

"That's the understatement of the century." Kalen grinned at him. Kyle cocked an eyebrow before continuing.

"Blaine was getting irritated with me and Rob was giving us a hard time about being so far behind. Kelly felt so bad for me that she purposely started playing badly to make me feel better. Rob was trying to be supportive of her even though he was so confused as to why she went from an above-average pool player to being on the same level as me. Blaine and I still lost but not as badly as we should've so Rob couldn't give us as hard a time as he would've liked to. Kelly was just so sweet and caring and she had such a good heart." He looked at Angelia and shook his head as he fought back his tears. She reached out to run her fingers down his cheek. He caught her hand and kissed the back of it quickly before clearing his throat and turning back to their friends.

"My favourite memory of Rob was um," he glanced quickly at Angelia before turning back to their friends, "it was while Lia was away for those four months. I thought she would come back after a month or two at the most. When it got to the third month, I started feeling a bit lost and I thought she was gone out of my life forever." He smiled at her as she squeezed his hand gently. "At one stage I literally went to work and came home to sit in my room and stare at the walls and the weekends I pretty much just stayed in there from Friday till Monday.

"So, one Saturday Rob came barging in and told me to get my sorry ass out of bed, he's tired of me sulking so we're going fishing. Now, I had never been fishing in my life but I thought Rob had. Turns out, he'd never been fishing either but he thought I had. So, in his infinite wisdom, he booked a trip for two on a deep-sea fishing charter. Rob, for those of you who don't know, suffers..." Kyle faltered for a minute and ran his hand over his eyes, "um suffered from motion sickness." He corrected himself. He took a calming breath before continuing with a slight smile. "I spent most of the trip on my ass because I kept falling over but I still managed to do a bit of fishing and caught a nice-sized fish." He laughed quietly. "As for poor Rob, he spent the entire trip hanging over the side of the boat going different shades of grey and green. Both of us were extremely happy to get back to land and swore we would never go fishing again. Kelly had to fetch us because neither of us felt up to driving after all that." He ended his story to a few chuckles from his friends.

"They were so perfect together." Kendra said wistfully. "I couldn't imagine them being with anyone else." She smiled sadly as Kalen wrapped an arm around her shoulders.

"I'll go next." Megs offered quietly. Blaine reached over and took her hand. She smiled at him and squeezed it gently. "I was dating Anthony a while back and I really liked him, not sure why." She chuckled wryly. "We went out a few times and then I didn't hear from him, he completely ghosted me. Then a few nights later he suddenly walked into Con's with his new girlfriend. I was fuming and I so badly wanted to walk up to him and punch him in his smug, arrogant, asshat face. Kel, the sweet soul that she was, stopped me and said, 'We don't get mad Megs, we get *even*' and insisted on taking their drinks to them. She 'accidentally' knocked an entire glass of red wine over Anthony's bright white pants." She laughed. "He was furious and convinced she did it on purpose, so he complained to Alex and Kel looked at him with those big beautiful blue eyes of hers and said so innocently 'But Alex you know how clumsy I am' and he knew she wasn't, she was the most graceful person ever. He covered for her and told Anthony, she really is very clumsy and it was obviously an accident."
She laughed. "My favourite memory of Rob was the first night we met him. I think it was our second or third shift at Con's and his first time working with us. He was so smitten with Kel from the moment she walked through the door. He ran circles around her all night, clearing plates, carrying drinks and just about anything she needed and *didn't* need him to do and she thought he was the most handsome and adorable man she had ever seen. They ended up kissing at the coffee machine while they were supposed to be making coffee for her customers." She shook her head smiling at the memory.

"I remember that night." Blaine looked at Kyle. "You and Rob finished shift around eleven and came back here. Mark and I were watching movies and we all ended up outside at this table chatting till sunrise. Do you remember Kyle?"

"Yeah, I remember. He sat here and said 'I met the girl of my dreams tonight. I'm going to marry her one day' I laughed and told him he was crazy because they had only known each other a few hours." Kyle chuckled and shook his head. "He turned around and said to me, rather arrogantly I might add, 'One day you'll see what I mean. You will hold a girl in your arms and when you kiss her your heart will whisper 'This is her, she's the one' and you'll find the piece of your heart that you never knew was missing'." He paused and swallowed back his tears before continuing. "I just shook my head at him and laughed as he gave me that smug look of his. Not even two months later I got home the one night and I had to phone that arrogant ass and tell him he was right." He turned to look at Angelia. "That was the night I met you, the love of my life." He said quietly. She looked at him in astonishment before leaning over to drape her arms around his neck. He wrapped his arms around her and pulled her onto his lap holding her tightly against him. Jarryd smiled and glanced at Christian who returned his smile.

"I don't want tonight to end." Megan said tearfully. "Sitting here like this I can just pretend that they're away for a few days or Kel's on shift and Robbie is sitting at the bar waiting for her to finish. Tomorrow I…" She trailed off as she burst into tears.

"Wherever they are Megs, they're together." Blaine said to her as he rubbed her back soothingly. "I know it's not much comfort but," He shrugged as he slid his arm over her shoulders and drew her closer to him.

"You're right, they are. It is a little comforting to know that they are together."

"It's how they would've wanted it. Together forever, just not how they thought." Kendra wiped her tears off her cheeks.

"Tomorrow is going to be an extremely emotionally and trying day." Christian sighed putting his arm around Ciara. "I know we should all have an early night but I just can't bring myself to leave."

"No one has to leave." Kyle spoke quietly. "Everyone can stay as long as they want and whoever wants to stay over, we will make a plan with couches and cushions and blankets. We all need each other right now and I would rather have everyone here than have someone off alone somewhere hurting on their own."

"Someone can always share a bed with JR." Angelia volunteered. "He has a whole double bed to himself."

"Oooh me. Can I please?" Kalen said in a falsetto voice.

Jarryd looked over at him. "Come near my bed Kalen and you'll be talking like that permanently." He warned him. Everyone laughed quietly as Kyle shook his head.

"Kalen, I just can't. Where the hell did we find you?"

"I ask my mother that on a weekly basis. It used to be daily so there has been some sort of improvement." Christian smirked at his brother.

Angelia sat up on Kyle's lap. "I have an idea."

"No more suggestions from you Lia." Her brother gave her a stern look.

"I was going to say we should go in and watch a movie. It was Rob's favourite thing to do. All of us being together, watching a movie and eating popcorn.

"I like that." Megan said quietly.

"Me too." Casey reached out to squeeze her hand.

"Let's go in and watch a movie then." Blaine said standing up and reaching for Megan's hand. She placed her hand in his and he helped her to her feet. They walked inside followed by Christian, Ciara, Kendra and Kalen.

"Jake," Jarryd called him as he started to walk past. Angelia shot a concerned glance at her brother. Jake turned as Jarryd held his hand out to him. "There are moments that define us and its often during tragic and trying times that a person's true character comes out. You've been a rock and a huge help to everyone and I think it's time that you and I put the past behind us." Jake reached out to shake Jarryd's hand.

"I'd like that." He said smiling. Jarryd patted him on the shoulder as they turned to join the others.

"Jarryd." Casey called him. "Can we talk? In private." He nodded and followed her to the pool table. Angelia stood and looked at Kyle. He rose to his feet and rubbed her arms gently. She put her hands on his cheeks.

"I love you."

"I loved you from the day I met you. As you heard earlier." He chuckled quietly. She wrapped her arms around his waist.

"All of this has made me realise how fragile and fleeting life is. A love like ours is different, and special. It's you and me, always." She whispered.

"I want to spend the rest of my life with you. There is no one else." He whispered gently. "You are the only woman I have ever truly loved, the only woman I want to love. You're right. It's you and me, always." His eyes swung to the door as Kalen swung it open and motioned to them. He gave a quick nod. "Right now, we have to go be with our family." She turned to smile at Kalen. Kyle held her hand tightly as they made their way inside.

"Blaine and I are making popcorn." Kalen announced as they walked in.

"I can smell that." Angelia responded as she reached past Blaine into the cupboard to grab some bowls.

"Hey, Kyle. Did I tell you about the time that Lia tried to make us popcorn?" Blaine asked laughing.

"No, you didn't."

"Don't you dare, Blaine." She pointed a finger at him.

"Lia set the kitchen on fire." Jarryd laughed as he and Casey walked through the door.

"Jarryd!"

"Ok, ok to be fair she set the pot, the stove, three cloths, and a bowl on fire, not the whole kitchen." Jarryd corrected himself.

"You really are a disaster, aren't you?" Kyle kissed the side of her head.

"And she's your disaster now." Jarryd sniggered as he patted him on the shoulder.

"Yes, she is." Kyle leaned down to kiss her quickly.

"What did we miss?" Christian enquired as the rest of the group joined them in the kitchen.

"I was telling Kyle about the time that Lia tried to make us all popcorn when our parents went out and everyone came over to watch movies." Blaine smiled.

"Wasn't that when she set the kitchen on fire?" Christian asked laughing.

"It was not the whole kitchen." Angelia protested.

"The entire house was full of smoke and we literally had every door and window open trying to get that awful smell out of the house." Blaine chuckled.

"Then we had to hide the charred remains of Mom's favourite cloths and the brand-new bowl that she bought to replace the one that Lia baked with." Jarryd added.

"We did manage to save the pot that time though." Christian grinned.

"Poor Mom, she hunted for those cloths for months." Blaine looked at his sister. "Do you know what my favourite Lia memory is though?" He asked as he reached over to flick her ponytail. She shook her head, smiling at him. "When I went through a rebellious stage and started smoking when I was fourteen or fifteen. One day I dropped my cigarette on the couch and burnt a hole in it. I was so scared about what our parents would do. When Mom saw the burn mark and asked what happened, you told her that it was you, that you had dropped a candle on the couch." He looked at her. "You got into so much trouble and you were grounded for three weeks. When I asked you why you did it, you hugged me and said 'Because you're my brother and I love you'. I know we tease you a lot about your cooking and driving but it's because we love you and we can't imagine our lives without you. You're the best sister anyone could ask for and I love you so much."

He sniffed, wiping at the tears in his eyes. She wrapped her arms around him and hugged him tightly.

"I love you too." She said softly. Christian looked at Jarryd who was watching them with tears glistening in his eyes. He wrapped his arms around the two of them before laughing.

"If that popcorn burns, I'm going to have two cooking disasters for family members." He pointed to pot on the stove. Kalen hauled the pot off and checked inside.

"Nothing burnt."

Angelia leaned back against Kyle. "Do you remember the time I tried to make bacon and eggs for Mom on Mother's Day?" She grinned at Blaine. He groaned and shook his head.

"Like it was yesterday."

"I haven't heard this one." Christian said raising his eyebrows.

"Let's grab the popcorn, get settled in the lounge and my brothers will tell you all about it." Angelia laughed while Jarryd grabbed two of the bowls and walked through.

Angelia caught Blaine's arm. "Are you ok hon?"

"Yeah, I just keep thinking, what if you had been in the car and it was you and not Kelly who..." He shook his head sadly, "I can't even imagine what Kelly's brothers are going through. Matt, Mikey and Wes, they don't get to hug or tease their sister again or tell her they love her or hear her tell them she loves them." Angelia hugged him.

"Let's go join them before they finish all the popcorn." She said smiling at him. Blaine grabbed the last bowl of popcorn and followed her to the lounge.

Angelia smirked as she saw Casey sitting on her brother's lap. Blaine dropped down onto the floor next to Kalen and set the bowl of popcorn between them as Angelia made her way to Kyle who was sitting on the single couch. She settled onto his lap and kissed his cheek.

"I've changed my mind. I'm not teaching you to cook anymore. It sounds far too dangerous." He chuckled as she rolled her eyes. Jarryd looked at the two of them and grinned.

"Kyle the last time I was here, Mark mentioned something about the night that there was a wet bath towel left in the kitchen. After all he has been through, I thought I would finally get him some answers to that little mystery. So, spill the beans you two. What's the story with the towel?"

"I have no idea what you are talking about." Angelia gave him an innocent smile.

"I remember that night." Kyle said with a smug smile. She turned to glower at him as he flushed. "I mean I don't remember that night. What wet towel?" He asked trying to hide behind Angelia.

"You are useless." She huffed as she rolled her eyes.

"Kyle." Jarryd looked at him. "You may as well tell us while Lia is here because she is going to give me another story when you are not around and you won't be there to defend yourself."

"I would never do that baby." She said fluttering her eyelashes at him.

"I have my doubts about that." He chuckled. "Well, it's, uh, not a bad story, I guess. We had a huge screaming fight at Chris's place so I left and came back here because I was fuming. I was in the shower when some persistent person rang the doorbell about a hundred times."

"It was four times drama queen." She rolled her eyes.

"Hey, who's telling the story?" She huffed and looked at Jarryd who smirked at her. "So, I open the door and its little miss attitude over here who went stomping into the kitchen. I followed her in and stood there helplessly as she proceeded to undress and seduce me." He shrugged.

"Excuse me?"

"You unhooked my towel." He looked at her indignantly.

"Yeah well, who answers the door in a towel?" She sneered at him.

"I was in the shower and *someone* was ringing the bell very persistently."

"Wait. So that's where you disappeared to? You told me you had a headache and you wanted to go home to sleep it off." Christian arched an eyebrow at her. "Meantime you came here to seduce poor Kyle."

"*Poor* Kyle?" She looked at him as her jaw dropped. "Poor Kyle wasn't moaning about it. Well, he was moaning, but not about that." She bit the side of her lip to hide her smile.

"Lia." Kyle ducked behind her as Jarryd burst out laughing before pointing a finger at him.

"So, I have had a little chat with all the shops in the vicinity and you and my sister have both been banned from the whipped cream aisle." He smirked at Kyle as he flushed red.

"You told your brother about the whipped cream?" He looked at her wide-eyed.

"No but Casey explained it to him five times, they used the entire can in one night."

"It was not five times Lia." Casey protested.

"It *was* five times." Jarryd corrected her.

"Ok, I guess it was five times then."

"You know it takes us a weekend to finish a can of whipped cream." Kyle looked incredulously at Jarryd.

"Can we *please* change the subject? I'm going to need serious therapy after this." Blaine complained dropping his head in his hands.

"Oh, is that right sweet brother of mine?" Angelia flashed an evil grin at him. He looked at her warily.

"What do you know Lia?"

"I packed away your socks the other day."

"You didn't." He looked at her horrified.

"Oh, but I did." She turned to Jarryd. "Want to know what I found in your sweet, innocent little brother's sock drawer?"

"I'm pretty sure I don't Lia, but you're going to tell me anyway."

"Angelia Ryan. You *will* regret it." Blaine warned her.

"Kyle will protect me." She said confidently.

"Yeah. No, he won't."

"Even if I promise to do that thing you like?" She asked innocently.

"Lia." Jarryd shook his head.

"Twice and you have a deal." Kyle smirked at her.

"Kyle." Jarryd sighed shaking his head again.

"Twice then." She rolled her eyes.

"Fine. No one touches Lia." Kyle narrowed his eyes at Blaine who shook his head.

"Traitor. What happened to Bros before h…"

"Blaine, are you about to call our sister a hoe?" Jarryd looked at him with a raised eyebrow.

"Yes."

"Ok, just checking." Jarryd chuckled as he drew Casey against his chest and grinned at his sister.

"Un-freaking-believable." Angelia scowled at him. They all turned to look as Kendra and Megan burst into uncontrollable giggles.

Megan tried to catch her breath after a few moments. "I'm so glad that we decided to stay and do this." She said smiling. "I really needed this. I think Rob and Kelly would be happy to see us like this."

"I think so too." Ciara said softly. Megan looked at Angelia.

"So, tell us what's in Blaine's sock drawer."

"Ah yeah, Megs, you don't want her to do that." Blaine cautioned, shooting her a quick look.

"It was black furry handcuffs." Angelia laughed. "Wait. What?" She gaped at Megan who had turned bright red. "Those are yours?" She asked shocked as Megan hid her face in her hands and nodded. Everyone laughed as Megan looked up and grinned at Blaine.

"I wondered if you kept them." They all sat in silence for a few minutes before Kyle cleared his throat.

"Um Blaine, if you're not going to be using them tonight..." He trailed off as he smirked at him.

"Kyle." Christian groaned as Jarryd burst into laughter.

"I was about to ask for them as well." He confessed with a wry smile.

"JR" Christian groaned again and shook his head. "You're supposed to lead by example, not join them."

"Guys it's nearly midnight. We need to get some sleep." Kalen said standing up. "Is everyone just going to stay here tonight?" They all looked around and nodded.

Blaine rose to his feet. "Chris and Ciara you take my room."

"No take ours." Kyle insisted as Blaine shook his head.

"Makes more sense for couples to take beds. I'm going to sleep on a big double bed by myself while Chris and Ciara or you and Lia squash up here on a chair." He shrugged.

"Thanks, Blaine." Ciara smiled warmly at him.

"Ok so Chris and Ciara, Case and I and Lia and Kyle will take the bedrooms. Who are we left with?" Jarryd asked.

"Kalen, Kendra, Megs, Jake and Blaine." Angelia replied.

"We're also a couple." Kalen protested as he put his arm around Kendra.

"Yeah, ok. You're right." Jarryd conceded. "Let me rephrase that. Couples who actually have a sex life will take the bedrooms." He grinned at Kalen.

"Excuse me." Kalen glared at him. "We have…"

"Kalen if you finish that sentence…" Kendra trailed off as she gave him a warning look

"We'll take the one double couch." Kalen grumbled giving Kendra a sheepish look.

"I'll take the floor on some cushions and blankets." Jake volunteered. "So, Blaine and Megs can take the other two couches."

"Everyone sorted then?" Jarryd asked, looking around as Kyle and Angelia walked back in with arms full of cushions, pillows and blankets.

"Yeah." Blaine made himself comfortable. "I'm going to put a movie on until we fall asleep." He said flicking through the channels. Angelia bent down and kissed him on the cheek.

"Do you know how much I love you?" She asked him quietly.

"As much as I love you."

She smiled and followed Kyle out the door to his room. Kyle pulled his shirt off and threw it on the chair over his shorts, he looked over at Angelia as she climbed onto the bed and smiled at him. He climbed in next to her and ran his fingers lightly over her stomach before moving to rest his body over hers. He brushed her hair back as he leaned down to press his lips against hers. Their kisses were soft and gentle and she sighed as she ran her fingers up and down his back slowly. He smiled lovingly down at her.

"I know we're normally fast-paced, intense and passionate. Tonight, I just want to hold you and kiss you and just be here with you, present in this moment. I love you so much."

"I like that." She whispered. "I love you, more than anything." She smiled as he leaned down to kiss her.

Chapter 19

Angelia took a deep breath as she looked at the church. Kyle squeezed her hand gently as their friends walked up to join them.

"I guess we should go in." Jarryd said quietly as he started walking towards the door.

"Jarryd, it's so lovely to see you again." Robbie's Mom hugged him. "I have asked them to keep the third and fourth row on the right-hand side for all of you." She smiled tearfully as she reached out to gently squeeze Angelia and Blaine's hands.

"Thank you, Mrs. H." Jarryd said giving her a sad smile as he ushered everyone in towards their seats. Kyle reached over and held Angelia's hand as they sat down. She squeezed his hand gently as she looked up at the photos of Robbie and Kelly in front of the stage. Tears welled in her eyes and she looked back down at her hands.

"I'm so glad you're here brother." She heard Jarryd say and looked up to see Kalen putting the brakes down on Mark's wheelchair. She smiled at him as he looked at her and returned her smile.

"I had to be here." Mark said quietly to Jarryd who nodded.

"Hi, Mark." Megan bent down to kiss him on his cheek. He caught her hand and held it tightly.

"Hey, Megs. How are you holding up hon?" He asked gently. She shook her head sadly as a tear trickled down her cheek.

"Megs, Mom wants you to come sit with us." She looked up at Kelly's older brother.

"Hi Mikey. I'll be there now." She said softly squeezing his arm gently. He nodded to the rest of the group and made his way to his family. "I'll see you all just now." She said as she turned to follow him.

"I can't imagine what Kelly's brothers are going through, losing their only sister." Jarryd glanced over at his own sister who was talking quietly to Blaine, she met his eyes and smiled sadly.

They all turned to face the stage as the pastor walked to the podium and started speaking. After opening in prayer, he called Dylan to address everyone. After speaking briefly, he looked up at the group of friends and gave them a brave smile.

"We asked two of Robbie and mine's longest-standing friends to sing today. Rob and Kel loved listening to them and would often sit in on our practice sessions. We thought it would be a wonderful way to pay tribute to them. Lia, Blaine, please." He said smiling sadly and motioning for them to join him. Jarryd turned to look at them in surprise as they stood and made their way up to Dylan. Blaine picked up his guitar from the back and sat down on a chair. Dylan gave Angelia a hug before handing her the microphone. She stood behind Blaine and rested her hand gently on his shoulder. He closed his eyes briefly to blink back his tears before running his fingers over the strings. Angelia looked at Jarryd and smiled bravely before she lifted the microphone and started singing 'Jealous of the Angels' with Blaine joining in softly for the chorus. They finished the song and Angelia handed the microphone back to Dylan as she wiped the tears from her cheeks. Blaine set his guitar down and hugged her tightly before they headed back to join their friends. Kelly's younger brother paid tribute to her before calling Megan up to join him. He placed his arm around her as she stood stoically recounting sweet memories of her friendship with Kelly.

Dylan made his way back up to the podium and cleared his throat. "I'd like to ask Robbie's best friend JR to please come up and say a few words now." Jarryd walked up to Dylan, hugged him and spoke to him briefly before heading to the podium. He took a deep breath as he glanced at his friend's casket. He cleared his throat and pulled his speech out of his pocket.

"Robbie told me once that you will make many friends during your life and that some of those friends will become family. Robs was one of those people for me. He was my friend, but he was also my brother. In all the years I knew him, I never met one person who had a bad word to say about him and I think that is a true testament to the amazing person he was.

"There was no distance too far or favour too big if you needed his help. He, uh, he loved…" Jarryd stopped and looked down at his speech. He shook his head before looking up at Angelia and Blaine. He cleared his throat and took a deep breath.

"Robs loved his family and friends and he never hesitated to let us all know. I have never once doubted how he felt about me, my brother, my sister and our group of friends because he always told us. He didn't believe in letting things go unsaid and I think that is something we should all learn from him.

"Losing Robs has shown me that you need to hold those you love close to you and tell them as often as you can how much they mean to you. Hug them like it's the last time you will hold them in your arms so that when something tragic like this happens, you will have no regrets.

"The only person Robs loved more than his family and friends was his Kelly." He looked at her family and smiled sadly. "I didn't know Kelly that long, only a few short weeks but for Robs to love her the way that he did, I knew she was an incredibly special person and I will be forever grateful to her for making him so unbelievably happy. He loved her from the first day he met her. Thank you for raising such a beautiful, kind and incredible woman, she was a true beacon of light and she will be sorely missed."

He turned to look at Robbie's family. "I want to thank you for my best friend, my brother, he meant the world to me, to us." He gestured to his friends. "He has left a huge void in our lives, but I am beyond grateful that I had the privilege of having him in my life for over twenty-two years. Thank you for giving him an amazing life and for raising him to be the caring, compassionate and loving man that he was, that we will always remember him being."

Jarryd took a deep breath and looked over at his friend's casket and then at the photo of him behind it. "Robs, my friend, thank you for the memories, thank you for your friendship but most of all my brother thank you for the never-ending love that will forever define our friendship. I know I will see you again one day and I will hold my memories of you in my heart until we meet again." He stepped away from the podium and made his way down to his friends taking his seat between Mark and Blaine.

***

"I knew today would be difficult, but it was brutal, way worse than I expected." Kyle spoke softly as they sat quietly at the kitchen table.

"It's not something I ever want to go through again." Jarryd looked at his siblings. "I felt a little blindsided today. Lia, Blaine I had no idea you could sing like that. I knew you guys played guitar but I have never heard you sing."

"It's because Lia's shy about it." Blaine reached over to squeeze her shoulder gently.

"It felt good to sing to Robs and Kel one last time." She said as she rested her head on Kyle's shoulder.

"Yeah, it did." Blaine agreed quietly.

"You must be happy to have Mark home." Jarryd smiled at Kyle who nodded.

"Yeah, I am. Especially after today. I'm grateful for a lot of things. I realised how much I take for granted every day and I'm going to be a little more thankful for what I have and who I have." Kyle kissed the top of Angelia's head.

"Me too." She mumbled softly smiling at Jarryd.

"Maybe that's the lesson in all of this. Stop being busy and caught up in everything and just take time to breathe and be happy and to appreciate the people you love." Jarryd sighed as he leaned back in his chair.

Kyle looked up as Mark called him from the lounge. "Let me go see what he needs." He said standing up and heading out the door.

"Are you going to be ok?" Jarryd looked at his sister with concern.

"Yes. Why?" She frowned.

"Kyle and I are both leaving in two weeks."

"I know. I have Blaine and Mark is going to need a lot of help. I'll be fine." She reassured him. He nodded as Kyle walked back in.

"Mark's hungry, especially after all that delicious hospital food, so I'm going to get dinner started. Why don't you guys go hang out with Mark in the lounge."

"I can't leave you to cook on your own." Jarryd protested.

"It's ok, I have Lia." Kyle rubbed her shoulder as Jarryd arched an eyebrow. "Oh no, she doesn't actually cook, she sits on the counter, drinks wine, criticises me and tries to seduce me." Kyle grinned at him.

"Sitting on the counter drinking wine is the safest thing for Lia to do in the kitchen." Blaine smirked.

"Are we seriously back to this?" She glared at him.

"Please don't let Lia near my food. I've suffered enough." Mark shouted from the lounge.

"Unbelievable."

Kyle laughed and rubbed her arm gently. "Love you." He smiled at her.

"Bite me." She huffed rolling her eyes at him.

"Definitely later baby." He gave her a smug look.

"Kyle." Jarryd sighed. "I like to think that we are friends because I do like you so I would hate to have to throw you in the pool now."

"Sorry." Kyle chuckled. "It's a habit."

"You get used to it after a while." Kalen spoke behind them. They turned to find Kalen, Christian, Kendra, Ciara and Megan standing in the doorway of the kitchen.

"No, you don't." Christian sighed. "You just try to pretend not to hear it."

"What are you guys doing here?" Angelia smiled at him.

"We decided we wanted to be with our family tonight. And we were hoping Kyle was going to cook." Kalen grinned.

"I am actually, I'll just have to run out quick and get some more food."

"No need to do that." Jake announced as he walked into the kitchen with packets of groceries. "Thanks for the help, guys." He gave Christian and Kalen a pointed look as he handed the packets to Kyle. "We weren't sure what you would need so we bought, cream, mushrooms, bacon, pasta, tomatoes, ham and chicken. We also brought dessert."

"Should I be expecting a small army to appear shortly?" Kyle raised his eyebrows.

"Wait. Who's we?" Angelia frowned.

"Me and Dyl." Casey said as they walked in. "I got dessert." She lifted the packet in her hand. "Brownies and my favourite ice cream." She smiled. "And, uh, a can of whipped cream." She grinned at Jarryd who grinned back at her as Angelia burst into laughter. "I got you one too Lia."

"Casey." Jarryd gave her a stern look as Angelia wrapped her arms around Dylan and hugged him tightly.

"I'll sneak it into the fridge." Casey stage whispered to Angelia as she walked past her.

"I heard that." Jarryd huffed as Angelia rolled her eyes.

"While you're all here, I wanted to ask if everyone wants to do family dinner this Sunday?" Kyle looked around at his friends. "If it's too soon…" He trailed off.

"No, that would be great." Megan said smiling. "I think that Rob and Kelly would want us to."

"I think so too."

"Alright, everyone out. I would like to eat before midnight. Kyle and I are going to make food quickly." Jarryd said pointing to the door.

"Just so you know, Kyle expects kisses and cuddles while he's cooking." Angelia grinned at her brother as she walked out the door.

"Yeah, that's not going to happen. No offense Kyle, you're just not my type." Jarryd grinned at him.

"Yeah, there's only one Ryan family member I like to kiss."

"How can I help?" Blaine asked gloomily as he dropped down on one of the chairs. Kyle lifted an eyebrow.

"Since when do you offer to help cook? Mark and I just about have to chain you to the table to get you to help with anything in the kitchen." He chuckled while Blaine sighed heavily.

"Mark sent me. He said I have to learn how to cook because you leave in two weeks and he's not going to be able to so that just leaves Lia."

"Yeah, cooking lessons start now." Kyle laughed.

"Anyone need a drink?" Angelia asked as she stood up.

"May as well bring for everyone Lia." Christian smiled warmly at her.

"Find out from the cooking crew when dinner is going to be ready, I'm starving." Kalen complained. She shook her head as she walked to the kitchen.

"The ingrates are comp…" She trailed off as she realised she was talking to an empty kitchen. "That's weird." She stuck her head out the door. "Kyle. Blaine. JR." She yelled up the passage. She frowned when there was no response. "Maybe they're outside." She opened the door to the entertainment area and shook her head. "Hey slackers. Aren't you supposed to be cooking?" She walked up to join them and wrapped her arms around Jarryd. He put his arm around her.

"The food is in the oven so we are taking a well-deserved break."

"Kalen's complaining." She shrugged.

"How is that different from any other day?" Kyle laughed.

"Why are you out here and not in there with us?" She asked looking at them suspiciously. Blaine looked down at his feet and shrugged. "Blaine?" She asked, letting go of Jarryd and wrapping her arms around him. He smiled and flicked her ponytail.

"Yeah?"

"What's going on?" She asked looking up into his eyes. He shook his head as Kyle shot a panicked look at Jarryd who met his eyes before looking back at his brother.

"Nothing LiLi." He laughed at her.

She narrowed her eyes at him. "You're lying to me." She accused him.

"I would never lie to you. I love you too much." He hugged her. "We just wanted some fresh air and to discuss what we are going to make for family dinner on Sunday." He explained smiling down at her.

"Ok. I'm getting drinks for everyone else. Can I get for you three as well?" She offered.

"I won't say no." Jarryd laughed. They watched as she smiled and headed back inside.

"Thanks for not saying anything Blaine." Kyle said quietly. "I know you hate keeping things from Lia."

"I don't tell Lia everything." Jarryd snorted and Blaine glared at him. "What?" He asked defensively.

"You tell her *everything*." He smirked.

"Yeah, I guess I do." Blaine smiled as Angelia walked back to them and handed them each a drink before putting her arm around Kyle's waist.

"The food is going to be ready in about ten minutes. Maybe we should start bringing plates out and getting everyone here." Kyle said as he rubbed her arm.

"That was incredible." Ciara sat back and smiled at her friends.

"Kyle knows his way around the kitchen." Jarryd agreed. "And I didn't even have to kiss and cuddle him once." He grinned at Angelia who rolled her eyes.

"Why would he want to kiss *you* when he can kiss *me*?" She asked him smugly.

"Are you trying to say that I couldn't get Kyle to kiss me?" Jarryd queried looking at her with a raised eyebrow.

"No, Kyle's saying that." Kyle laughed as he shook his head. "No offense, I'm sure you are a great kisser JR, but Lia is the *only* Ryan family member I will be kissing, thanks." He grinned at him.

"I rest my case." Angelia sniped at her brother.

"Are you trying to say that you are more kissable than I am?" Her brother asked with a raised eyebrow.

"Yes." She smirked.

"You are in denial."

"These dinner conversations seem to get progressively worse." Christian sighed shaking his head.

Jarryd looked at him and grinned. "If you can't beat them join them."

"I'm glad everyone is here together. This is what life is about. Time with family." Blaine said quietly. "It's something I will never take for granted again." He smiled at his friends as he raised his glass. "To family."

"To family." They chorused as they all smiled at each other.

"Does everyone have plans for tomorrow?" Kendra asked looking around.

"JR, Blaine and I are going to do a grocery run quickly in the morning for family dinner on Sunday but other than that we have no plans." Kyle shrugged. Angelia's eyes shot to Jarryd before going to Blaine. She looked up at Kyle who looked back at her and smiled.

"I'll stay here with Mark." She beamed at him before looking at Mark. "We can watch a movie, I'll make us popcorn."

Mark groaned and shook his head. "There goes the kitchen." He sighed.

"It's microwave popcorn you ass." She glowered at him. "I bought a few boxes the other day. It's so much quicker than making it on the stove."

"And safer." Megan piped up.

"Bitch." Angelia narrowed her eyes at her.

"LiLi." Megan pulled a tongue at her.

"Don't call me LiLi." She moaned as she dropped her head in her hands.

"We may need to get a new microwave while we're out tomorrow guys." Kyle sighed, Angelia's jaw dropped as she turned to look at him.

"Don't *you* start." She glared at him. "No sex for you." She said moving away from him.

"Oh please. Like you can resist me." Kyle looked at her smugly.

"Excuse me." She gave him a pointed look.

"I just need to pull you close, kiss your neck and you'll melt into my arms."

"You can sleep on the couch tonight." She huffed as she picked up her drink.

"It's my bed, *you* sleep on the couch." He countered.

"Fine, I'll sleep on the couch." She sniffed. Kyle burst out laughing.

"I give you half an hour and you'll be climbing into my bed." He smirked at her.

"Kyle." Jarryd sighed heavily.

"We all know it's true." He chuckled as he took a swig of his beer and looked at his girlfriend.

"He's not wrong." She laughed.

"Lia." Her brother shook his head and sighed again.

She pointed a finger at him. "You are not innocent brother of mine." She smirked as he looked at her. "No sex on my couch you two. Again." She raised an eyebrow as Casey blushed.

"Technically only one of us was on the couch." Jarryd grinned as he took a sip of his beer.

"JR" Christian groaned as dropped his head in his hand.

"I'm still going to have to have it steam cleaned." She grumbled as she leaned back in her chair.

"Oh yes, Mark. I solved a mystery for you." Jarryd gave him a snide smile. Mark arched an eyebrow.

"What mystery is that, Nancy Drew?" He sniggered.

"The mystery of the wet bath towel in the kitchen." Jarryd grinned.

"Do I want to know?" Mark asked frowning. "Alright, let's hear it."

"Apparently, Lia and Kyle had a huge fight at Chris's place." Jarryd explained as Mark nodded.

"Yes, I remember that."

"Afterwards my little sister drove over here and seduced poor, innocent Kyle in the kitchen."

"Poor innocent Kyle? Really?" Angelia sniped at her brother.

"What have I told you two about having sex in the kitchen." Mark gave them a disapproving look before turning to Blaine and Kalen. "I told you we needed to sanitise that table."

"Technically Lia only undressed me in the kitchen." Kyle corrected his brother.

"How is it undressing when all you were wearing was a towel?" She raised an eyebrow at him.

"Hey, I was completely covered so it was definitely undressing." Kyle gave her a smug look. She rolled her eyes and turned to Kendra.

"Please excuse the rude men in my life. Is there something you want to do tomorrow?"

Kendra burst out laughing. "No, I was just wondering what everyone is up to."

"We could always come here and keep you and Mark company." Megan looked at her innocently. "Maybe we could do a girls pamper day." Mark swung his head to look at her as she gave him an evil grin. "Mark won't mind. Will you Mark?"

"Mark will." He stated solemnly as the girls laughed.

"You could do with a makeover." Angelia gave him a sweet smile. Mark turned to Jarryd.

"You are *not* leaving me here alone tomorrow."

"Girls, please do not wax Mark." Jarryd said in a stern voice. "However, you *can* do his nails and eyelashes."

"I thought we were friends." Mark gave him a disappointed look as he shook his head.

"And take lots of photos." Jarryd added with a grin. "Send them to us while we're shopping." Mark groaned as Angelia and Megan gave him matching angelic smiles.

***

"Hey guys, come help carry plates through, the food is almost ready." Jarryd shouted from the door. Blaine and Kalen followed him inside. Christian stood and started clearing phones and towels from the table.

"Baby, won't you please grab the champagne from the fridge." Kyle said as he poured pasta into a bowl.

"Anything for you sugar lips." Kalen replied in a high-pitched falsetto. "Ow. Lia." He glared at her as he clutched his arm.

"I don't sound like that Kalen. And I have never called him sugar lips." She scowled at him.

"Kalen, I...you know you just...I don't know where your mother found you." Kyle sighed as he handed the bowl of pasta to Blaine who sniggered and walked out the door.

Jarryd looked at Kalen. "What is wrong with you?" He asked shaking his head.

"You got three days?" Christian chuckled as he grabbed a stack of plates and headed back out the door.

"I make things interesting."

"You make things scary." Kyle muttered as he took glasses out of the cupboard.

"Did you buy champagne glasses babe?" Angelia frowned as she looked at the glasses on the counter.

"I figured we're adults, we should have at least six champagne glasses and six wine glasses in our cupboard."

"You are so weird sometimes." She leaned up to kiss him.

"Only sometimes?" Blaine asked snidely.

"Hey. Do you want to be homeless?" Kyle asked as Blaine chuckled, grabbed some of the glasses and walked back out.

"You look so damn sexy." Angelia whispered huskily as she wrapped her arms around Kyle's neck and pressed her lips against his. She pressed her body up against him and he moaned softly as he reached down and pulled her up into his arms and wrapped her legs around his waist.

"I may be wrong but I'm pretty sure that I heard Mark say something about no sex in the kitchen." Jarryd interrupted them from the doorway. Kyle flushed and set Angelia back down on the ground. "Oh, Kyle. You look so cute when you blush." Jarryd grinned at him.

"Shut up." Kyle mumbled as he shot Angelia a look and picked up the last bowl of food.

"I'm looking for ice buckets for the champagne. I thought it would be best to have it after dinner so we need to keep it cold." He gave Kyle a quick look.

"Please show him where they are babe." Kyle said as he ducked out the door. Angelia smiled as she reached into the cupboard and pulled out two ice buckets and handed them to her brother. He set them down on the counter and leaned against the door to look at her.

"Are you happy Lia?" He asked her quietly. She looked up at him wide eyed. "All I have ever wanted, was for you to be happy."

"I am. I never thought we would get to this point and I know he's leaving in two weeks and the long-distance thing is going to be difficult but we can make it work."

"If anyone can, it's the two of you." He said smiling as he picked up the ice buckets and headed out the door.

"Can I have everyone's attention for a minute please?" Kyle asked as everyone turned to look at him. "Thanks." He put his arm around Angelia and took a deep breath. He glanced at Jarryd and Blaine and gave them a quick smile. "This last week has been very challenging and heart-breaking. Saying goodbye to our two friends was tragic but it made me realise a few things. We need to be a lot more thankful for what we have and appreciate the amazing people in our lives. I'm extremely grateful for each person here today because your love and support for Mark, for me and for each other is something very rare and I am glad that all of you are here today. I love every single person here but," He turned to Angelia and smiled at her "there is one person that I love slightly more."

"Sure, only *slightly*" Kalen smirked. "Ow, JR." He glared at Jarryd as he rubbed his side. Kyle chuckled as he shook his head.

"Kalen is right, for a change. It is a lot more than slightly. Babe, we have been on a rollercoaster the last few years and somehow through everything, we always find our way back to each other. You are my rock, my calm in the storm and so, so much more. I cannot imagine my life without you. I loved you from the first night I met you and my love for you has only grown stronger."

He looked over at their group of friends and smiled. "With all the sadness we have had recently, I thought that we needed a bit of love and a bit of hope and I wanted everyone I love, *we* love, to be here together today."

Kyle took Angelia's hand and kissed it before smiling at her and dropping down to one knee. "Angelia Ryan, would you do me the incredible honour of being my wife?" She stared at him as she held a hand over her mouth, tears welled in her eyes as she nodded.

"Yes." She laughed. He slipped the ring onto her finger and stood up to hug her as their friends clapped and smiled.

"Congratulations you two." Angelia looked up at Blaine. She smiled as she hugged her brother tightly.

"Hey, I also want a hug." Jarryd laughed as he wrapped his arms around them both. He let go and reached out his hand to Kyle. "I'm really happy for you two. You have been through so much to be together, you deserve your happy ending." He smiled at them as Kendra wrapped her arms around Angelia and hugged her tightly. "I'm going to help pour the champagne."

"That's why you bought glasses. When did you buy this?" Angelia asked looking at the beautiful and delicate ring.

"Yesterday morning." He admitted. "I looked at rings a while back and there was one that caught my eye. It was still there but I wanted your brothers' opinions so I asked them to come with me."

"Blaine knew? He didn't say anything to me."

"It was supposed to be a surprise." Kyle laughed. She looked up at him with tears in her eyes.

"It was. I love you so much."

"I love you too. Do you like it?" He held her hand up to admire it. "You can change it for another one if you don't."

"It's perfect." She looked away as Jarryd made his way to them with two glasses of champagne. "Thank you." She took her glass. She smiled at Blaine as he joined them and handed Jarryd a glass.

"I would like us to raise our glasses to my beautiful sister and a man I already consider my brother. To Kyle and Lia." Jarryd said raising his glass.

"To Kyle and Lia." Everyone chorused raising their glasses. Angelia looked up at Kyle as he leaned down to kiss her.

***

"Kyle." He looked up as he heard a familiar voice call his name.

"Brianna." He exclaimed in surprise. She reached out and put a hand on his arm.

"It's so good to see you. You're looking so tanned and handsome." She beamed at him.

"Um, thanks. You look great too." He gave her an uncomfortable smile. "You here with someone?" He asked looking around.

"No, just some girls from the office. I'm not seeing anyone at the moment. Are you? Seeing anyone?" She asked giving him a flirty smile.

"Brianna." Angelia snarled in an icy voice as she placed her hand on Kyle's back and glowered at her. Kyle curled his arm around her and kissed the top of her head as he pulled her against his side. Angelia looked up and smiled at him before turning back to glare at Brianna again.

"You two are still together?" She tried to hide her disappointment.

Angelia gave her a snide look. "Yes, we are Brianna, despite your best efforts to tear us apart."

"Why are you two out here and not inside?" Jarryd asked as he and Casey walked up to the couple.

"Brianna." Casey scowled at her. "What the hell are you doing here?"

"I'm meeting friends for dinner." She snapped defensively as she glanced at Casey before looking back at Kyle.

"Clearly I missed something here." Jarryd looked at Casey for an explanation.

"Brianna's the one who tricked Kyle into believing she was pregnant and made him kick Lia out of his life." Casey explained as Kyle looked over at them.

"Let's just go inside guys." He said warily as Jarryd turned to look at Brianna, anger flickered across his face.

"So, you're the one who hurt my sister." He said quietly. She looked at him in surprise.

"You know what? It doesn't matter, that is all in the past. Tonight is a celebration of hope and love and the future." Angelia smiled up at Kyle as he bent down to kiss her. "Our future." She reached up to run her fingers gently down his cheek.

"You're engaged." Brianna blurted out as she saw the ring on Angelia's finger. Kyle caught Angelia's hand and kissed it while looking into her eyes.

"Yes, to the love of my life." He whispered never taking his eyes off his fiancée.

"I am so in love with you." She smiled lovingly up at him and sighed.

"Uggh. You two are just beyond sickening." Kalen grumbled as he walked past.

"Come on you two, let's go join the others." Jarryd laughed as he patted Kyle's shoulder and headed to the restaurant. Casey glared at Brianna one last time before slipping her hand in Jarryd's and following him inside.

Angelia watched as Brianna and her friends walked past them to a table directly opposite theirs. She exchanged an irritated quick glance with Casey.

"Please can you bring us two bottles of champagne." Kyle asked as the waiter handed their drinks out.

"Kyle, you do realise you are going to be cooking for the rest of your life." Jarryd laughed as he took a swig of his beer.

"I will do it happily as long as my lovely lady agrees to sit on the counter, drink wine and criticise me while I cook."

"Don't forget the kisses and cuddles in between cooking." Blaine added as Angelia leaned over to kiss Kyle on the cheek before shaking her head at her brother.

"Yeah, those kisses and cuddles in between ended in us eating burnt food on more than one occasion." Mark grumbled before chuckling.

"It's still better than Lia's cooking." Kalen sniggered as she glared at him.

"I have a question I am dying to ask." Megan looked at them with a smile as she reached out to hold Mark's hand. Kyle raised an eyebrow.

"It's going to be inappropriate, isn't it Megs?"

"How many cans of whipped cream are you guys going to take on your honeymoon?"

"Megan." Jarryd sighed as he looked at her. "It takes them two to three days to finish one can so I'd guess about seven." He grinned at Kyle who chuckled.

"I don't know what concerns me more. You participating in the conversation or that you've actually done the maths." Kyle sat back and smirked as Jarryd burst out laughing.

The waiter returned with their champagne and looked at Kyle who nodded at him. He opened and poured the champagne, handing everyone a glass. Kyle picked up his.

"Stand if you're going to make a speech."

"Seriously?" Kyle groaned giving Jarryd a pained look.

"Yes." Mark replied as Jarryd nodded.

"Fine." He sighed as he stood. "I just wanted to say how incredibly grateful I am to have all of you here tonight to celebrate with us." He gave them a sad smile. "We are missing two of our family who I know would have loved to be here and I know that we are all missing them very much. So, I would like us to raise a glass to Rob and Kelly." He raised his glass. "To Rob and Kel." He said softly.

"To Rob and Kel." They all clinked glasses and sipped their champagne. Kyle turned to look at Angelia and reached for her hand to pull her to her feet. He kissed her hand gently as she stood up.

"Babe, we have been to hell and back so many times. There were moments where I genuinely thought I had lost you for good and by some miracle you kept coming back to me. I honestly don't deserve you and I am so honoured that you keep choosing me and I promise to keep choosing you for the rest of our lives or for as long as you'll have me."

"How does forever sound?" She smiled back at him.

"I could live with forever." He placed his hand on her cheek and bent down to kiss her. She curled her hands around his neck and rested her forehead against his before reaching up to brush his hair back off his forehead.

"Then forever it is." She said softly as he bent down to kiss her again.

"I think they've forgotten we're here." Megan laughed. Angelia turned to smile at her, she caught Brianna glaring at her before she turned back to look at Kyle who flushed.

"Um, I kind of forgot where I was going with this." He admitted as he played with the collar of his shirt and gave his friends a sheepish grin.

"See, Lia kisses him and his brain goes to mush." Ciara giggled.

"Ciara." Angelia exclaimed. Kyle grinned at her as he shrugged.

"She's not wrong babe."

"I'd like to say a few words." Jarryd spoke up. "If you don't mind Kyle."

"Go right ahead." Kyle consented as he and Angelia sat back down. Jarryd rose to his feet and picked up his glass as he looked at the couple.

"Kyle I just want to start by saying that Blaine and I are incredibly grateful to you for making our baby sister so happy and loving her the way that you do. I know that our dad would have loved more than anything to be here tonight giving this speech for his baby girl. I'm going to do it on his behalf." He smiled at Angelia as she wiped at her tears. "My Lia, we are so proud of you, of the woman you have become. Blaine and I are honoured to be the brothers of a woman who has more compassion, love and integrity than anyone we know. It has been a privilege to have watched you grow up from this sweet little girl to an amazing young woman who I know is going to do great things. We love you more than you will ever know.

"My parents would have loved you Kyle and they would definitely approve of the two of you. The last time I was here Lia told me that despite what was happening between you, your love story wasn't over. That the love and connection you two share is so unique and so strong that it keeps pulling the two of you back together. I must admit that I had my doubts until the first time I saw the two of you together. In amongst the tragedy and the chaos we were faced with, I witnessed a love that was so powerful and encompassing I was in awe of it. You love, respond to and protect each other in a way I have never seen before and I finally saw what Lia was talking about. Looking at the two of you has made me realise that as long as we have love, we have everything because love truly does conquer all. To Kyle and Lia." He raised his glass.

"To Kyle and Lia." Their friends chorused as she leaned over to kiss his cheek.

***

"I've come to the conclusion that we spend far too much time out here." Jarryd chuckled as Casey leaned back against his chest.

"Yeah, somehow we always end up back here either swimming, playing pool or just chilling and talking." Blaine grinned at his brother.

"It's almost like we're drawn here." Megan agreed as she flashed a quick smile at Mark.

"Lia. Kendra." Kyle leaned back in his chair. "Do you two want another drink?"

"Yes please." Kendra replied.

"They're here on the table. Come fetch." He pointed to the ice bucket with drinks on the table.

She pulled her sunglasses down and looked at him. "Please bring them here."

"I'm not your waiter Kendra." He sighed. She pouted and glanced over at Angelia.

"Get him to bring them here."

"He's not my waiter either." She grumbled.

"Kyle, Lia says she'll do that thing that you like if you bring us our drinks." Kendra grinned at Kyle.

"I said no such thing."

"Twice and you have a deal." Kyle smirked at her.

"Done." Kendra laughed.

"Did you seriously just prostitute me for two drinks Kendra?"

"Yes, I don't feel like getting in the water right now." Kendra grumbled. Angelia shifted on her floating lounger, slid her hand under Kendra's and flipped it over. Kendra came up spluttering.

"I can't believe you did that you bitch." She glared at her friend as she laughed and slid off her own lounger into the water.

"You deserved it." Angelia floated in the water and grinned at her.

"I really don't feel like flying back tomorrow." Jarryd sighed as he watched Kendra and his sister chat in the pool.

"Me neither." Kyle said smiling at the two in the pool before looking back at him. "It's going to be hard leaving her behind."

"It's just six more months, right?" Jarryd looked at him. Kyle nodded. "What's half a year for the two of you after everything you have been through? If anyone can make it work, it's the two of you."

"Yeah. Six more months and then we have the rest of our lives together."

"What are you talking about?" Angelia wrapped a towel around herself before snaking her arms around Kyle's shoulders and kissing his neck.

"I'm not looking forward to going back tomorrow but it's just six more months babe." He reached up to squeeze her arms gently. She draped herself over his lap.

"I was thinking about that."

"You were?"

"I'm going to do all the paperwork to join you for the last three months. Then we can come back together. What do you think?" She asked.

"I think I love you even more." He grinned at her as she gave him a quick kiss.

"You can show me later how much you love me." She whispered huskily as she trailed her fingers down his chest.

"Lia." Jarryd sighed and shook his head. She turned her head and pulled a tongue at him before standing and picking up two drinks and heading back to Kendra.

"What do you have planned for tonight?" Blaine looked over at Kyle who gave him an evil grin.

"I was thinking of a candlelight dinner with romantic music, a bit of dancing, and clothing optional. And for dessert…"

"McAllister before you finish that sentence just remember that you're talking about defiling my innocent little sister." Blaine looked at him with a raised eyebrow.

"I have bad news for you Matthews, she's not innocent."

"Are you going to let him talk about our baby sister like that?" Blaine gave Jarryd a pointed look. He sighed and shook his head.

"Unfortunately, I think Kyle's right. Between the whipped cream revelations and the sexual favours for gossip and drinks, I think Blaine may be the only innocent sibling I have left."

"I am not innocent." Blaine protested.

"Blaine was the one with the furry handcuffs." Kyle pointed out as Megan went bright red. "Oh right, they were Meg's handcuffs."

"What furry handcuffs?" Mark arched an eyebrow.

"I'll show you later." Megan smirked at him.

"Yeah, you need to get them back from Lia and Kyle first." Blaine chuckled.

"Not a chance." Kyle laughed. "I need them for tonight."

"Kyle." Jarryd groaned, shaking his head.

"Yeah, I'm not using anything that comes out of Kyle and Lia's bedrooms." Mark sighed. "Where's Cara these days?"

"The whole thing with Robs and Kel was too much for her. She broke up with me."

"Sorry, Blaine." Kyle gave him a sympathetic smile.

"So, what are our plans for tonight?" Angelia asked as she dropped down in the chair next to Kyle.

"Your fiancé is making dinner for you, and you are going to be his dessert." Jarryd laughed.

"Did you buy whipped cream babe?" Angelia grinned at Kyle as Jarryd groaned.

"Lia."

"I actually don't have anything planned. Should we call everyone over and have a family dinner or do you want to do something with just you and me." He ran his fingers lightly across her shoulders.

"Why don't we all do something together but have an earlyish night to spend some time alone." She suggested.

"I think that's a great idea." Casey smiled.

"Yeah, that sounds kind of perfect." Megan agreed.

Chapter 20

"Did Lia say anything to you about why she is coming back early and without Kyle?" Mark looked at Blaine. He shook his head as he indicated to change lanes.

"She sounded really upset though." He sighed as he pulled up at the airport. "There she is." He climbed out and waved to Angelia before heading over to her. "Hey, Lia." He said as he hugged her.

"Hey, Blaine." She said softly as she hugged him back. He grabbed her suitcases and headed to the car. Angelia climbed into the backseat and gave Mark a despondent smile.

"Hey Mark."

"Hey Lia. Is everything ok hon?" He asked, looking at her in concern. She shook her head and sat back in her seat. He sighed heavily as Blaine climbed in and gave him a quick look.

"Do you want to stop off anywhere?"

"I just want to go home." She said quietly. He nodded and pulled off into the road.

"What happened Lia?" Blaine glanced at her in the rearview mirror. "You were going to stay with Kyle until he moved back here."

"He's not moving back." She said quietly as she stared out the window. Mark frowned as he turned to look at her.

"What do you mean?"

"They want him to sign on for another four years. They're promoting him and giving him a huge raise. It's an incredible opportunity."

"Then why are you back here?" Blaine asked.

"I hate it there; my work visa was declined, so I couldn't work and I was stuck in the apartment every day bored out of my mind. Kyle was so sweet telling me I don't have to work and that he'll support me but it was so hard being in a strange place and everyone I met was so rude." Tears ran down her cheeks. "I knew he would leave there and move back here for me because I was so unhappy, and I couldn't do that to him. He loves his job, he loves being there and he's been trying to get a job here and he can't get anything. His company's office here where he was working has had to close off some of their departments and let people go so, he can't go back there. I couldn't let him give up his dream job and move back here for nothing, so I broke up with him." She burst into tears.

"Lia, why would you do that?"

"I love him that much. I would rather let him go and have him stay there and be happy than come back here and be miserable."

"Don't you think that should be his choice?" Blaine asked her.

"He would choose me and move back here. It's not fair on him." She said sadly. "And I can't stay there. I tried, I really tried to be happy there but he works so hard and we were fighting all the time."

Mark's phone rang, he glanced at the screen and sighed. "Hey, Kyle. Yes, she's here with us. Let me check." He held his phone against his shoulder. "Do you want to speak to Kyle?" She nodded and reached for the phone.

"Hello." She listened for a moment before replying. "I love you Kyle, I will always love you. There will always be a piece of my heart that will belong to you but somewhere along the way, I fell out of love with you. I need to figure out who I am without you. You have been a part of my life for so long that I don't know who I am anymore. No, Kyle. Maybe one day in the future we will find our way back to each other. If we are truly meant to be then there is no force in this world that could keep us apart. Yes, this really is goodbye." She ended the call and burst into tears as Blaine pulled up into the driveway. He climbed into the backseat and held his sister as he looked worriedly at Mark who shook his head.

"Did you mean what you just said to Kyle?" Blaine asked gently.

"No but it was the only thing I could think of to stop him from getting on a plane to follow me." She sobbed into Blaine's shoulder.

"Oh, my Lia. Do you know how much I love you?" He asked softly. She nodded sadly as he rubbed her back. She looked out the car window and frowned.

"This isn't my apartment." She looked accusingly at Blaine.

"Yeah, I'm not leaving you on your own. You're going to stay with us for a while." He explained as he helped her out of the car. She squeezed his hand as she walked inside. She walked into the lounge and stopped dead.

"Hi." She said quietly as she looked at her friends' faces. Kendra stood and hugged her.

"Come sit Lia." She said quietly as she pulled her down onto the couch with her. Angelia wrapped her arms around her friend's shoulders and burst into tears as Megan rubbed her back gently and looked sadly at Casey.

"What happened Lia?" Casey reached over to squeeze her friend's hand.

"He was offered a great opportunity and I want him to take it." Angelia said stiffly. Casey looked up at Blaine who shook his head.

"There's more isn't there?" She asked gently as Angelia stiffened for a moment before shaking her head and looking up at Casey.

"No." She looked back down at her hands as she fought her tears. Blaine clenched his jaw and stalked to the kitchen.

"She's lying or she's holding something back." Blaine stated irritably as he reached into the fridge to grab two beers.

"What makes you so sure?" Mark frowned.

"Because I know my sister better than anyone."

Mark pressed dial to call his brother, it went straight to voicemail.

"Kyle, please call me when you get this." He said before ending the call. Megan came through and poured a glass of water. She put her arm around his waist and kissed him. "How is she?"

"She's not saying much. Just that Kyle was offered a contract and she broke up with him to get him to take it." Megan sighed as she rested her head on Mark's arm.

"Not buying that either huh?" Blaine asked darkly.

"I know Lia and her love for Kyle and I do believe she would walk away from him if she felt she was in the way of something great for him. But yeah, I do get the feeling that she's not telling us the full story." She sighed, she looked at Mark as his phone rang.

"It's my brother." He glanced out the kitchen door before pressing answer and putting the call on speakerphone. "Hey Kyle."

"Hey Mark." Kyle's tired voice came through. "How is she?"

"Heartbroken."

"She's heartbroken? She just fucking broke up with me with no explanation, packed her shit, left her ring and ran." Kyle snarled through the phone as Mark looked at Blaine in confusion. "I'm done. I can't do this with her anymore." Kyle ended the call as Megan frowned.

"This makes no sense." She sighed as she picked up the glass of water and headed to the door.

"Megs, don't say anything to her." Blaine sighed as he scratched his jaw. She shook her head quickly and headed back to the lounge.

"What do we do now?"

"Play along until she's ready to tell us what's really going on. You know how stubborn she is. If we push for answers she'll shut down and if she feels trapped she'll run again, probably to JR." Blaine ran his hand over his eyes and sighed heavily.

"How are you feeling?" Mark asked softly as he took a seat next to Angelia. She smiled sadly.

"Like my world just ended."

"Speak to Kyle, what you've done is very drastic." She shook her head. "What's really going on hon because when I spoke to Kyle earlier, he didn't mention that he was offered another contract or that you told him to stay. Speak to me Lia." He rubbed her back soothingly.

"He doesn't know that I found out about the job offer. I am so scared that he is going to move back here and be miserable. I know at first he will be happy to be here and be with me and our family but my biggest fear is that he will grow to hate me because he'll feel trapped here. I would rather hurt him and have him angry with me than have him hate me."

"That makes a lot more sense but you don't know that will happen for definite." He said gently.

"There are no jobs here, everyone is battling. Even over there jobs are not easy to get. It's crazy for him to give up a well-paying job that he loves for the uncertainty he will have here. The contract they are offering him is a dream come true for him, I had to let him go so he would accept it." She said tearfully. Mark pulled her into his arms and rubbed her back comfortingly.

"Oh Lia. You love him so much." Mark sighed as she nodded forlornly. She stood up and wiped her eyes.

"I'm going to go home now, I need to unpack and take a shower." She gave him a small smile.

"Why don't you stay here? With Blaine, Megs and me. Stay for dinner at least. I'm making your favourite pasta dish."

"That sounds great. Can I help?" She offered. He eyed her warily.

"That depends."

"On what?" She asked with a slight smile.

"How much cooking did you do over there?" He arched an eyebrow as she rolled her eyes.

"None. I was banned from the kitchen," She sighed dramatically. "He kept mumbling something about not getting his damage deposit back."

"Well, you can sit on the counter, drink wine, criticise my cooking and keep me company. How does that sound?"

"That sounds kind of perfect." She laughed softly as she followed him into the kitchen. Blaine looked up from the packet of mushrooms he was inspecting.

"I don't think these are edible." He sighed as he handed them to Mark. "They smell damp."

"There is nothing wrong with these Blaine, I bought them yesterday." He laughed. "They're a fungus, I'd be concerned if they didn't smell damp."

"Oh. Right." Blaine said as he turned his attention to his sister. "You coming to help cook Lia?" He flashed her a cheeky smile.

"No, she is going to sit on the counter, drink wine and keep us company." Mark explained as Angelia opened the fridge to take out two beers and a bottle of wine. Blaine placed a glass down on the counter and she smiled warmly at him as she filled it. He took a sip of his beer before putting his hands on his sister's waist and lifting her up onto the counter.

"Hey." She looked at him with a raised eyebrow. "Maybe I wanted to sit at the table and watch you guys cook." She protested.

"Did you really?" Mark asked her smugly.

"No." She rolled her eyes as she took a sip of her wine. She gave a small smile as she watched the two of them bicker about the correct way to chop vegetables. "Thank you." She said softly as they both looked up at her. "For convincing me to stay." Blaine leaned over to kiss her cheek.

"I love you." He said quietly as she reached out to squeeze his shoulder.

"I love you too." She said with a sad smile.

CHAPTER 21

Angelia sighed contentedly as the delightful warmth from the sun made her feel lazy. She turned her head to look at Kendra.

"Kenz, should we go to the movies tonight?"

"I can't, I have plans." She mumbled. Angelia frowned and squinted at her.

"Plans with whom may I ask?" She arched an eyebrow.

"An old friend." Kendra said vaguely.

"Who?" Angelia asked feeling slightly irritated.

"It's an old friend from college." Kendra answered evasively.

"Does your friend have a name?" Angelia's irritation crept into her voice.

"It's no one you know Lia." Kendra sighed. Angelia looked up into the clear blue sky as she frowned. It was the first time in the month since she arrived back that she felt like going out.

"Ciara, how about you? Movies with me tonight?"

"Sorry, Lia. Chris and I have dinner plans." Angelia sat up and looked around at her friends.

"Is anyone free to go to the movies tonight?" Mark and Megan shook their heads.

"Sorry, Lia." Kalen replied as Casey shook her head. Blaine got to his feet and stretched.

"I have to go see Cara now." He announced.

"You guys back together?" Kalen looked at him. He smiled happily as he nodded.

"I'll pick you up at seven Lia." Blaine tugged his shirt over his head. Angelia looked at him confused. "Movies? Tonight? You and me." He grinned at her.

"Don't you have plans with Cara?"

"You're more important." He shrugged as he reached over to flick her ponytail.

"Thanks, Blaine." She smiled at him before shooting an irritated look at Kendra. "I will see you at seven." She smiled serenely as she lay back down.

"Yeah, make sure you're ready on time little miss fashionably late." He chuckled as he pulled his keys out of his pocket.

"Bite me." She said with a grin.

"Love you too little sister, love you too." He laughed as he headed into the house.

***

"Hey Kenz, the gate was open. I brought that…" Angelia trailed off as she came face to face with Kyle.

"What are you doing here?" She turned to look at her best friend. "Kendra?"

"Ummm, hi Lia." Kendra was examining her fingernails as her cheeks flushed crimson red.

"Hey guys, do you know…" Kalen trailed off as he looked at Angelia. "Uh, hi." He said as Angelia gave him an icy smile and waved her fingers at him. She looked to the right as Mark, Christian and Megan walked out of the games room, they stopped in their tracks as they spotted her.

"Hmm," Angelia said as she nodded. "This is why no one wanted to go to the movies with me tonight."

"Lia." Christian said cautiously.

"Wow. Just wow." She said quietly as she blinked back tears. Mark took a few steps closer and reached out to catch her arm. "Don't touch me." She hissed as she snatched her arm away from him. Mark shook his head and sighed.

"Don't take this out on them Lia." Kyle said softly. "If you're going to be angry with anyone, be angry with me. I asked them not to tell you that I was going to be here."

"How noble of you." She snarled her voice dripping with venom. "I wasn't aware that everyone felt like they had to take sides but clearly a line has been drawn somewhere and everyone has decided who they are siding with." She fought to keep her tears out of her voice.

"It's not like that, Lia." Kyle explained as he pulled his keys out of his pocket and jingled them in his hand.

"Why don't you stay?" Mark asked her gently.

"No. Thanks anyway." She gave him an insincere smile. "I'm not staying where I am clearly not wanted." She spun on her heel and stormed out the door. Kyle shook his head and chased after her.

"Lia just stop for a minute." He shouted out to her. She turned around and folded her arms.

"What Kyle? What could you possibly have to say to me?" She snapped at him.

"You are infuriating." He threw his car keys down on the table.

"Me? You didn't even tell me that you were coming back. I came here by pure chance to drop some stuff off for Kendra. If I hadn't Kyle, was I ever going to find out that you were here?"

"I didn't think you would care considering that you just packed up all your stuff and disappeared on me." He yelled at her.

"I don't care." She shouted back at him.

"Are you sure about that? Because you sure are acting like you care."

"Those are my friends Kyle, *my* family, how could you ask them to lie to me?" She asked furiously.

"I know that's the way it seems but it's not the way it is. I came back here to run some ideas past them. I didn't think I needed to get your permission, and I didn't want to upset you because I'm still not sure why you left other than you telling me that you don't love me anymore." He gave her a hurt look before shaking his head.

"So, you came all the way here to discuss things with everyone but me, like I meant nothing to you." She glared at him.

"Try to see things from my perspective Lia."

"From your perspective? If you could stop being so self-involved, you might actually notice that there is an entire world out there that does not revolve around you. I am so sick and tired of putting my life on hold while you try to figure out what it is that you want. Do you want to stay in New York, or do you want to move back here? You told me that you were moving back home and then I find out that they offered you a four-year contract that you accepted and were signing without even discussing it with me." She shouted at him as he looked at her in surprise.

"How did you find out about that?" He asked quietly.

"Your friend Shayna stopped by to personally tell me about the contract and how excited they were to have you sign on for the next four years." She looked up at him with tears in her eyes. "You made that choice without even discussing it with me. We were supposed to be planning a wedding and our future together. Now what? We put our lives on hold for another four years? And after that Kyle? Will it be *another* four years?"

"Lia." He took a cautious step towards her.

"Don't, Kyle. Just don't. I can't do this anymore. I am tired and I am over it and I am over you. Stay away from me. Go back to your wonderful life in New York." She said bitterly as she climbed into her car, reversed into the road and sped off.

He sighed in frustration and ran his hands through his hair, as he watched her drive off. He felt Kendra appear at his side.

"You really screwed up this time." She sighed.

"Thanks, that was extremely supportive."

"Why didn't you just tell her?" He looked at her and shook his head.

"I don't know."

"If you're planning on turning down the promotion in New York to move back here to be with her, you may want to tell her at some point." Kendra gave him a sharp look.

"I don't know if she's ever going to speak to me again."

"Of course she will," Kendra said confidently.

"How can you be so sure?" He gave her a sideways look.

"Come on. It's you and Lia, everyone knows you two are meant to be together."

"Yeah, everyone but Lia." He sighed sadly. "I'm going to head home."

"Are you still flying back tomorrow afternoon?"

"Yeah, I need to make a decision. I either need to pack up my apartment and move back here or finally sign that contract, they're pressing me for an answer and I can't delay any longer."

"What are you going to do?"

"Honestly, Kenz, I don't know."

"What do you want Kyle?" She looked at him.

"I want Lia. I want to be back here with all of you. It's been tough being away the last few years. I want to be back with my family, but…" He trailed off as he shook his head.

"The main reason you are coming back is Lia."

"Yeah." He sighed. "If she doesn't want to work things out then I may as well go back to New York."

"I won't take it personally that you don't love the rest of us enough to stay." She sniffed.

He laughed and shook his head. "You know I love all of you."

"It will just hurt too much to be here and be around her if she won't be yours?" Kendra asked quietly as she looked at him.

"Yeah." He sighed sadly as he picked his keys up off the table. "See you tomorrow, Kenz." He gave her a quick smile as he climbed into his car.

Kyle opened the oven, shoved the tray of food in and sighed irritably. He looked up as the doorbell rang.

"It's open." He shouted. "Probably not the smartest thing to leave the damn thing unlocked all the time." He grumbled to himself as he placed dirty dishes into the dishwasher before slamming the door shut.

"Kyle."

He spun around. "Lia." He exclaimed in surprise. She looked at him in silence for a moment. "Come here, baby." He held his arms out to her. She flew into his arms and he held her tightly. He put his hand under her chin and tilted her face up to his. She bit the side of her lower lip as she looked up at him. He smiled as he bent down to kiss her.

She draped her arms around his neck as he moved her against him. "I missed you so much." She whispered between kisses.

"I missed you too Lia." He let go of her to reach over and switch the oven off before pulling her back into his arms. He lifted her up and set her down on the counter. She parted her legs so he could stand between them as he moved her closer to the edge so she was pressed against him. He trailed kisses down the side of her neck as she moaned quietly. He lifted her shirt off and dropped it on the counter beside her before placing his hands on her waist.

"Kyle." She sighed softly.

"Yeah, baby." He whispered.

"I think a car just pulled up." He glanced at the kitchen door and nodded.

"I think Mark might be home." He hefted her over his shoulder and grabbed her shirt as he headed to his room.

"This is so romantic. Caveman style." Angelia giggled as he shut the door behind them and lay her down on the bed. She looked up at him and exhaled softly. He removed his shirt before unzipping her shorts and tugging them slowly down her legs. He slipped his shorts off and threw them over his chair. He ran his hands gently up her legs to her thighs before placing a light kiss on the inside of her thigh.

"Baby." She moaned quietly.

"What do you want, Lia?" He trailed gentle kisses up her stomach.

"I want you." She whispered seductively. He smiled as he ran his hands lightly over her stomach and up to her shoulders, then bent down to kiss her tenderly.

"You have me." He whispered back as he wrapped her legs around his waist.

"Lia?" Kyle squinted up in the dark. "Where are you going, babe?"

"I have to leave Kyle."

"Stay the night with me. Please." He pleaded softly.

"I can't. Nothing's changed." She mumbled as she pulled her shirt on and paused at the door.

He clicked on the light. "What do you mean nothing has changed?" He asked flatly.

"I didn't want things to end like that between us. After everything we've been through and the love we have shared, I didn't want you to go back to New York hating me." She spoke softly as her tears threatened to spill.

"I could never hate you, Lia. I just don't understand what's happening between us." He said despondently.

"I know. I'm sorry."

"I'm turning down the promotion and moving back here." He said quietly.

"You shouldn't." She said firmly as she fought back her tears.

"What? Why?"

"You should take the job. There is no reason for you to come back here." She said, shaking her head vehemently.

"Lia."

"I'm not in love with you anymore Kyle. I'm sorry." She stepped out and closed the door behind her. She held her hand over her mouth to stifle her sobs and made her way rapidly down the passage.

"Lia?" Blaine asked confused, as she went past the kitchen. She looked at him and froze in surprise before she raced towards the front door. "Lia, get back here right now." Blaine yelled as he ran to the entrance of the kitchen.

"Blaine. Stop her." Kyle shouted as he tried to zip up and button his shorts. Blaine looked up at him startled for a second before turning to bolt after his sister.

"Lia." He shouted as she sped off.

"Fuck." Kyle snarled angrily as he ran out in time to see her drive down the road.

"What the hell is going on?" Blaine glared at him.

"I have no fucking idea." Kyle answered angrily. "I came back to tell everyone that I'm turning down the job I was offered in New York to move back here. I had a few business opportunities that I wanted to discuss with them. I asked everyone to keep it quiet because things with Lia and I are on shaky ground at the moment. I wanted to make dead sure that this was the right move for me. For her. For us. She walked in and flipped out at everyone before storming off. Then she arrived here and we kissed before we…uh, I'm sure you can guess what we did next." Kyle shook his head. "Next thing I know she's getting dressed and trying to sneak out while I'm half asleep. She keeps telling me to go back to New York because there is no reason for me to move back here. She is the most frustrating and infuriating person I have ever met."

"So, what are you going to do now?"

"Right now? I'm going to get dressed and track down your crazy sister so I can talk some sense into her." He snapped as he stormed inside. Blaine stared after him before chuckling. Kyle came racing back out pulling his shirt over his head.

"You're going to move back here for her?"

"I love her Blaine. I would give up everything for the chance to make her happy but for some reason she seems determined to either be unhappy or push me away. She keeps telling me that she doesn't love me anymore." Hurt echoed in his voice.

"She loves you, Kyle. I don't know why she is saying she doesn't, but I know she does." Blaine assured him. Kyle smiled sadly as he climbed into the car and drove to Angelia's apartment.

"Lia, open the door." Kyle knocked loudly then listened for any sounds. "Lia please, I need to know what's going on." He sighed and leaned against the door as he pulled his phone out and dialled her number. Angelia picked up her phone as it buzzed on her lap. She leaned back against the wall as tears streamed down her cheeks. She watched the door as Kyle knocked again. "Please Lia, I need you." He pleaded. "I need to understand why you're doing this. I love you Lia, please just let me in."

She held her hand over her mouth to stifle her sobs as she felt her heart shatter. "Lia, I'm leaving at two tomorrow, please I need to see you before I go." He rested his head against the door. "Please my Angel Lia. I love you so much." He whispered softly.

Chapter 22

Angelia groaned and dragged her pillow over her head.

"Go away." She shouted at the person who was persistently knocking on the door.

"Angelia Ryan. Open this door. Right now." Kendra shouted back.

"Arrgghh," Angelia growled as she climbed off her bed and stormed to the front door. She swung it open and gave her soon-to-be former best friend a scathing look before spinning on her heel and skulking back to her room. Kendra sighed dramatically and followed her into the darkened room. She walked straight to the curtains and yanked them open.

"Time to get up and face the world, Angelia. We're going to the beach. Get up and get dressed or so help me you will go in your pyjamas." Kendra stood next to the bed with her arms folded as Angelia glowered at her.

"When did you get so bossy?" She snapped as she got up and walked to her closet. She rummaged through her shelves before pulling out a pair of shorts and a tank top.

Kendra smiled sweetly at her. "I'll give you a minute." She announced as she waltzed into the bathroom to hunt for her friend's beach towels.

"Alright. I'm dressed." Angelia stated grumpily. Kendra appraised her friend's outfit and smiled. Her shorts accentuated her muscular legs and the vest hugged her curves.

"Not bad, you could've put a little more effort in though. Let's go." She grabbed Angelia's hand and hauled her out the door before she had a chance to change her mind. She opened the car door. "Get in."

"Oh, is that how cars work?" Angelia sniped sarcastically. "All this time I thought you had to walk next to them."

"Do you want to sit in the passenger seat or the trunk Lia? You are seriously testing my patience right now." Kendra scowled at her.

"Fine." Angelia snapped as she climbed in and put her seat belt on. She turned the radio up full blast as Kendra pulled out into the road. They arrived at the swimming beach within a few minutes, the traffic was always lighter on Sundays. They made their way down to the beach. Kendra waved at Kalen who was standing with his feet in the water speaking to Dylan. He waved back to Kendra and gestured for them to join him. She shook her head, grabbed Angelia's hand and dragged her along the beach.

"Come. We're going for a walk." She explained as they walked down to the water's edge and made their way along the beach to the rocks. Kendra headed to the spot that she knew her friend always went to when she wanted to think. She spread out the towel, sat down and patted the space next to her. Angelia sighed impatiently and sat down.

"You're wrong, you know." Kendra said quietly as she looked out at the ocean.

"You don't know that."

"He loves you Lia and you love him. The two of you finally have a chance to be together. Here in the same place. No more long distance, no more obstacles."

"You mean no more speed bumps."

"Yeah, no more speed bumps." Kendra chuckled.

"I'm sorry that you ended up being one of those speed bumps." Angelia gave her an apologetic smile.

"Serves me right for trying to get between two soulmates." She shrugged.

"I can't hold him back."

"That is his choice to make, but Lia you need to give him the chance to make that choice. You cannot make it for him."

"I can't." Angelia sniffled as a tear trickled down her cheek.

"Why Lia?" Kendra watched as she wiped at the tears threatening to spill.

"I don't want him to give up the job of his dreams, it would be really hard for me to know that he had to do that for me. But what I think would be even harder is giving him the chance to choose and he doesn't choose me." She turned to Kendra who was taken aback by the pain and sadness she saw in her friend's eyes.

"Why would you think he wouldn't choose you?" She asked confused.

"You wouldn't understand," Angelia whispered as she stared out at the horizon.

"What wouldn't I understand? What really happened in New York? Lia, did he hurt you?"

"Not the way you're thinking." Angelia laughed mirthlessly. "But yes, he did hurt me. He did some things that seriously made me question if he truly loved me. I would rather push him away because if he chose his job over me, it would destroy me, Kenz. I'd rather not leave the choice to him."

"Give him the chance to choose, then at least you would know. Do you really want to spend the rest of your life wondering what if? What if this time you could have made it work? Do you really want him to walk out of your life thinking you don't love him anymore?" Kendra glanced quickly at her watch. "Kyle wanted me to give you this." She reached into her bag and pulled out a small, flat square box and handed it to Angelia who looked at her in surprise.

She reached up to her chest and ran her fingers over the angel pendant that rested there before taking the box from Kendra. She opened it and gave a small gasp when she saw the beautiful heart pendant inside. She took it out gently and ran her fingers over the K and L engraved on the front. She turned it over where the words 'I'll love you forever, Kyle' were engraved on the back. Tears filled her eyes as she placed it back in the box.

"He leaves for the airport soon. Can I take you to him?" Kendra prodded gently. Angelia nodded silently as she rose to her feet. Kendra pulled her keys out of her pocket and followed her friend back to the car as Kalen ran up to join them. "You're covered in sand Kalen." She grumbled as he gave her a sheepish grin and climbed into the car. Kendra slid her phone out of her pocket and made a quick call. "We're on our way now, have you spoken to him?" She asked quietly. "Ok, let's do this." She sighed before ending the call.

"Kyle." Angelia called out as she walked up to him.

He leaned casually against the car door and watched her as she tucked a strand of dark hair behind her ear and bit the one side of her lower lip. The familiarity of it made his heart ache. He cleared his throat and she looked up at him.

"So, it comes back to this, the proverbial fork in the road that has defined our relationship for the last five years." He said softly.

"Every path we have taken away from each other always seems to lead us back here, back together." She sighed as she shook her head.

"So, what do we do now?"

"The same thing we have always done. Walk away."

"Why? Let's finish this. Let's figure out why, after all these years and all the fights and breakups we have had, everything leads back to us."

"It's just something that always happens." She shrugged.

"But why? Why does it always happen, Lia?"

"What? Are you suggesting that fate keeps bringing us back together? No offence, but fate has had some pretty lousy timing." She laughed sadly.

"Meaning?"

"There's always been, to quote you, the proverbial spanner in the works."

"Uh-huh." He looked at her as he folded his arms over his chest.

"Girlfriends." She looked up at him.

"Boyfriends." He smiled.

"Secret fiancées." She laughed as he groaned and shook his head. "Maybe all these complications and roadblocks were fate's way of telling us that we were never meant to be."

"Or maybe it was fate's way of saying it wasn't our time then."

"And it's our time now?"

"Can you think of any reason why we can't be together?"

"There are probably a million reasons."

"Give me one Lia. Just one that makes sense and I will get on that plane, go back to New York and never call you again."

"I can't let you throw away everything you have built and achieved for something we can't define. For a relationship that we can't seem to get right. We don't get the happy ending, Kyle, but we get a love that will last into eternity. A love that will never end because we will hold it in our hearts until the day we die."

"I'm not throwing anything away. I am choosing the woman I love, the only woman I have ever loved. You said once that you were at a crossroads trying to decide whether to stay or leave to save our relationship. To save us. Well, this is *our* crossroads, Lia. The crossroads of us. So, what is it going to be? Are we going to stay and fight for us or are we just going to walk away? I want to fight for us babe, what we have is worth fighting for. The love I have for you, the love I hope you have for me, it's worth fighting for, but I can't fight alone."

"I will always love you, Kyle. There will always be a piece of my heart that will belong to you, but I am not in love with you anymore."

"Then what was last night?"

"Last night was just this insane physical attraction we have for each other. It's not love Kyle, it's just sex."

"Not for me." He protested.

"Well, that's what it is for me." She shrugged as she tried to keep her voice calm and steady.

"I don't believe you." He said as he fought back his tears.

"I don't know what you want me to say."

"Tell me you love me. Tell me you want me. Tell me to not get on that plane because you can't live without me because that's how *I* feel about *you*." He moved away from the car to stand in front of her.

"I'm sorry Kyle. I can't give you what you want, I can't give you a reason to stay." She said quietly as she fought back the pain that was coursing through her body. "You need to go now. You're going to miss your flight." She gave him a small smile. He closed the gap between them.

"I want you to keep this." He said holding her ring out to her. She shook her head. "Take it Lia." The pain in his voice shattered her already broken heart even more. She reached out and took it from him. "I don't understand why you're doing this but one day when you're ready to admit that you still love me, I want you to put that ring on and come back to me. I love you, Lia. I will never stop loving you." He cupped her cheek with his hand before turning around and climbing into the car. Mark glanced at her in the rear-view mirror before looking at his brother.

"Kyle." He said softly.

"Just drive." Kyle ordered him as he fought back his tears. Angelia stood in the road watching them drive off as tears streamed down her face.

"I'm doing this because I love you that much." She said quietly.

"Lia." She looked up at Blaine as he wrapped an arm around her waist and held her until her sobs subsided.

"Why are you doing this Lia?" He asked her. "You do love him, more than anything, so why would you let him go?" He pulled away from her and put his hands on her shoulders.

"I let him go because I love him that much." She looked up at Blaine. "Because I realised that he would give up everything to stay here with me and he shouldn't have to choose between me and his job. He loves being there and I can't ask him to stay here. I'm scared that he'll end up resenting me. I love him so much that I won't let him make that choice." She said sadly as she started crying again. Blaine sighed deeply.

"Let's go inside Lia. You need to be around your family right now." He slipped his phone into his pocket as he hugged her tightly. "Why don't you go wash your face and join us outside." She made her way to the bathroom. She washed her face and sighed as she looked at her reflection. She dried her face and looked towards the door as she heard slamming doors and voices. She took a deep breath before exhaling and drying her face. She ran a hand through her hair and smiled miserably at her reflection. She picked up her engagement ring and looked at it before closing her fingers around it and walking outside to join her friends.

"Hey." She said quietly as she walked outside and looked at her brother and their friends.

"Where's Kyle?" Kendra asked as she glanced over her friend's shoulder.

"He's on his way to the airport." Angelia replied softly. "I let him go."

"And he just left?" Megan asked.

"I lied and told him that I didn't love him anymore so that he would leave." She looked down at the ring she was clutching in her hand. She slid it onto her finger as tears streamed down her cheeks.

"Do you know how much I love you?" She heard a voice ask behind her. She wiped the tears from her cheeks as she turned around.

"As much as I love you." She whispered in surprise. Kyle dropped his phone onto the table and wrapped his arms around her. He looked up at Blaine and nodded before resting his head on top of Angelia's.

"I don't want to leave baby. I want to stay here, with you." He whispered into her hair. She looked up at him and smiled.

"Then stay." She said softly. "Stay here with me." He held her face in his hands.

"That's all I ever needed to hear you say Lia." He bent down to kiss her.

CHAPTER 23

Blaine's head shot up as he heard the front door slam loudly and heated voices drifted through the house. He looked at Mark and raised his eyebrows. Mark frowned and shook his head as Blaine placed his cards on the table and walked to the door to open it.

"I'm so tired of your jealousy Lia. What is your problem now?" Kyle snapped at her.

"You were flirting with the waitress in front of me and you expect me not to get jealous?" Angelia shouted at him.

"Where was I flirting?"

"Oh, I don't know. Maybe when you turned to say 'You have such pretty eyes' to her." Angelia snarled at him.

"I was paying her a compliment." He snarled back.

"Well, she thought you were flirting. She even wrote her number on the receipt." She threw the crumpled paper at him.

"I never asked her for it."

"I just can't do this with you. I'm going home."

"Oh, you're running, what a surprise. It's one of the few things you're good at." He snapped at her.

"Oh, that's rich coming from you." She snatched her keys off the counter as she stormed to the door.

"Lia, wait." Blaine shouted to her as he headed down the passage, pausing briefly to glare at Kyle. He followed his sister out to her car where she stood fighting back tears. "Let's go somewhere for coffee little sister." He took her keys and opened the passenger door for her.

"Ok." She said quietly as she climbed in. Blaine started the car and pulled out onto the road.

"You want to go to Give Me Coffee?" He asked giving her a troubled look. She nodded before turning to look out the window.

"What's going on Lia?" Blaine asked concerned as he sipped his coffee.

"I don't know." She looked at him tearfully. "The last six months have been so incredible. Just having Kyle home and finally having the chance to be together, but these last two weeks we've been fighting constantly. He goes out of his way to say nasty things and flirt with other women which he knows pisses me off and then he denies it and makes out like I'm unreasonable. I love him so much, Blaine and we're getting married in less than three months, this is supposed to be a happy and exciting time. I'm trying to plan this wedding and he just shuts down when I try to discuss it. Do you think he's changed his mind about marrying me or do you think maybe he doesn't love me anymore?" She looked at her brother tearfully.

"I don't know little sister. He moved here to be with you, I doubt he's changed his mind. Maybe he's still adjusting to being back here. Give him some space. Maybe you should stay at your place tonight and he should stay at our place. Take some time apart from each other." Blaine suggested as she nodded.

"Yeah ok." She sniffed as Blaine stood and helped her up.

"Do you want me to stay with you for a bit?" He asked as they walked out together and headed towards her apartment block.

"Yeah please." She said quietly. "Maybe we could watch Pretty Little Liars or Gossip Girl." She gave him a weak smile as he sighed.

"You really are pushing the boundaries of my love for you." He shook his head as she giggled.

"Yeah, I know. We can watch a movie instead."

"That does sound better." He chuckled. "I can stay for dinner. As long you don't cook." He grinned at her.

"Don't be an ass." She sighed. "We can order pizza or burgers."

"Pizza sounds good." Blaine smiled as he held the elevator doors open for her.

"Kyle." She exclaimed as they got to her door to find Kyle sitting on the floor against the wall with his head and arms resting on his knees.

"Lia." He looked up at her before quickly rising to his feet. "I'm so sorry baby." He pulled her into his arms. "I didn't mean to hurt you. I've just been so frustrated at work and I took it out on you." He cupped her cheeks in his hands. "I love you more than anything. I'm so sorry." He said as he kissed her gently.

"I love you too." She smiled at him.

"I'm gonna head home then." Blaine said, giving them a concerned look. Kyle looked at him and nodded.

"Take Lia's car. We'll swing by to collect it tomorrow."

"Sure." Blaine nodded. "I'll talk to you later little sister." He smiled at her before turning to leave.

"Yeah. You know I love you." She said to his retreating back.

"Love you too." He glanced at her over his shoulder.

"So, um, can I take you inside and do bad things to you?" Kyle whispered seductively into her ear before brushing his lips along her neck. She felt her heart start racing.

"Uh-huh." She whispered back before pressing her lips to his and running her hands up to the back of his neck. He reached out to open the door before hooking his arms around her legs and picking her up.

"This is so romantic." She sighed as he walked through the door and chuckled. He pushed the door closed with his foot before heading to the bedroom.

"I'm practicing for our honeymoon." He grinned at her before lowering her onto the bed.

"So, you still want to marry me?" She asked nervously as he pulled his shirt over his head before unzipping his jeans.

"More than anything my Lia." He whispered as he reached down to pull her dress over her head before climbing onto the bed with her. "More than anything." He sighed as he pressed his lips to hers.

"Should I make dinner, or should we go out somewhere?" Kyle murmured as he kissed the side of Angelia's head.

"Let's stay in tonight. You can cook or we can order food for delivery." She smiled contentedly as she cuddled up to him.

"I'll cook something." He sighed as he rolled over and stood up.

"Oh ok." Angelia frowned as she sat up. "Why don't we cuddle for a bit, we can eat later."

"I'd prefer to cook early." He mumbled as he pulled his boxers on and searched for a pair of shorts in the cupboard. Angelia sighed and got up before pulling her dress back on as Kyle headed out the door. She glanced at the bedside table as his phone buzzed. She picked it up and frowned. "What are you doing?" She looked up at Kyle as he took his phone from her.

"Why is Kayla messaging you?" She huffed irritably.

"She's been asking questions about the files I worked on before I left New York. She just needed some additional info." Kyle replied with an edge to his voice. "Why are you going through my phone?"

"I wasn't. I heard it buzz, and I picked it up to bring it to you. I just happened to see Kayla's name on the screen." She replied coolly.

"Kayla is a friend of mine Lia; she can message me if she wants to. She's in New York, I'm here with you. I am really getting tired of your constant irrational jealousy." He replied angrily as he headed back out the door with his phone in hand. Angelia fought back tears as she walked into the bathroom and closed the door loudly behind her. She sat down on the edge of the bath as she wiped tears from her cheeks. Her fingers trembled as she pulled her ringing phone out of her pocket and pressed answer.

"Lia?" She heard her brother's voice.

"Hi JR." She said softly.

"What's wrong?" He sounded concerned.

"Nothing." She said sadly. "I miss you, it's good to hear your voice."

"I know my baby sister too well. What's wrong Lia." He sighed heavily.

"I don't know. Kyle and I are fighting all the time, and I don't know what to do." She said forlornly. "I know relationships take work but it feels like we're in the middle of a war. Love shouldn't be this hard."

"Why don't you come here Lia? For a holiday. Come visit and stay with me for a while."

"I can't right now. Do you have any advice for me big brother?"

"Oh, my Lia. All I can say is give him space. He needs to adjust to life back home now. I know you were both excited about him moving back but now you two need to settle down and adjust to being around each other so much. Remember that you two are used to only being around each other for a few weeks or a few months at the most. It's going to take time for you both to settle, be patient little sister." He paused for a moment. "But Lia if things don't improve it may be time to re-evaluate your relationship and think of closing that door and moving on for good. Not every love story has a happy ending."

"Lia." She looked up as she heard Kyle knock gently on the door. "Can I come in?"

"Yeah, you can." He opened the door and looked at her.

"Have you been crying?" He asked concerned as he walked up to her and put his hand on her cheek. She nodded as his eyes moved to the phone in her hand. "Who are you speaking to?" He frowned.

"JR." She replied as she put the phone back to her ear. "I love you, big brother, I miss you." She said softly.

"I miss you too Lia. I am always here for you." He said sadly. "I love you so much."

"I'll speak to you soon."

"Yeah, you will. Bye." He said as he hung up.

"Bye." She whispered as Kyle took the phone from her and put it down on the counter. He pulled her up onto her feet and into his arms.

"Don't cry babe. I didn't mean to snap at you." He tilted her face up to his. "I love you and I can't wait to marry you. I feel so unsettled living between two places. I think we need to decide whether we're going to live here or at my place." He brushed his lips lightly across hers as she smiled up at him.

"Move in here. We'll have more privacy, no housemates." She laughed.

"That does sound more appealing." He chuckled as he pulled her closer for a kiss. "You going to sit and drink wine and kiss me while I cook for us?" She nodded as she flashed him a shy smile. "I love you, Lia." He sighed as he ran his fingers through her hair. "Why don't we lie and cuddle for a bit like you wanted to. I'll make us dinner a little later."

"I'd like that." She whispered softly He reached for her hand and led her out of the bathroom.

"I said let's cuddle." Kyle sighed and shook his head in mock exasperation as Angelia giggled.

"I'm sorry." She looked up at him wide-eyed. "It's just that when I see you shirtless, I can't control myself."

"You have no restraint, Lia." He gave her a disappointed look.

"Excuse me?" She arched an eyebrow at him.

"Only you could turn innocent cuddles into sex."

"Is that right? Are you trying to imply that I seduced you?"

"Oh, I'm not implying it. I was lying here innocently holding you in my arms and you just took total advantage of me." He sighed.

"Really?" She scowled at him. He chuckled and pulled her against him.

"No. You are just too damn irresistible woman." He laughed as he ran his hand gently up and down her back.

"We can do this. Right? You and me? We can get it right this time?" She looked up at him as she blinked back tears.

"We have to babe. I think we've run out of last chances now. You are the love of my life, Lia and I want to spend forever with you. I can't lose you again." He whispered as he pulled her against him. "We're going to get married and be happy. This is what we have fought for babe. This is what the last five years has been about. All the heartache and pain was worth it if it meant we get to be together, to get married and have a happy life together."

"I don't want us to keep fighting. I love you and I honestly don't think my heart could take losing you or watching you walk out of my life again."

"I'm not going anywhere Lia. I promise you. I will never leave you again."

"Ok. Will you stop fighting with me all the time?" She raised an eyebrow at him.

"I will try but you can be very infuriating."

"Excuse me?" She asked indignantly.

"I will stop fighting with you all the time." He laughed. "I told you, I just feel unsettled. Once I move in with you, things will be better. You'll see." He smiled as he trailed his fingers along her back.

"Promise." She looked at him hopefully.

"I promise." He chuckled.

"Good. I love you so much, Kyle. I have wanted us to live together for so long and I don't want anything to ruin this." She looked up at him as tears brimmed in her eyes.

"Don't cry. Nothing is going to ruin this, Lia. I am exactly where I want to be. Where I need to be. With the woman I love. No more secrets, no more lies, no more drama, no more speedbumps." He sighed as he pulled her right up against him.

"Yeah, just you and me babe. No more lies and no more secrets." Angelia whispered as she looked over his shoulder at the wall before closing her eyes and biting her lip.

"I love you, Lia. I always have." He smiled as he kissed the top of her head tenderly.

"I love you too." She whispered as she planted soft kisses along his neck.

www.ingramcontent.com/pod-product-compliance
Lightning Source LLC
Chambersburg PA
CBHW051558010526
44118CB00023B/2739